HELP YOURSELF
TO HAPPINESS

Help yourself to happiness

through Rational Self-Counseling

by
Maxie C. Maultsby, Jr., M.D.

Foreword by Albert Ellis, Ph.D.

Institute for Rational Living, Inc.
45 East 65th Street, New York, N.Y. 10021

Third Printing

Copyright © 1975 by Maxie C. Maultsby, Jr., M.D.
Library of Congress Catalog Card Number 75-15057
Cloth ISBN 0-917476-07-7
  (formerly ISBN 0-89046-056-6)
Paper ISBN 0-917476-06-9
  (formerly ISBN 0-89046-005-8)

Published by the Institute for Rational Living, Inc.
45 East 65th Street, New York, N.Y. 10021

Manufactured in the United States of America.

DEDICATION

I dedicate this book to Warner Slack, M.D., Albert Ellis, Ph.D., and Arnold M. Ludwig, M.D., the three giants who were kind enough to let me stand for a while on their shoulders, and to my wife and kids who were patient enough to see me through it.

TABLE OF CONTENTS

FOREWORD

People often object to what they call "rationality" because they identify it with unemotionality and with lack of creativity. How wrongheaded! And how irrational!

Rationality, as beautifully shown on almost every page of this book, intrinsically includes a highly emotive, humanistic outlook. Dr. Maxie C. Maultsby, Jr. has not only pioneered in the developing of effective therapeutic and training methods, but he has also explicitly stated what makes physical and emotional behavior rational: namely, its getting based on objective reality or the known relevant facts of a life situation; its enabling people to protect their lives; its helping them to achieve their goals most quickly; its assisting them in keeping out of significant trouble with other people; and its enabling them to prevent or quickly eliminate significant personal emotional conflict.

If Dr. Maultsby correctly outlines these goals of human rationality — as I think he does — they boil down to the achievement, by a "rational" individual, of two basic values or purposes: (1) remaining alive, or surviving, for a goodly number of years and (2) remaining *happily* alive — with a maximum of joy, pleasure, satisfaction, and self-fulfillment and with a minimum of needless or gratuitous pain, dissatisfaction, discomfort, and self-defeat. Rationality, in other words, does not exist in any pure or absolute form. It has no thing-in-itself essence or substance. It consists of a tool invented and used by humans — and used, of course, in the service of their continuing to live and to enjoy themselves. They first decide (or choose) to live and to remain alive. Then they decide to remain *enjoyably* alive. Once they make these two decisions, they implement them by trying to behave rationally, sensibly, intelligently, or efficiently. And they do so because they believe — at least, Dr. Maultsby and I believe — that this kind of behavior, rational behavior, will *help* keep them alive and enjoying.

Rational, then, does *not* mean unemotional, mechanical, or uncreative. Quite the contrary! Thinking and acting, when truly rational, produce appropriate or happiness-creating emotions. They help you go after what *you* really want in life, in accordance with your *own* basic interests. Because they keep you in the realm of desiring and preferring, and get you to give up the absolutes of needing and demanding, they keep you particularly *human.* For when you think and act grandiosely and absolutistically, you deny your essential human fallibility: you pretend that you really do command others and run the universe and that you can act perfectly yourself. Well, lots of luck! Whether you like it or not, you will remain human and fallible. And the world will not perfectly cater to your preferences.

Once you decide, in other words, that you strongly prefer living and enjoying yourself, your rationality tells you how to do so more effectively. You could, of course, decide not to live — to kill yourself. And you could decide to live miserably — with enormous anxiety, depression, and self-downing. If so, you could rationally achieve these goals by using your head and acting in a logically self-defeating manner. But few of you would ever choose to do this. And those of you who did would probably have short lives and few offspring — so that your biological and environmental influence on future humans would prove minimal. The fact that you remain alive today and try, at least in many ways, to live happily, probably shows that you do have the two basic human goals of survival and enjoyment. As well you may!

As Dr. Maultsby nicely shows in this book, we usually achieve rationality in human affairs in two basic ways: (1) by seeing that we logically follow the goals (survival and happiness) that we start out by choosing; and (2) by making reasonably sure that these goals do not go seriously against the facts of empirical reality. Suppose, for example, you choose to live a long and happy life but you also choose to win the perfect approval of your peers, who happen to accept only the kind of people who continually smoke, drink, and overeat. Your goal of pleasing these peers by indulging, with them, in continual smoking, drinking, and overeating will most probably prove incompatible with your goal of living long and healthfully. So *if* you really choose the first of these goals, you'd better not logically also choose the second. The two seem at odds, for the most part; and the question arises: Which do you want more, assuming that you can't have both?

Even aside from the problem of your having to please your peers by engaging in life-destroying and health-sabotaging behavior, you have another serious consideration: If you crave the perfect, complete, absolutely guaranteed approval of these peers, can you truly devise *any* way of getting this kind of acceptance? Most probably not. For even if your peers approve you enormously, how can you feel sure that they accord you *perfect* approval? How can you ensure that their acceptance of you will ever achieve *completeness*? And even, if by some almost miraculous chance, you somehow got the perfect and complete approval of your peers, how could you ever *absolutely guarantee* that you would forever keep it? Obviously, you couldn't!

As a human, then, you desire and choose to remain alive and to feel happy, and relatively free from acute pain, much of the time. Why do you choose these paths? Probably *because* of your humanness — and because people, in order to perpetuate themselves, damned well better choose to stay alive and to feel pretty good about their aliveness. If they chose to kill themselves, or to let unfortunate conditions (such as famine, disease, fire, and warfare) kill them, the human race obviously would not survive. And even if they chose to survive, but didn't give sufficient consideration to surviving happily, they would soon enough probably feel aimless and purposeless and would *therefore* find little reason for keeping themselves alive, and would tend to die out. Their strong decision, or urge, or desire to keep themselves *both* alive and happy enables them, as individuals and as a group, to perpetuate their existence.

Once they do aim for survival and happiness, humans almost always go for the five goals that Dr. Maultsby considers rational. (1) They observe the real conditions around them — the state of the world and of other people in it — and they discover the relevant facts of the life situation (such as a job or a marriage) which exists for them. (2) They protect themselves from severe injury or death. (3) They decide on major and minor subgoals — such as living in a certain community, getting along with other people, intimately relating to a few people, and engaging in productive and creative work and recreational activities — and they try to achieve these goals efficiently and quickly. (4) They see how they can avoid getting into significant trouble with other people, especially those with whom they have steady contact. (5) They observe their own emotional difficulties and feelings of extreme upsetness and they try to prevent or minimize or eliminate their emotional conflicts. All these goals prove rational *because* they usually help people survive happily — and not because rationality immanently and absolutely exists in its own right and has some eternal definition.

Why, then, do humans have so much trouble thinking and behaving rationally and thereby existing in a relatively happy manner? Because, I would say, they have both powerful rational *and* irrational tendencies; and because both these tendencies have biological as well as sociological bases. That humans have profound predispositions toward rationality would seem evident from their very history of survival and by their ability, often, to survive happily even in the face of fairly dire environmental conditions (such as poor climate, barren soil, and a plethora of people-destroying animals). That humans also have strong predispositions toward irrationality would appear evident from the high incidence, throughout history, of emotional disturbance, fanaticism, crackpotism, extreme cruelty, superstition, dogmatism, rabid religiosity, etc. Even rational psychotherapy, as I noted in *Reason and Emotion in Psychotherapy* and as Dr. Maultsby accurately keeps pointing out in this book, has its limitations, partly because of the "natural" and easily maintained irrationality of us humans.

More specifically, virtually all men and women (not to mention children and adolescents!) tend to escalate many of their important desires, preferences, wants, and wishes into absolutistic shoulds, oughts, musts, necessities, have to's, and got to's. Karen Horney saw this clearly many years ago, when she wrote about the "tyranny of the shoulds." Fritz Perls also inveighed against the shoulds and the supposed to's that we impose on ourselves. My own writings, especially my revised editions of *How to Live with a Neurotic* and *A New Guide to Rational Living*, particularly stress the demandingness and commandingness of humans, and the resulting emotional disturbance that thereby ensues. Although we often call such disturbance by the high-sounding technical names of neurosis, character disorder, borderline psychosis, and psychosis, we probably would do much better in understanding and dealing with them if we more accurately called them states of whining. For that remains their essence: whining about how nobly and outstandingly we *must* perform ourselves — and thereby producing feelings of anxiety, depression, despair, and self-downing; whining about how considerately and kindly others *must* act toward us — and thereby making ourselves angry and enraged when they don't; and whining about how the universe *must* make things nice and easy for us — and thereby creating our feelings of low frustration tolerance, self-pity, apathy, and inertia when it provides us with hassles.

Emotional disturbance, then, consists largely of *musturbation* — of not only appropriately wishing and desiring that we and others behave better, but of whiningly commanding that we and they *must* so behave. Because, as Dr. Maultsby correctly shows throughout this book, humans remain essentially fallible and imperfect, and because the universe runs itself according to the laws of probability rather than those of necessity, *musturbating* will almost always (though not, of course, necessarily) get us into emotional trouble. It does!

To return to my opening theme. Some of the most rationally oriented therapists have belied the proverbial, and usually false, picture of "rationality" and have proven themselves exceptionally creative, unmechanical, and artistic. I think in this connection of such outstanding contributors to the field as Alfred Adler, Aaron Beck, Eric Berne, Raymond Corsini, Gerald Davison, Rudolf Dreikurs, Cyril Franks, William Glasser, John Gullo, Marvin Goldfried, Robert Harper, Paul Hauck, George Kelly, William Knaus, Arnold Lazarus, Donald Meichenbaum, and Julian Rotter. To this distinguished list, I think we may definitely add the name of Maxie C. Maultsby, Jr. For although he has stayed rigorously within the classical field of the rational-persuasive method (as handed down to us by Epictetus and the Greek Stoics and as developed over the years by a long line of distinguished philosophers, from Confucius to Bertrand Russell), Dr. Maultsby has invented, created, imagined, and cultivated a number of special therapeutic methods that emerge as both ingenious and unusually effective. He has pioneered in adapting my ABC's of understanding and treating emotional disturbance to the self-counseling area. He has added to and enhanced the homework-assigning techniques of Alexander Herzberg, Andrew Salter, and my earlier writings. He has created a particularly potent therapeutic tool in the technique of rational-emotive imagery (REI). He has originated exceptionally useful rational disputing techniques that distinctly improve upon some of the previously used methods. Although I have now actively employed rational-emotive therapy (RET) or what Dr. Maultsby usually calls rational behavior therapy (RBT) with literally thousands of individual and group clients during the last two decades, I have learned many new and valuable things from talking with and reading the writings of Dr. Maultsby during the last eight years with which we have maintained our association. Other rational therapists with whom I have had contact have also helped me develop my own thinking and practice of psychotherapy. But none more than Maxie Maultsby.

Let me say in conclusion: rational counseling offers no magic. As Dr. Maultsby continually points out in this book, it requires a great deal of persistent, hard work for you to use it effectively. But for those readers who will truly attend to the following pages and will make an honest effort to follow Dr. Maultsby's sage and sane procedures, I can almost guarantee that you will help yourself immensely. Not that you *have to;* not that you *must.* But you most probably will!

Albert Ellis, Ph.D.
Institute for Advanced Study in Rational Psychotherapy
New York, N.Y.

ACKNOWLEDGEMENTS

Because I try to be thoroughly undefensive about my writing, when I began to write seriously, I didn't hesitate to ask, plead and even badger my many friends, acquaintances and even a few foes, to read and critique my writing. That fact makes too numerous to list all the people who deserve sincere appreciative acknowledgement. With full knowledge that I will unwittingly overlook some, I want to acknowledge and thank: Solomon Kuperman M.D., Carolyn Slack, Charles Slack Ph.D., Mary Gutman Ph.D., Joyce Gram, Lynda Brodsky M.S., Leanna Steifel Ph.D., Connie Walling, Sister Antonia Lutz, Ruth Stone, Elizabeth Oien B.A., Mary and Michael Logan M.D., David Graham M.D., Jack Chosey M.D., Allie Hendricks M.S., Linda Carpenter, M.S., Ailene and Cindy Ludwig, Sylvia Wrobel, Jessie Pedigo, Alice Rudolph, Anne Beamon, Lori Whiting, Sharri K. Wright, Marsha McGee, Lela Denman, Harvey and Eilene Gram, Earl Glosser Ph.D., William Carlson E.ED., Tom Mooney Ph.D., Joan Jones R.N., Martha R. Small R.N., David Goodman, Mary Smith, April Cowan, Joseph Cunneen, Vicki Bigish and Melissa Jelm.

INTRODUCTION

What does it mean if you sometimes can't sleep at night, or you wake up anxious, dreading the day? What if a rejection seems to cut a hole in your stomach, or you have a mild panic the moment your boss sends for you? Should you worry about painful jealousy if you know it's silly? What about continuing in roles, jobs or relationships you hate; or eating more than you mean to and sometimes drinking more than is good for you?

Relax! It probably just means that you're perfectly normal. Normal people often behave in such ways, causing themselves needless trouble, useless worry, and emotional pain.

What else does it mean? Probably that like many other normal but often unhappy people, you have learned those habits well, by practicing them over and over, month after month. Naturally they now *seem* to be the right way, if not the only way for you to behave.

Fortunately, that appearance is wrong. Most people have much more control over their habits than they believe they have and usually more emotional choices than they ever realized.

It's not your boss who makes you worried, but your own thoughts about your boss. The man in the car causing the traffic jam isn't really making you angry. You are making you angry. And it's just one more of many examples of the useless anger normal people cause themselves. You and they would be better off with less of it. But if you are like most people, you are likely to continue as you always have — even if you give yourself high blood pressure.

Does that mean you have an unconscious death wish? Probably not; not if you are normal and sane. Such behavior is typical of normal, sane people who don't understand how their brain creates and controls their emotions. If your useless anger is giving you high blood pressure, it probably just means that you are a normal person, born with the tendency to react with that symptom to chronic but useless emotional stress. Still, high blood pressure will shorten your life, and you'd be better off without it.

Before you say that I don't know your boss, or that the man causing the traffic jam is enough to make even me mad, let me tell you about a self-help method that can help you control your own useless as well as harmful emotional stress. The method is called *rational self-counseling*. It's based on the most recent learning theories of human behavioral scientists.* Rational self-counseling consists of two easy-to-learn self-help techniques — rational self-analysis and rational emotive imagery. Anyone who has average intelligence can readily learn to use both techniques.

Rational self-analysis shows you how and which of your habits of thinking force you to have useless as well as potentially harmful emotional reactions. Rational emotive imagery helps you get rid of those habits fast, through reprogramming your brain for more desirable and pleasant emotional reactions. Both techniques have proven effective for hundreds of normal and even not-so-normal people.

Rational self-analysis (RSA) and rational emotive imagery (REI) are used routinely in rational behavior therapy.† As the director of the psychiatric outpatient clinic of the University of Kentucky Medical Center, each year I supervise instruction in this technique to over 150 medical students and graduate students in psychology, psychiatric nursing, psychiatric social work, pastoral counseling, and counseling education. In addition, each month my staff and I conduct an intensive training course in rational behavioral therapy for working mental health professionals from all parts of this country and Canada.

Even so, *neither* we, *nor* the professionals we help train, can see all the people who could use help. In fact, if all the mental health professionals in America were to work day and night, they would not be able to see even a fraction of the 40 million normal adults who repeated studies estimate could benefit by improving their mental and emotional health. That's why books like this one are useful. They teach normal people how to understand themselves better and how to deal effectively with useless, harmful, or otherwise undesirable emotions.

As I have stated, anyone with average intelligence can readily learn and use rational self-counseling. Clinical research has shown it to be effective in helping mental health clinic patients, normal high school and college students, as well as normal adults who just want to obtain more personal satisfaction from life.

Rational self-counseling has also proven acceptable and useful in the rehabilitation of inmates in state and federal prisons.

---

*Rotter, Skinner, Mowrer, Hebb, and Ellis are a few. For others, see the suggested reading list at the end of this book.

† Rational behavior therapy is also known as rational emotive therapy (Ellis, 1963).

They particularly like the ever-increasing sense of self-mastery that rational self-analysis gives them.

Family physicians in this country and Canada have read my articles on the value of using rational self-counseling for treating emotionally distressed medical patients. Many of those physicians were surprised to learn that they can do more than merely give such patients the three P's — a pill, a platitude, and a pat on the back. Consequently, I receive numerous requests from medical doctors for more information about the use of rational self-counseling in medical practice.

In 1970, I founded a non-profit organization of lay people and mental health professionals who were dedicated to teaching the use of rational self-counseling for the common problems in daily living. This group has grown rapidly from the original thirty to over 1500 members in all parts of the United States, and a few in Mexico and Canada. Called the Association for Rational Thinking, Inc. (ART for short), the address of ART's national headquarters is P.O. Box 159, Lexington, Kentucky 40501. In November, 1973, the Johnson Foundation sponsored ART's first national conference at Wingspread in Racine, Wisconsin. One of the main discoveries of that conference was the need ART members saw for this book you are now reading.*

By forming self-help study groups using rational self-help books and articles written by me and other rational therapists, ART members from different racial, religious, and educational backgrounds increase their joy in living through rational self-counseling. The most important discovery ART members make is that they themselves are their most dependable source of their own happiness. This book describes in detail how any normal person can make that discovery.

The first half of this book teaches you how your brain and emotions work. Using those facts, it then shows you why and how you can use rational self-counseling to make personally desirable emotional change.

In the second half of this book you will get practice in doing rational self-analysis (RSA) in the safest way possible — practicing on someone else's problems.

At the end of each chapter you will find emphasis questions highlighting the most important facts in the chapter. Emphasis

*For the complete history of ART and a detailed description of some of its success stories, see Section V, Chapters 16 and 17.

questions are made easy on purpose. They aren't to test you, but to help you remember. If you miss more than five of them you probably read the chapter too fast. Rereading it more slowly will be helpful. But if the questions seem easy and obvious, that means you have understood the material well.

What should you expect from this book? Nothing, unless you are willing to make a sincere effort to use rational self-counseling to help yourself. A sincere effort means spending at least a month using RSA (rational self-analysis) and REI (rational emotive imagery) every day. After that month, your increased happiness will probably convince you that the rational way really is the best way. Then you will continue to use it simply because of the personal rewards it gives you.

But that first month may be hard. That's because you've probably spent most of your life believing some things that disagree with some of the facts described in this book. Expect that. Don't get upset because of it. If you already knew and believed everything in this book, you wouldn't be able to help yourself with it. Remember, new facts usually appear strange and sometimes downright silly when you first hear them. For example, no doctor in his right mind would deliver a baby today without thoroughly sterilizing his hands first. But just 150 years ago, doctors laughed at Dr. Lister when he suggested they should sterilize their hands before delivering babies.

In the same way, many of the statements in this book may feel wrong to you when you first read them. Expect that too. But don't immediately reject them. Instead, look at the evidence that supports them. Then ask yourself: "Just for the sake of an objective experiment, what would I lose, if for one week, I assumed that even though my feelings are real, I am mistaken in having them and the ideas in this book are really right?" The answer will usually be: "I'd have nothing of personal value to lose." Then ask yourself: "Could I gain anything by making and acting on that assumption?" I think you will usually answer: "Yes, I will gain greater freedom from *unhappiness.*" Such great odds in favor of more personal happiness usually gives most normal people the courage they need to give rational self-counseling at least a sincere, one week trial.

Remember, by giving some aspect of rational self-counseling a one-week trial, you will have everything to gain and nothing of personal value to lose. And if you don't like the results, you can always go back to your old ways and the unhappiness that you know they cause. But, I don't think you will.

SECTION I
RATIONAL SELF-UNDERSTANDING

We all have our own self-understanding, and we use it to explain our emotional feelings and actions. Because we believe our self-understanding we usually use it even though using it may be causing us the disadvantages of needless emotional pain and self-defeating actions. Typical examples of both types of disadvantages are: (a) unproductive anger, resentment and depression; (b) chronic procrastination or irrational withdrawal, excessive eating, drinking and use of addicting drugs.

To avoid those and other common unhappy life events, you need a useful self-understanding: one that is based on facts about human emotions, one that helps you get what you want for yourself — most quickly, and keeps you out of undesirable conflict with other people, plus lets you feel the way you want to feel emotionally. I call that type of self-understanding, RATIONAL SELF-UNDERSTANDING.

describe in detail how to get rational self-understanding.

CHAPTER 1

RATIONAL SELF-COUNSELING AND WHY IT'S RATIONAL

Rational self-counseling is a practical method of emotional self-help. Like most professional counseling methods, rational self-counseling is based on proven facts about how the human brain works and a research-tested concept of human emotions. In addition, rational self-counseling has the same limitation that all professional counseling methods have. No method of counseling works unless the person being counseled decides to use it. Regardless of where people get advice, whether from a psychiatrist, a psychologist, a friend, a family member, or from a book such as this one, each person must decide whether or not to act on the advice. Because of that fact, the *only* effective counseling is self-counseling.

Unfortunately, effective does not always mean beneficial. With no help from anyone else, you counsel yourself every day and act upon your counsel. That's how you decide either to continue what you are doing or to change it. Because your self-counseling causes you to act, it always works. But, when your self-counseling is based on irrational thinking, it may work against you rather than for you. Let's look at two real-life situations and see the difference between rational and irrational self-counseling.*

Twenty years before Mr. McVey died (at the age of seventy-eight) he learned that he had high blood pressure. He announced one day that his doctor had just told him to stop eating salt and lose thirty pounds. Then he added: "That's exactly what I'm going to do." And that's exactly what he did.

The doctor gave the advice all right, but Mr. McVey counseled himself to accept the advice and follow it. In my opinion, that was rational self-counseling.

---

*All the case histories in this book are (or were) real people. But I've changed names and other identifying data to protect their privacy.

But not all patients act that rationally. Before I became a psychiatrist, I practiced family medicine for nine years. During that time I gave many patients the same advice Mr. McVey received. But in spite of my advice, some of my patients counseled themselves quite differently from Mr. McVey, and in my opinion, quite irrationally.

Their thoughts ran something like this: "Dr. Maultsby is a good doctor, but sometimes he's just like a nervous Nelly. High blood pressure can't be that bad; my mother had it and she lived to be eighty. I'm no fatter than Mama was, and fatness runs in my family. And I couldn't possibly eat my food without salt; that's all there is to it. Anyway, what the hell, you have to die with something."

In short, they counseled themselves against following my advice. Both types of self-counseling were effective, but Mr. McVey's was rational while the other patients' was not.

Now the patients who ignored my advice weren't trying to spite either me or themselves. They sincerely thought they were behaving rationally; in addition, they sincerely believed their actions were "right." What they needed, and what rational self-counseling supplies, was a good set of rules for deciding if their behavior was rational or not.

Both physical and emotional behavior is rational when it obeys at least three of these five rules:

(1) It's based on objective reality or the known relevant facts of a life situation.
(2) It enables people to protect their lives.
(3) It enables people to achieve their goals most quickly.
(4) It enables people to keep out of significant trouble with other people.
(5) It enables people to prevent or quickly eliminate significant personal emotional conflict.

Looking at these rules, you can see that Mr. McVey based his self-counseling directly on the objective reality, or the relevant facts about his health described to him by his doctor. The other patients based their self-counseling on *irrelevant* facts and their subjective opinions about the objective reality concerning their health. Mr. McVey's self-counseling caused him to protect his life and enabled him to achieve many of his other personal goals. It kept him from being unnecessary trouble to his doctor, family, and friends, (all of whom were concerned about his health and well-being), and Mr. McVey's self-counseling made him feel as comfortable as possible, both physically and emotionally. The self-counseling done by the other patients usually had exactly the opposite effects.

Not all decisions are as clear-cut as deciding to follow good medical advice. To avoid confusion in using the five rules for rational behavior you need clear insight into the concepts of "significant trouble with others" and "significant personal emotional conflict."

In almost any decision-making situation some conflict is inevitable, and some trouble with others is possible. But "significant" conflict or trouble is the amount that you don't want to have; it serves no useful purpose, and you will act to avoid it. The most important insight though, is that you alone must decide for yourself how much trouble or conflict is significant for you.

To make this point clearer, let me contrast myself with the late Dr. Martin Luther King. I hate the thought of being arrested so much that I rarely even jay-walk. The most minor arrest would interfere with my professional and personal goals and cause me significant personal emotional conflict: "Why ever did I *do* such a foolish thing? What effect will it have on my family, career, friends? How am I going to get out of this mess without being hurt?" Because I don't want to deal with any of those worries, personal behavior that keeps me from being arrested is rational behavior for me. And behavior that would cause me to be arrested would be irrational behavior for me.

But Dr. King's goals were best achieved by his getting arrested, as often and as publicly as possible. He set out to get arrested, and he usually succeeded. Naturally, he experienced some personal emotional conflict — no good citizen likes going to jail — and the trouble with other people that getting arrested caused Dr. King was broadcast on television all over the United States. But neither his emotional conflict nor his trouble with other people was "significant" to Dr. King; both were necessary for him to achieve his goals most quickly. Therefore, the personal behavior that got him arrested was rational for him.

What is rational for you one day may not be rational another. Even I might well find myself quite rationally seeking arrest at some future date if, for example, I were to join a movement similar to the one led by Dr. King. And as you find yourself in new situations with different goals, what is then rational for you will often be new and different. But you will always have the same responsibility to decide it for yourself. Rational self-counseling helps you make such decisions with ease and confidence.

How Rational Is Enough?

Because all human beings are fallible, you can't be perfectly rational all of the time; so don't expect that of yourself. Of course, the more of the five rules for rational self-counseling your self-counseling obeys, the better. But you can call your self-counseling rational if it just obeys at least three of the five rules for rational self-counseling. That is usually rational enough to enable you to prevent or quickly solve most of the emotional problems in daily living.

Objective Reality and the Camera Rule of Thumb

When someone walks in front of your car, you may yell: "You crazy fool, you could have gotten yourself killed!" That would be a logical response because it simply isn't rational to walk in front of moving cars. You can get yourself killed. For that reason, you don't usually step into traffic. You have formed the sensible habit of protecting your life.

The other rules for rational behavior often are not that clear-cut. And the rule that most people have the most trouble using is the first one: objective reality. That is especially true when they don't like the particular objective reality they are facing. Then, they often ignore or deny it. Doing that is one of the main reasons people act irrationally and cause themselves all kinds of emotional pain and trouble with other people. Instead of calmly looking at objective reality and reacting directly to it, such people react to what they believe the reality means. For example, my former medical patients ignored my advice (to lose weight and give up salt) and reacted to their belief that my advice meant I was a nervous Nelly.

Spelled out, the first rule for rational self-counseling requires your thoughts, feelings, and physical actions to be based *only* on what is actually happening at the time — that is, what could be recorded with a camera, tape recorder, or some other recording device. Like Jack Webb used to say in Dragnet: "We just want the facts, ma'am, just the facts." Remember how weary he always sounded? That was because even though normal people usually start out with the facts, often they quickly mix in so many of their fears, hopes, or beliefs that they honestly can't tell the facts from their sincere opinions about them.

Sincere opinions are personal and familiar and cause strong emotional feelings. Naturally, such opinions seem factual and true. But reacting to sincere but mistaken opinions, rather than directly to the facts, can make emotional and physical behavior be completely irrational. That is because sincere but mistaken opinions usually influence your view of facts in one of these four ways: They cause you to deny or ignore the facts. They cause you to distort the facts. They cause you to see the facts as being opposite to what they really are. They cause you to see different facts as all being the same.

My former medical patients in the McVey example either denied or ignored the objective facts of their health situation, then focused on their subjective opinions about me as a doctor, and confused what they wanted to do — keep salting their food and eating too much — with what was most healthy for them to do. The following examples will demonstrate the three other ways sincere but mistaken opinions can influence your view of objective facts.

A tired, irritated mother yelled at her teenage daughter, "Mary, your room is a mess. I want you to clean it up this minute and no but's about it." A camera would have verified that the room was a mess. The second statement about the mother's desire was true. So the objective facts in this situation were: the girl's room was a mess, and the mother wanted her to clean it up.

But the teenager's thoughts ran something like this: "She's always picking on me. Why can't she ever leave me alone? I can't stand to live in this hell-hole another minute. I've got to be free to live my own life."

Feeling increasingly angry and trapped, she ran away later that night. After hitchhiking a ride from a stranger, Mary was beaten up and raped. By the time the police finally returned her to her parents, she was on the verge of a nervous breakdown.

Mary's decision to run away after her mother's complaint seemed perfectly rational to her. Actually though, her decision was perfectly irrational.

First of all, it was not based on the objective reality of the situation. A camera would not have verified her thoughts; it would have contradicted them. A camera would have shown only a tired, irritated mother yelling at her daughter in a nice looking house (with a messy teenager's room). It would not have shown a mother always picking on her daughter, a mother who never left her daughter alone, nor a hell-hole. But a camera would have shown Mary staying in the house several hours after she said she could not stand it another minute. And her running away certainly didn't free her to live her own life at that time. So none of Mary's thoughts described the objective facts; they described only her opinions, fears, and anger about what she thought the facts meant.

By acting on her confused self-counseling, Mary violated the other four rules for rational behavior:

(1) Her actions might well have gotten her killed.
(2) They did not achieve her goals.
(3) They got her into significant trouble with others.
(4) They caused her significant emotional conflict.

Even had Mary used the five rules for rational self-counseling after her mother yelled at her, she may still have gotten angry. But by quickly giving up the idea of running away, she would have spared herself the other serious trouble and unnecessary emotional pain. Had she been in the habit of using rational self-counseling, she probably wouldn't have thought of running away in the first place.

Two loving parents refused to let their young child watch any more television because it was time for the child to go to bed. The child became furious and screamed, "You just hate me. That's why you won't let me have any fun. You just make me sleep, sleep, sleep all the time, while all the other kids have fun! I wish I had somebody to love me sometimes." He then ran to his room and cried himself to sleep.

The child's sincere opinion caused him to see the facts as being opposite to what they really were. Still his view was all he had to react to. That's why his reaction violated the first, third, and fifth rules for rational behavior.

As the next example shows, the rules for rational behavior are especially important in dealing with the changing objective reality of various situations.

Having grown up black in America, Michael had had many real life experiences with racial prejudice. Although he didn't have any more such experiences than most other American blacks, Michael was super-sensitive. He saw racial prejudice everywhere: where it was and where it was not. He saw it when white people looked at him and when they didn't look at him. If waiters gave him a table out front, Michael thought that they were just trying to hide their prejudice by showing him off. If they gave him a table to the side, he thought that meant they didn't want the white customers to see him there. No matter what happened, in Michael's mind it just proved his sincere but incorrect opinion: "All whites hate blacks." And Michael not only hated them back, he caused himself serious trouble by acting out his hate. Therefore, his self-counseling violated all five of the rules for rational self-counseling.

Are Negative Emotions Ever Rational?

In each of the last three examples, sincere but mistaken opinions caused intense but irrational negative emotions. Those negative emotions caused irrational physical behavior. That raises the question: Are negative emotions ever rational? Yes! They often are; but often they are not. Only you can objectively decide which is the case for you. When you are in doubt, the following rational insight into negative emotions will help you make a correct decision.

Negative emotions have the same function as physical pain. Both are important warnings. Physical pain tells you that something physically or medically wrong needs to be corrected. Negative emotions tell you that something mentally or emotionally wrong needs to be corrected.

If either physical pain or negative emotions *fail* to cause you to correct what is wrong, then they both are merely irrational suffering. That's why rational self-counseling forces you to analyze your negative emotions objectively. When negative emotions violate three or more of the five rules for rational emotions, those negative emotions are irrational. You will probably be better off if you get rid of them. The following real life example demonstrates those insights into negative emotions.

Bob, a bright graduate student, had been working hard to get all A's. But he panicked on one oral exam and got a C in that course. Naturally he had some negative feelings about that. The next semester, however, Bob used rational self-counseling to get rid of his exam anxiety. But he also continued to study just as hard as ever. At the end of this semester he got all A's. Now, were Bob's negative feelings about himself and the C grade rational?

Only Bob can say for sure. However, if he had not been somewhat disappointed and irritated with himself he probably wouldn't have done anything to eliminate his exam anxiety. Therefore, it's reasonable to say that the negative emotions that caused Bob to learn rational self-counseling and eliminate his exam anxiety were definitely rational. But any more negative emotions than were needed for that (for example, depression, anger, guilt, shame, self-hate, etc.) would have been irrational.

They would *not* have helped Bob earn his A and having them would have meant suffering for nothing. Then, in addition to his exam anxiety, Bob would have had the unnecessary problem of getting rid of his irrational negative emotions. Rational self-counseling would have been a big help with that problem too.

What Rational Self-Counseling Does and What You Must Do

Rational self-counseling enables you to get rid of undesirable emotional habits without outside help or drugs. And you're always in control. You change the emotional habits you want to change, and keep the others. At the same time, you make yourself relatively independent of other people for almost all of your psychological and emotional support.

The process of rational self-counseling occurs in two stages. The first is rational self-analysis (RSA) and the second is rational emotional re-education. Before beginning stage one (RSA), you first need to learn these three things: How your brain works, what your emotions are, and how they work.

The next three chapters give you that information. Then you will be able to learn rational self-counseling quickly.

Summary

Rational self-counseling is a practical, easy-to-learn method of emotional self-help that has the same essential features professional counseling methods have: It's based on proven facts about how the human brain works and a research-tested concept of human emotions. To counsel yourself rationally, you must know the five rules for rational behavior.

(1) It will be based on objective reality, or the known relevant facts of the situation;

(2) It will enable you to protect your life;

(3) It will enable you to achieve your goals most quickly;

(4) It will enable you to keep out of significant trouble with other people;

(5) It will enable you to prevent or quickly eliminate significant personal emotional conflict.

Rational physical and emotional behavior will meet at least three of these five rules.

Emphasis Questions

Remember, this is not a test. The questions were made easy on purpose. Answers are on the pages shown in parentheses.

(1) Rational self-counseling is a practical method of emotional _____-help.   (P-7)

(2) Rational self-counseling has the two essential features that professional counseling methods have.
True   False   (P-7)

(3) These two features are: It's based on proven facts about how the human _____ works, and it uses a research-tested concept of _____ emotions.   (P-7)

(4) The only effective counseling is _____ counseling.   (P-7)

(5) A negative emotion is rational when it causes you to _____ something that is _____.   (P-13)

(6) A negative emotion that serves no useful purpose is irrational.   True   False   (P-13)

(7) What are the five rules for rational self-counseling?

   1.

   2.

   3.

   4.

   5.

   (P-8)

(8) Rational self-counseling will meet at least _____ of the rules given above.   (P-8)

(9) It is possible for you to be completely rational all of the time.   True   False   (P-10)

(10) What is rational self-counseling for one person may not be rational for another.   True   False   (P-9)

(11) The five rules for rational self-counseling apply to your _____ feelings as well as physical _____.   (P-8)

(12) Some personal emotional conflict and some trouble with other people is possible in most decision making situations; but the amount of conflict or trouble that serves no useful purpose is called a _____ amount.   (P-9)

(13) _____ _____ -counseling will help you decide what is rational for you.   (P-9)

(14) One very common cause of irrational behavior is failure of people to base their behavior on the _____ _____of a situation. (P-10)

(15) Objective reality means what could be shown in a situation by a_____or tape_____or other recording device. (P-10)

(16) If you choose to react to your opinions rather than the facts, your behavior will often be_____. (P-10, 11)

(17) Opinions have *no* influence on how you view facts. True   False   (P-10, 11)

(18) The process of rational self-counseling occurs in _____stages. (P-14)

(19) The first stage in rational self-counseling is _____ self _____ and the second is rational _____ re-_____. (P-14)

(20) To learn to do rational self-counseling well, you must first learn how your_____works and what your_____are and how they_____. (P-14)

CHAPTER 2

YOUR BRAIN AND HOW IT WORKS

Your Brain Controls Your Emotions But You Direct It

Your brain lets you perceive yourself and the outside world. It makes mental images of your perceptions, keeping some and discarding others. Your brain then combines its stored images with your beliefs about them and makes you feel and act accordingly. But since you choose the beliefs you hold, you direct your brain.

For example, one day I was driving to an important meeting with my boss. I was speeding because I was late. Suddenly I noticed flashing red lights in my rear-view mirror. I thought: "Damn! A cop! Just my rotten luck! Now I'll really be late. Damn!" I felt miserable. But as I pulled over, the police car darted around me and kept going. Then I thought: "How about that! He's not after me. That's great! Now I can just about make it." I felt really great. My panic was gone in a flash.

Most people would say that it was the police car that made me upset. That isn't true. In reality, I upset myself with the upsetting thoughts I believed about what I saw. When I saw the police car behind me, I thought and believed angry thoughts, and they made me feel angry. When I saw the police car speed away, I thought and believed happy thoughts, and they made me feel happy. My brain did all the work. But I directed my brain with my thoughts.

When you don't have a brain disease and you are not on drugs, you direct your brain. Therefore, you control your emotions. To control your emotions rationally and enjoy your life more, you need to know a few basic facts about your brain: what its main parts are; how they interact; and how your brain works like a camera.

The two main parts of your brain that control your emotional and physical reactions are:

(A) the neocortex (or thinking part), and
(B) the limbic system (or feeling part).

Millions of nerves link your neocortex and limbic system with each other and with your sense organs (eyes, ears, skin, etc.). Your sense organs cause your brain (neocortex and limbic system) to make you notice and react to yourself and the world. If you first understand how your neocortex and limbic system work separately, you will more readily understand how they work together.

The Neocortex or Thinking Part of Your Brain

This is what you'd see if you took away your skull bones. This is where you notice and form images of yourself and the world. It's also where you think and understand, and where you start, maintain and stop your emotional and physical reactions.

The following fact is very important. Remember it well. Normally your neocortex forces you to notice, be aware, make images and think. *But it doesn't force you to do any one of them in the most rational manner for you.* My experience with the police car shows how easily you can have mistaken thoughts, causing unnecessary emotional upsets. Unfortunately, the neocortex treats mistaken thoughts as if they were factual, if you believe them. If you let that happen to you often, you will suffer needlessly, and enjoy life less than you otherwise would.

The Limbic System or Feeling Part of Your Brain

Your limbic system is deep inside of your brain. Normally it forces you to have emotional feelings; but it lets you choose the ones you have. That's why rational self-counseling can enable you to choose the emotional feelings you *want* to have.

You may be thinking: "Hey! That can't be right. I don't want to feel worthless and afraid of rejection, but I do. I choose to feel worthwhile and unafraid of rejection; but I don't. Explain that to me."

You choose your emotional feelings by your choice of thoughts to believe. In the police car example, I definitely would have preferred *not* to have been needlessly upset when I saw the police car. But, by my mistaken choice of thoughts, I chose to be upset. I didn't have to think and believe: "Damn! What rotten luck!" I could have just as easily and much more rationally thought: "Well, I took a calculated risk and lost. No point in getting upset about it. Next time I'll pay more attention to my schedule or look out more carefully for cops or both."

This is an important point. Remember it! If you are having undesirable emotions, that usually means you are making irrational choices of thoughts. But that doesn't prove that you *want* to feel bad. Instead, it probably means that for as long as you can remember, you have always thought the way you think about yourself and the world. Because of that, you learned the strong emotional feelings you now have.

You probably don't remember ever thinking or feeling differently from the way you do now. So it seems to you that you have no choice in the matter. Or, you may know you have other choices of thoughts and feelings, but your present habits are so strong that you don't think of your other choices at the time you need to make them. In any event, you don't usually make choices you don't see, or think about at the time. Rational self-counseling teaches you to look at all your emotions and change any of them that you want to. That's how rational self-counseling helps you enjoy your life more.

How Your Neocortex and Limbic System Work Together

As the police car example showed, before you have a complete emotion you first notice something; the nerves from your sense organs (eyes, ears, skin, etc.) send nerve impulses to your neocortex. Your neocortex changes those nerve impulses into images and impressions that cause you to see, hear, or physically feel something. Those images and impressions trigger thoughts about what you notice. Your neocortex takes the thoughts that you believe and types them as being:

(A) relatively positive;
(B) relatively negative;
(C) relatively neutral; or
(D) some mixture of those three.

Your thoughts then cause your limbic system to make you have logical feelings for what you believe. In the police car example, when I was thinking and believing angry thoughts, I felt angry. When I saw the police car speed away, I thought and believed happy thoughts and felt great. Later, I thought: "I wonder where he was going?" But I quickly added: "What do I care? It's got nothing to do with me." Because I thought and believed those neutral or indifferent thoughts, my neocortex caused my limbic system to make me feel neutral or indifferent about where the police car was going.

The Human Brain Can Work Like a Lousy Camera

A camera makes picture images of objects and events in the outside world. Your brain makes mental images of them. You can choose to notice and react to the picture images your camera makes, or you can ignore them completely. You can also prevent your camera from making images by leaving the film out. But if you are physically healthy, you don't have those choices with your brain. If you're awake and have a healthy brain, you almost always have to have mental impressions. You also have to notice and react logically to the thoughts you believe about them. If you don't, you'll become thoroughly confused — you may even go completely crazy.

A camera uses light rays from the outside world to make its picture images. In making its mental images, your brain uses nerve impulses. The light rays used by a camera have to come from the world outside the camera. That means every picture image a camera makes stands for something that actually exists in the outside world. Your brain is not that limited. It can get nerve impulses to make its mental images from the outside world, from your memory, and also from your imagination. In addition, your brain doesn't automatically separate the impulses from the outside world from those from your memory or from your imagination. Depending upon how well you direct your brain, it may treat impulses from those three different sources differently; but it may also treat all of its nerve impulses as if they came from the same source. So, if you don't direct your brain carefully, it may work like a lousy camera and make faulty images. Then you may end up reacting to mental images that have very little to do with your real life situation. That's an important insight. Remember it!

Objective reality is the first rule for rational self-counseling. Since your brain can be so unreliable, you need a good way (like the camera rule of thumb) of checking your mental images. Otherwise, your brain may use incorrect images to control your emotional and physical reactions without your realizing it.

Many people find that fact hard to believe. They say: "If I'm looking at something right before my eyes, how can my mental image be wrong?" *Easily*, if you ignore these facts:

(A) What you see is *not* right before your eyes — it's a mental image of it, formed by nerve impulses in the back of your neocortex.

(B) Those nerve impulses may all be coming from what's right before your eyes, but they don't have to be. Many may be coming from your imagination and memory.

(C) Your brain doesn't automatically tell you where its nerve impulses are coming from. You have to direct it to do so. If you don't, needless suffering can result.

For example, Mr. Nathorne lost every penny he had when the banks went broke in the thirties. Everyone on our block knew that. But no one liked to talk about banks to Mr. Nathorne; he'd get upset, and that was bad for his heart. His face would turn red; his breathing would get fast, as if he were about to die; but he would talk on for hours, if someone would listen. He'd say: "I can see it clear as day. There I was with my friends banging on the bank doors. They didn't pay no attention to us. We did it every day for a week, but they didn't open — wouldn't give us our money. Then one day the police came, ran us off and told us not to come back. They said we were disturbing the peace."

Even in the 60's when Mr. Nathorne saw a real bank, or just heard the word "bank", his brain still formed an image of a bank. But the image was thirty years old. The nerve impulses for it came primarily from Mr. Nathorne's memory. He still saw a locked bank door and he and his friends being driven away by the police. And that's what he reacted to. That shows what a lousy camera the human brain will work like, if you don't check it against objective reality.

Lousy camera or not, Mr. Nathorne's mental images of banks were real, vivid and familiar to him. They seemed so real, he never bothered to check them against the real world of modern banking. So it seemed to him that he had no other emotional choice than to hate and distrust banks.

His hate and distrust for banks made Mr. Nathorne keep all of his money in secret hiding places in his house. The neighbors all knew this, but they thought nothing of it — until the day they found Mr. Nathorne murdered, his house turned upside down, and his money gone.

A Healthy Brain Is Not Enough

Many people think that a healthy brain is all they need for good mental and emotional health. They think that a healthy brain will guarantee them rational thoughts. They are wrong; but since they don't even suspect it, they usually react to their sincere beliefs without question. When their beliefs are irrational however, reacting to them causes those people much useless emotional pain. Even so, they usually continue to react blindly to their sincere beliefs.

Jeffrey, a bright, good-looking high school football star, is a good example of such people. He was the kind of teenager about whom people said, "Gee, if I had his brains, talent and looks, I would be Mr. Everything." Yet out of class or off the football field, Jeffrey was a dud.

Three of Jeffrey's friends decided to teach him to play bridge. Jeffrey agreed and started lessons with high hopes of learning how to have fun. But from the first lesson, he was miserable. Everytime he'd make a mistake, he'd get mad at himself and call himself "stupid." Later at home, he'd sit for an hour or two rethinking his mistakes. The more he'd rethink them, the madder he'd get at himself. He'd think: "I should have seen that coming. How could I have been so stupid? What a dumb ass I am! They must really think I'm a blue ribbon dunce. I'm too dumb to learn this game. I may as well face it; I'm just plain dumb."

After the third lesson, Jeffrey began to get depressed at just the thought of bridge, so he stopped thinking about it between lessons. After the fifth lesson, he told his friends: "I've lost interest in bridge. It's just as well because I can't learn it anyway. So why beat my head against a brick wall? I've decided to drop the lessons." So he quit — a victim of his believable but irrational thoughts.

Jeffrey's thoughts were irrational because they:

(A) were *not* based on objective reality;
(B) kept him from reaching his goal of having fun playing bridge;
(C) caused him to have emotions he *didn't* want to have — self-hate, depression, and feelings of inferiority.

Jeffrey's high school offered a course in rational self-counseling. He took it and immediately started to use it on himself. One of the first things he learned was the big difference between merely believable thoughts and rational thoughts. He first saw that difference when he used the five rules for rational thinking to rethink his attempt to learn bridge. This time he thought: "It was foolish of me to expect to play expert bridge from the very beginning. I needed practice and lots of it. I could start taking lessons again and keep at it even if it kills me to make mistakes. But that wouldn't be fun, so that's out. I know I'm not a dumb ass, so it's dumb to call myself that, especially if I turn around and feel as if I believe it. I could take the time to practice more than I did before. I could practice the same amount of time, but be more patient with myself. I could combine both ideas and get the best of all possible results."

Jeffrey continued to think and react to those rational thoughts. That gave him the courage to try bridge again. His more rational thinking quickly stopped his negative feelings about making mistakes, and soon he was playing bridge as well as his friends most of the time — sometimes even better. But whether he played well or not, he now enjoyed playing, and his friends enjoyed playing with him.

Summary

Jeffrey's case clearly shows the value of knowing what your brain does and what you do. Your brain controls your emotional and physical reactions. But you direct your brain with your thoughts. Your brain can't tell if your thoughts are believable but irrational, or believable and rational. You have to do that. Your brain will use either type of thoughts with the same ease and speed in controlling your emotions and physical actions. Rational self-counseling makes your brain favor believable and rational thoughts.

Emphasis Questions

(1) Your _brain_ controls your _emotions_ but you direct it.   (P-17)
(2) What you think and _believe_ about what you notice makes you _feel_ and act the way you do.   (P-17)
(3) The two main parts of your brain for controlling your emotional and physical reactions are your neocortex, or the _thinking_ part of your brain, and your limbic system, or the _feeling_ part of your brain.   (P-17)
(4) You notice and form images of yourself and the world in your _neocortex_ or thinking part of your brain.   (P-18)

(5) You also understand, start, maintain and stop your emotional and physical reactions by using your neocortex.
True   False   (P-18)

(6) Your _neocortex_ or thinking part of your brain forces you to notice, be aware of, and make images and think, but it doesn't force you to do any of them in the most correct or rational manner.   True   False   (P-18)

(7) It is very easy to make mental mistakes and have useless, irrational emotional upsets.   True   False   (P-18)

(8) If you make mental mistakes without realizing it, you may _suffer_ needlessly.   (P-18)

(9) Your _limbic_ or feeling part of your brain forces you to have emotional feelings, but it lets you _decide_ the ones you have.   (P-18)

(10) You choose your emotional feelings by your _choice_ of _thoughts_ (P-18)

(11) If you are having more undesirable emotions than you want, that usually means that you are making irrational choices of thoughts.   True   False   (P-19)

(12) Your neocortex types the thoughts that you believe as being either correct or incorrect.
True   False   (P-19)

(13) The human brain can work like a lousy camera.
True   False   (P-20)

(14) If you don't direct your brain carefully, it will make mental images using impulses from your memory and imagination without your realizing it.
True   False   (P-20)

(15) What you see is right before your eyes.
True   False   (P-20, 21)

(16) If you have a healthy brain, you will be guaranteed good mental and emotional health.   True   False   (P-21)

(17) If people sincerely believe their thoughts, they will often act on them without questioning the validity of them.
True   False   (P-22)

(18) At first Jeffrey made himself a victim of his _believable_ but irrational thoughts.   (P-22)

(19) Rational self-counseling helped Jeffrey see the difference between merely believable and rational thoughts.
True   False   (P-22)

(20) Jeffrey's new way of thinking met at least ___3___ of the five rules for _rational_ thinking.   (P-22, 23)

1. objective reality
2. protected his life
3. achieved his goals
4. kept him out of trouble
5. prevented personal emotional conflict

CHAPTER 3
THE ABC'S OF HUMAN EMOTIONS AND HOW THEY WORK

Part I
COMPLETE HUMAN EMOTIONS

Introduction

Human emotions are one of the most talked about yet most misunderstood of all human behaviors. Most people have the sincere but incorrect belief that an emotional feeling is the whole emotion. They are wrong. The feeling is only one-third of a complete emotion, and it's the least important part.

To most easily see why that is true, think again about the emotions described in Chapter 2. They were all complete emotions. But before those people had their emotional feelings, they first were aware of something. They saw, heard, or physically felt something. Their awareness was their perception. Next, they thought and believed something about their perception. Then their brain (neocortex) automatically evaluated those thoughts, giving them one of four general ratings: relatively positive, relatively negative, relatively neutral or some mixture of all three. That rating was a cue for the limbic system to trigger one of those four types of emotional feelings. That feeling was experienced as an inner urge to act in a corresponding positive, negative, neutral or mixed way.

Suppose you hear this news report on the radio: "Next year the city government plans to double the landing fee for all private airplanes at the local airport." Let's say that you think: "How could they do such a lousy thing! It's unfair! They charge too much already."

Each of those statements implies the unspoken evaluating belief: "It's bad for me." Because of that your brain would evaluate those thoughts negatively. And, if you really believed them, they would trigger negative feelings or urges in you toward that plan. You would feel bad and, if you knew how, you'd act to get that plan stopped.

But suppose you think: "That's great! It's been long overdue to make those free-loading private plane owners pay their fair share of airport expenses."

Every one of those statements implies the unspoken evaluating belief: "It's good for me." Because of that, your brain would evaluate those thoughts positively. And if you really believed them, they would trigger positive feelings or urges in you toward the plan. Then, if you knew how, you'd act to put the plan into action.

Suppose you think: "Who cares? I don't. You couldn't pay me to own a private plane." Each of those statements implies the unspoken evaluating belief: "It's irrelevant for me or I'm neutral about it." Consequently, your brain would evaluate those thoughts neutrally or indifferently. If you were sincere, those thoughts would trigger neutral or indifferent feelings or urges in you toward the plan. Then even though you had the power to stop it, or to put it into action, you'd do neither.

The final possibility is mixed thoughts about the plan — partly positive, partly negative, and partly neutral. In that case your feelings or urges to act would be mixed. If you took any action, you probably wouldn't be as committed to it as you would have been in one of the other three cases.

The important insight to make here is: almost every thought you have implies one type of evaluation. It's your implied or stated evaluation that directs your neocortex (brain's thinking part) to control your emotion.

In the process of growing up most people are taught that it's selfish and bad to always think in terms of themselves first. So by their early teens most people drop the "for me" and soon forget they ever had it after their "It's good, bad or irrelevant," evaluations of their conscious self-talk or thoughts. But whether people know or admit it or not, based on their past experiences, their brains automatically evaluate and rate all of the thoughts they *believe* as having personally positive, negative, neutral or irrelevant meaning for them as people or for their self-concept. Because the brain makes its evaluation automatically, as often as not, people don't notice or they don't bother to describe the evaluations to themselves. But their automatic emotional reactions and sincere physical actions reveal the type evaluations their brain has been (or is being) programmed to make.

The clinical research of Dr. David Graham (now Professor and Chairman, Department of Medicine, University of Wisconsin) demonstrated those facts about human emotions and enabled Dr. Graham to formulate this simple yet scientific definition of human emotions. Human emotions are your physiologic or emotive reactions (i.e. "gut feelings" or inner urges to act) based on what you think, believe and want to do about your perceptions.

Figure 1

The ABC's of Complete Human Emotions

A Complete Emotion { (A) your perceptions
{ (B) your evaluating thoughts
{ (C) your emotive feeling

Again, however, the most important insight to keep in mind here is: Basically there are only four ways you can react — relatively positively, negatively, neutrally, or with some mixture of those three.

Thanks to Dr. Graham's scientific discovery, you can avoid the common confusion that results when you don't know what or who causes your emotive feelings. *You* do it. You do it with the thoughts you believe about your perceptions. Though Dr. Graham proved this fact scientifically less than twenty-five years ago, that knowledge is not new. The Greek philosophers knew it over two thousand years ago. About that time Epictetus said: "It's not facts and events that upset man, but the view he takes of them."

Because Epictetus' idea really was a basic insight into human emotions, it's as true today as it was two thousand years ago. It means that you are mistaken when you say, "He (she or it) makes me mad (or makes me happy, depressed, etc.)." You have those emotions merely because of your learned habit of having them.

Rational self-counseling makes you realize that *you are not a robot!* You don't have to habitually react to yourself or to others like a puppet on a string with useless painful anger, guilt, depression, etc. You have at least three other emotional choices in every life situation. The next three examples demonstrate that is true even when the situation causes you physical pain.

Your Emotional Choices

Imagine that you are on a crowded elevator. A stranger steps on your sore toe, but he immediately apologizes and seems sincere. You'd perceive the pain in your toe and the sincere apology. You'd probably think: "I wish the hell people would pay more attention to where they step. Oh well, he probably didn't mean to do it. He seems to feel as badly about it as I do. I'll just pass it off and forget it. The pain is almost gone now anyway." By choosing to believe those moderately negative-to-neutral thoughts, you'd trigger moderately negative-to-neutral emotive feelings. These feelings would be inner urges to do nothing. So you'd probably label your emotions: mild irritation that turned quickly to calm or forgiving indifference or neutrality.

Now, suppose that instead of a sincere apology, the stranger gave you a dirty look and said, "Put your damn foot in your pocket." Even though your pain would be the same, you'd proba-bly now think or say something like: "You damn idiot, I was standing here out of everybody's way, trying to protect my sore toe and like a blind bull you stomped on it! And now you have the gall to try to put the blame on me! I ought to beat your brains out, you dirty louse." By choosing to believe those strong negative thoughts, you'd trigger strong negative emotive feelings. These feelings would be inner urges to strike out, harm, destroy. So you'd probably label them "anger."

Finally, imagine another stranger stepping on your sore toe, but this time he says nothing and acts as if he doesn't know or care about your toe. Your first thoughts would probably be pretty much the same as above. You'd probably think: "You blind idiot! Why don't you look where you're going?" But then you notice that the man *really is blind*! Now you'd probably think something like: "That poor guy. He really can't see where he's going. Maybe I should have been a little further back out of the way. What the hell. How can you be angry at a blind man? It didn't hurt that bad anyway. I'll just forget it." By choosing to believe that line of thought, you'd go immediately from strong negative emotive feelings to moderately negative feelings to neu-tral feelings. You'd probably describe them as: first anger, then irritation, then indifference or neutrality.

Suppose while you were angry, someone had asked: "Why are you angry?" If you are like most people, you probably would have said: "He made me angry" or "It made me furious when he stepped on my sore toe." The widespread, *incorrect* belief that human emotions are controlled by external forces is so effec-tively taught and so thoroughly learned that even many otherwise objective scientists stubbornly cling to it. Yet the simple, two-thousand year old truth is: There is no magical "He", "She", or "It" that can make you feel any specific emotion against your will. Only if there really were magic could that happen. The simple truth is, when you are angry, glad or whatever, you alone do it. That was true two thousand years ago, and it's still true today.

That is a very important fact. If you remember it, you'll avoid or quickly eliminate most of your useless and otherwise irrational negative emotions. Why? Because negative emotions are painful. Most intelligent people refuse to voluntarily cause themselves needless or useless physical pain; but many of those same people willingly suffer needless, useless anger, depression, and other kinds of emotional pain, primarily because they refuse to admit that they themselves are causing it. They stubbornly accuse "he", "she", or "it" of causing it or doing it to them. But, as soon as these same intelligent people sincerely admit to causing their own suffering, they quickly cut down the amount they have. Why? Because it's irrational to sincerely and knowingly cause yourself needless, useless suffering.

Suppose in the previous example you had accidentally bumped your own sore toe against the wall of the elevator. You might have felt irritated at yourself; you may even have called yourself stupid, dumb, etc. But, you wouldn't have gotten nearly as angry at yourself as you would have gotten at the guy in the second example who said, "Put your damn foot in your pocket." Why not? Because anger is a painful emotion. You don't like to suffer. So you *wouldn't* choose to cause yourself useless emotional pain, if you knew beforehand that would be what you'd be doing. You have that same emotional choice when other people do things that you don't like.

At this point, people often ask: "Dr. Maultsby, do you mean to say that you wouldn't get angry if somebody stepped on your sore toe and then told you to put your damn foot in your pocket?" *No*, I do not mean to say that at all. I might well get angry. But, that wouldn't mean that I couldn't keep from getting angry. In addition, it doesn't matter that I or most people might get angry in such a situation. That fact doesn't mean that anyone of us would have to do it. Instead, it merely means that we have the well-learned habit of doing it.

Many people then ask: "Are you saying that people

shouldn't get angry?" No, *I'm not* saying that people shouldn't get angry. All I'm saying is that people have three choices about their anger:

(1) when to get angry,
(2) how much to get angry,
(3) how long to stay angry.

They also have those same choices about any other emotion. Again, I want to emphasize that rational self-counseling does *not* try to teach you which emotions you should or shouldn't have. It merely teaches you what your emotional choices are.

Anger is a negative emotion. Useless, negative emotions are the most common reasons people don't enjoy their lives more. That's why it is good to keep in mind that you always have at least four personal choices about your emotions.

Emotional Ignorance as a Cause of Needless Pain

When I was in the U.S. Air Force, I was sent to Japan. I liked Japan and began to study Japanese. At first, the Japanese people could understand what I said to them much better than I could understand what they said to me. One night I wandered into a Japanese nightclub where Americans were not welcomed. I didn't know that then. Since no one there seemed to speak English, I thought it would be a good time to practice my Japanese. I quickly started talking to two pretty hostesses. They smiled and talked back to me. Everything seemed great. Other customers close by joined in the conversation. Soon a group of us were laughing and talking and having a good time.

Although I was able to make myself understood, I didn't understand much of what the others said to me. But everybody seemed to be having fun, so I didn't think much about it.

In terms of what emotions are made of, I noticed smiling faces and people talking and joking with me. I thought: "Oh Boy! What a lucky break for me! Such friendly people, helping me practice my Japanese." My positive thoughts triggered positive emotive feelings and I felt really happy.

Immediately after my daily Japanese class the following day, I asked my teacher to translate some of the words I had heard but hadn't understood the night before. To my surprise, many of the words were not good; some were frankly insulting to me and the American military in general.

I immediately got angry; I mean, I was furious. I had a strong inner urge (anger) to go back to that nightclub, tear it up and everybody in it. I don't know when I was that angry before. Lucky for me, though, I wasn't so upset that I was blind to the deep trouble I would be in if I acted the way I felt.

Before my teacher told me what the people had said, I had positive beliefs about them. I felt good every time I thought about them and that night. After I found out what they had said, I had negative beliefs about them. I felt miserable every time I thought about them and that night. I then thought: "Those dirty SOB's! How could they do that to me? They made a fool out of me. They made me look like a perfect ass. That was a dirty rotten trick to pull on me," etc. With beliefs like that, I couldn't help but feel miserable. If I had not felt miserable, my thoughts would have seemed meaningless. But my thoughts were extremely *meaningful* to me; so I had to feel miserable.

My anger triggered another emotion — fear, fear of getting into real trouble. My fear kept me from acting on my anger. So all I did was feel hopelessly and helplessly miserable.

I suffered because I was ignorant. I sincerely believed that they — the people in the nightclub — were making me feel miserable. I never dreamed that I was doing it. That's why I *didn't* immediately make myself feel better.

By refusing to act out my anger, I proved that an emotion is merely an inner *urge* to act; you *don't* have to act on it. Since I wasn't going to act on my angry feelings, they were useless to me. I would have been much better off without them.

Unfortunately for me, I didn't know then about rational self-counseling. But if I had just had the habit of applying the first rule for rational thinking to my thoughts, I might have looked more at the facts of the situation and less at my opinions about it. Then I could have seen right away how silly it was of me to blame the people in the nightclub for the way I felt. They had *neither* fooled me *nor* made a fool out of me. I had fooled myself. So I was angry at them for what I had done to myself. But my most painful mistake of all was believing that I had no other emotional choice than to feel miserable.

Granted, the behavior of the other people toward me made it easy for me to fool myself. And most people who understand as little Japanese as I did then would probably have made my mistake. But that fact is irrelevant. The important facts are:

(1) I fooled myself.
(2) I, alone, made myself feel the way I felt.
(3) If I had known what my emotional choices were, I would have felt differently about the event.

But people can't act on knowledge they don't have. So I did the only thing I could do; I counseled myself like most people counsel themselves.

After a week or so of feeling miserable, I decided: "This is ridiculous. I have suffered enough. I refuse to let it bother me anymore. I will just put the whole damn thing out of my mind, pretend it never happened, forget I'm even in Japan." I quit my Japanese lessons, ignored my few sincere Japanese friends, and stayed on base for seven straight weeks. And as long as I was busy and didn't think about the incident, I felt almost normal most of the time. But when I was alone with nothing to do, I felt depressed. It was a mild depression though, and I could easily distract myself most of the time. Still, I was suffering more than I wanted to.

About three months later, I decided to stop pretending the event had never happened. Instead, I turned it into a big joke. I began to tell funny stories about it to anyone who would listen. Soon, I became completely indifferent to the matter. Then I got bored with it and began to forget about it, first for days, then weeks and finally months at a time.

Summary

The ABC's of a complete emotion are:

(A) your perceptions,
(B) your evaluating thoughts, and
(C) your emotive feelings.

Since you control your thoughts, you alone control your emotional feelings. How rationally you control them is your personal choice.

Part II
ABBREVIATED EMOTIONS

Introduction

After most people read about the ABC's of complete human emotions, they have some reservations. They say: "That's fine as far as it goes. But that can't be the whole story for all of my emotions. Many, many times, I just have feelings and I'm not thinking about anything in particular. Some mornings I just wake up feeling anxious or depressed and that's all there is to it. So there must be more than the ABC's to my emotions." Those people are right. The ABC's tell the whole story *only* about complete emotions: that is, your emotions as they are when you first learn them.

Your Attitudes, Beliefs and Abbreviated Emotions

The key word here is *habit*. When you habitually think the same type of positive, negative or neutral thoughts about your similar specific perceptions or images of external events, you began to get the same type of positive, negative or neutral emotive feelings about those perceptions or images. Then your brain is doing two important things: (1) It's converting your emotional habits into basic or relatively permanent personality traits. (2) It's producing basic or relatively permanent attitudes and beliefs.

Figures 2 and 3 below enable you to see the relationship between your complete and your abbreviated emotions.

Figure 2	Figure 3
Your Complete Emotions	Your Abbreviated Emotions
(A) Your specific perceptions	(Specific A's & Habitual B's)
(B) Your habitual evaluating thoughts	or
	Attitudes or Beliefs
plus	plus
(C) Your habitual inner urges or emotive feelings	(C) Your habitual inner urges or emotive feelings

The key insight to make here is: Your attitudes and beliefs are merely different mental forms of your habitually paired perceptions and thoughts. But their difference in form causes you to be both emotionally flexible and spontaneous.

Attitudes cause people to go from "A" in Figure 2, to "C" in one step. Because of this, most people get the mistaken impression that the external event, perceived at "A" causes their emotive feelings at "C." In reality, it's always their own well learned attitudes about their perceptions at "A" that cause their feelings at "C".

Beliefs cause people to go from "B" in Figure 2, to "C" in one step. That's why you can sit at home and imagine or remember an external event and get a logical feeling at "C."

Most people have negative attitudes and beliefs about child molesters and positive attitudes and beliefs about their favorite movie stars. Consequently, at the mere sight of a child molester, most people react automatically with negative emotions; and at the mere sight of their favorite movie star most people react automatically with positive emotions. In both cases, their attitudes trigger their emotions without there being time to think first. And because beliefs are merely different mental forms of attitudes, those people will have the same emotions described above if they just believe that a child molester or their favorite movie star is in their neighborhood. Their beliefs will make it *unnecessary* for these people to have to see anyone before having their usual emotional reactions.

The following examples of how children form some of their basic or life-long emotional habits will make those facts about attitudes and beliefs easier to see. When most children are learning their basic or abbreviated emotions (between two and ten years of age), they usually learn that receiving smiles from others usually means: "They are friendly; they like me; they want to be my friend," etc. And whether children actually think it or not, "That's good for me" is the usual evaluation their brain gives those types of thoughts.

Naturally then, children get into the habit of feeling good when they receive smiles. Usually normal children, in normal families, quickly reach the stage of basic or abbreviated emotional reaction to smiles. Then, just the sight of a smiling face usually triggers an automatic good feeling; there is no need to think about it first. In addition, just the thought of a smiling face will trigger good feelings, even though no smiling face is in sight. Those abbreviated emotions mean the children have formed friendly attitudes and beliefs about smiling faces.

Because the human brain can work like a lousy camera, it isn't necessary to have objectively good, bad or neutral real life experiences for children (or adults) to form corresponding attitudes and beliefs. For example, most young children *don't* fear snakes. Two year olds will pick up a snake if they can catch it. But most adults are usually afraid of snakes. Even if a toy rubber snake is dropped in their lap, most adults will automatically be frightened, without having had time to think first. Yet *very few* adults have ever had an objectively dangerous experience with a real snake. How then have most adults learned to fear snakes even though they have never had a dangerous experience with a real one? Easily! They learned by practicing feeling afraid in response to their fearful beliefs about snakes.

From the time most children begin to talk, almost every statement they hear about snakes is a fearful statement. When children are young, they can immediately have a logical emotion for almost any thought they think. So when they think or say: "Snakes are dangerous. They kill people. Oh! They're scary! They're sneaky! You have to watch out for them," children immediately feel afraid. Having the same feeling over and over in response to the same thoughts is one of the most rapid ways to form strong beliefs. Consequently, by the time most children reach age ten, just the thought of a snake being close to them triggers an automatic fear, even though no snake is in sight. Most people continue that habitual fear reaction into adulthood.

This is an important point. Remember it! Each of those statements about snakes implies the second unspoken statement: "That's bad for me." That evaluation, (i.e. unspoken belief or attitude) was always implied, no matter what sentences those children thought or said about snakes. So, at the same time the children were learning to feel afraid at the mere sight of snakes, they were also learning to feel afraid at the mere thought of one.

Figure 4	Figure 5
Complete Fear Reaction to Snakes	Abbreviated Fear Reaction to Snakes
(A) Sight of snakes	(A) Sight of snakes
(B) Evaluating Thoughts	There are *no* "B's" (evaluating thoughts) now. The brain has made them a part of its habitual image of a snake, indicating that an attitude has been formed.
(1) Snakes are dangerous!	
(2) They are scary!	
(3) etc.	
(C) Inner feeling of fear	(C) Inner feeling of fear

In other words, when your brain forms an attitude, it can skip your old B's (Figure 4) forcing you to go from A to C (Figure 5) in one step.

Equally as important, when your brain forms a belief, it can skip your old A (Figure 6 below), forcing you to go from B to C (Figure 6) in one step.

Figure 6
(A) Perceptions — None
(B) Evaluating Thoughts
   (1) Snakes are dangerous!
   (2) They are scary!
   (3) etc.
(C) Inner feeling of fear

In summary, it is not the snake that makes you feel afraid. The snake may not even be there. The causes of your fear are your fearful attitudes or beliefs about snakes. Although most adults cannot remember reacting in any other way to snakes, their fear is nevertheless a learned reaction which has become an abbreviated emotion: see or think snake and feel fear.

What you call your personality or nature is nothing more than your abbreviated emotions. The chef who explodes if you criticize his cooking, or a beauty who gets depressed about a five pound weight gain — both people are merely practicing their well learned abbreviated emotions.

Remember the two thousand year old observation about human emotions: "It's not facts and events that upset people, but the view they take of them." That ageless insight is what makes rational self-counseling both possible and practical.

A Personal Example of How Attitudes and Beliefs Work

My nightclub experience in Japan (Part I of this chapter) was a good example of that. In the Japanese nightclub that night, I heard the insulting Japanese words for "dirty American military swine," but I didn't get angry. Not knowing what the words meant, I didn't know how to evaluate them. But I saw people smiling when they talked to me. In my past experiences, my brain had formed a friendly attitude using images of smiling faces. That friendly attitude triggered friendly, happy feelings in me, even though to have felt insulted, angry or embarrassed would have been more logical for the real situation.

Even though my friendly attitude automatically triggered my friendly feelings without me needing to think friendly thoughts first, abbreviated emotions can't maintain themselves. So to keep my friendly feelings going I had to quickly start thinking and mistakenly keep believing happy thoughts.

Figures 7 and 8 below show the relationship between my abbreviated happy emotions in the nightclub and my old complete emotions (from my early childhood) which originally caused and kept my friendly feelings going that night.

My friendly attitude (Figure 7) consisted of mental images of smiling faces — plus the now implied or unspoken "That's good for me," part of B in Figure 8. Because that evaluation had been understood for so long, I no longer needed to actually think it, nor the old thoughts formerly associated with it.

Figure 7
AN ABC DIAGRAM OF MY
ABBREVIATED HAPPY
EMOTIONS

A — Facts and Events
   Smiling Japanese people.

At first, there were no
B — evaluating thoughts or
self-talk. My long standing but
now unspoken friendly
beliefs, i.e. my friendly
attitude toward smiles caused
my feelings at "C" below.

*C — Emotional Consequences
of A & B*
Happiness, friendliness
(felt good)

Figure 8
AN ABC DIAGRAM OF MY
COMPLETE HAPPY
EMOTIONS

A — Facts and Events
   Smiling faces

*B — Evaluating Thoughts or
Self-Talk*

(1) They are friendly, and
    that's good for me.

(2) They like me, and *that's
    good for me.*

(3) They want to be friends,
    and *that's good for me.*

*C — Emotional Consequences
of A & B*
Happiness, friendliness
(felt good)

The next day I immediately got angry after I learned the negative things the people in the nightclub had actually said to me. I was then reacting to my negative beliefs about what I thought they had done to me. And again, to keep my anger going, I immediately had to add angry thoughts. I thought: "Those dirty SOB's made an ass of me," and all such irrational nonsense as that. But because I sincerely believed my irrational nonsense, from then on, when I thought about that night in the nightclub, my negative, angry *beliefs* triggered negative, angry feelings (at "C" in Figure 9) even though I was no longer hearing nor seeing those people.

Figure 9
MY ABBREVIATED ANGRY
EMOTION DEMONSTRATING
HOW BELIEFS WORK

*A — External Event (the
nightclub)*
Not present; I had only my
memory of it plus my
evaluating thoughts or

B — Evaluating Self-Talk

(1) Those SOB's. How could
    they do that to me? That's
    terrible.

(2) They made an ass of me.
    That's bad.

(3) They were unfair to me.
    That's awful . . . etc.

C — Emotion
Anger, embarrassment, insult
(I felt miserable.)

That explains how beliefs (i.e. a memory or an imaginary external event plus your actual thoughts) carry you from B, (the thought or self-talk part of your abbreviated emotion) to the C or feeling part of it, without needing a real external event. But you alone still direct and therefore control the whole process.

Summary

Your well-learned attitudes and beliefs trigger your well learned habitual emotional feelings automatically. But you have to add logical, corresponding conscious thoughts to keep those feelings going.

Regardless of how your emotions get started, you can still change them by changing your conscious thoughts and their implied attitudes or beliefs. Your sincere thoughts reflect or indicate what your attitudes and beliefs are. This is an important fact. *Remember it well!* You will make use of it when you are learning to do rational self-analysis of your abbreviated emotions (Chapter 14).

Figure 2	Figure 3
Complete Emotions	Abbreviated Emotions
(A) Perceptions	(A + B)
(B) Evaluating thoughts plus	Attitude or Belief plus
(C) Inner urges or your emotive feelings	(C) Inner urges or your emotive feelings

Emphasis Questions

(1) Human emotions are the _____ talked about yet most _____ of all human behavior. (P-27)

(2) Three types of mental evaluations or ratings that your brain automatically makes of every one of your perceptions are: relatively _____, relatively _____ or relatively _____. (P-27)

(3) You prove that this is a fact every day when you feel _____ in response to your positive beliefs and you feel negatively in response to your _____ beliefs, and you feel neutral or indifferent in response to your _____ beliefs. (P-28)

(4) A complete emotion is composed of your _____ and your evaluating _____ and your emotive feelings. (P-29)

(5) Is the statement, "He made me mad," a rational statement?   Yes   No   (P-31)

(6) Rational self-counseling tries to teach you the emotions you should and must have.   True   False   (P-32)

(7) Rational self-counseling tries to teach you never to get angry.   True   False   (P-32)

(8) Useless _____ emotions are the most common reason people are unhappy. (P-32)

(9) When people are ignorant of the scientific facts about their emotions, they often experience needless emotional pain.   True   False   (P-32)

(10) If you're not going to act on your miserable feelings, then they are probably useless feelings to have.
True   False   (P-33)

(11) If someone fools you, that means that they have made a fool out of you.   True   False   (P-33)

(12) Even though you get upset about something, that does not mean that you had no other emotional choice.
True   False   (P-32)

(13) Even though we demonstrate every day that we control our emotions, most people still stubbornly cling to the incorrect belief that their emotions are controlled by some magical, external "it" or by other people.
True   False   (P-31)

(14) Even though you may hate feeling depressed, if you are ignorant about who controls your emotions, you may suffer needlessly.   True   False   (P-33)

(15) Needless suffering is the price you pay for being ignorant of the facts about how your emotions work.
True   False   (P-33)

(16) The ABC explanation of human emotions tells the whole story only about complete emotions.
True   False   (P-35)

(17) By practicing complete emotions year after year, you transform them into abbreviated emotions.
True   False   (P-35)

(18) The "B" part drops out of your complete emotions when you form attitudes.   True   False   (P-37)

(19) When your attitude triggers your emotions, you seem to go from A to C in one _____.   (P-37)

(20) Attitudes and beliefs are merely well learned pairs of old perceptions and thoughts.   True   False   (P-35)

CHAPTER 4
NEW EMOTIONAL LEARNING AND EMOTIONAL RE-EDUCATION

Introduction

Whether you're learning new physical habits or new emotional habits, you use your brain in the same way. Understanding the stages and process of any new learning will help you to understand the stages and process of new emotional learning. Understanding both types of new learning will help you quickly understand emotional re-education.

New learning occurs in four stages:

First, your neocortex (your brain's thinking part) gives you intellectual insight into the action to be learned and a mental map of it.

Second, your neocortex uses that mental map to direct you in the correct practice of the new action.

Third, while you are practicing, your neocortex causes your limbic system (your brain's feeling part) to make your new action feel right; that is, it gives you emotional insight — the correct normal, natural, emotional feeling state for the new action.

Fourth, with emotional insight plus consistent practice, you turn the new action into a relatively permanent personality trait.

NEW LEARNING

Intellectual Insight

That's merely understanding what you are to learn. For example, on my first day in driver's ed class, I was supposed to learn the correct way to start a car.

My teacher said, "Watch me closely as I tell you and show you each step in starting a car. The first thing you do is put your left foot on the brake pedal; next, push the gear stick as far to the left as possible; then the car is in park. Even though it looks like it's already in park, push the gear stick to the left anyway. You want to get in the habit of doing it without thinking about it. Next, put your right foot on the gas pedal and the key in the ignition. Then turn the key to the right as far as possible and hold it there until the engine catches. Next, release the key while pressing lightly on the gas pedal. You got it?"

I said, "Yeah."

That's how I got intellectual insight into the driving actions I was to learn.

My Mental Map

He then said, "Okay, close your eyes and picture yourself in your mind doing it as you repeat after me: "When I get into a car, the first thing I do is put my left foot on the brake pedal . . .", etc. He talked me through each step while I kept my eyes closed and pictured myself in my mind doing those things.

Then he said, "Okay, open your eyes and go through it for real and start the car. Pay attention to the feel of doing each step right."

I went through the whole routine without a mistake.

Emotional Insight

That's getting the correct emotional feeling for what you are learning so that you will *feel* right when you are acting right. You can get it in two ways:

    (A) doing actual practice; and
    (B) doing mental practice called emotive imagery.*

After I had started the car correctly a couple of times, my teacher said: "Now, close your eyes and repeat each step in your mind, and this time make yourself feel exactly the same way you felt when you actually did it right, a minute ago."

That was emotive imagery: practicing the feeling state (emotional insight) for the action I was learning. After I practiced that a couple of times, the teacher had me start the car again. Then we were ready for the next lesson — driving and stopping. And with that and every new lesson, we repeated the same four steps:

---

*Actual practice is really a combination of emotive imagery and real life action.

first, intellectual insight with a mental map;
second, correct practice;
third, emotional insight;
fourth, emotional insight plus consistent practice.

Now let's look at what was happening in my brain.

Every time I drove the car correctly (actual practice) my neocortex caused my limbic system to make me feel right: have the same correct, normal, natural emotional feeling that goes with correct driving actions. Also, when I merely thought about the correct way to drive (emotive imagery), I'd get the same correct emotional feelings. By combining physical practice with emotive imagery, I learned to drive in the fastest way possible.

In emotional learning, the learning process is the same. For example, let's look again at how Jeffrey, (the high school bridge player in Chapter 2), learned the new emotion of hating bridge.

Jeffrey's understanding or belief (intellectual insight) was that only a stupid dumb ass would make the mistakes he made. He also believed that a stupid dumb ass should feel bad. He had a well-learned mental map for feeling bad about his mistakes. So every time he made a mistake at bridge, he'd call himself a stupid dumb ass. His mental map in his neocortex for feeling bad would cause his limbic system to make him feel bad. But his bad feeling felt right, i.e. appropriate, logical, correct.

That's an important point. Remember it well. Jeffrey felt bad, but right. Every time he repeated that bad feeling, he was learning to associate playing bridge with feeling bad. But what was worse, he was practicing his habit of feeling bad every time he made a mistake.

Later, when Jeffrey would sit in his room thinking about his last bridge lesson, he'd feel bad all over again. That was mental practice (emotive imagery) in feeling bad when playing bridge as well as when making mistakes. Because he felt bad both when playing bridge and when just thinking about it, he was learning to dislike bridge in the fastest way possible. Soon, real bridge games or just the thought of them would trigger an automatic bad feeling in Jeffrey. That's when he incorrectly decided that bridge wasn't for him: but his decision felt right.

Whether people are learning to drive a car in the fastest way possible or learning to hate bridge in the fastest way possible, their neocortex and limbic system work together.

EMOTIONAL RE-EDUCATION
or
REPLACING AN OLD HABIT WITH A NEW ONE

Introduction

You use your brain in the same way whether you're replacing an old physical habit or an old emotional habit with a new one. That's *the most* important insight you need for quick success in rational emotional re-education. But, it is a little harder to get rid of a lifelong emotional habit than it was to learn it.

When you are learning your first habit of emotional reaction to a new event (say, driving a car), that's emotional *ed*ucation. You have only four clear cut learning stages to master, and you rarely get confused. But replacing that first emotional habit with a new one is a little bit different process: it's emotional *re-ed*ucation. You have five learning stages to master — the same four in emotional *ed*ucation *plus* a new third stage called cognitive dissonance.*

Most people don't know about cognitive dissonance. That's why they usually get confused and frustrated by it when they try to replace unwanted emotional habits, without professional help. In their frustration they usually end up concluding that they can't succeed at emotional re-education. Then they go back to their old emotional habit, even though they don't want it, and they are made miserable by it. To avoid that fate, you must clearly understand cognitive dissonance.

What Is Cognitive Dissonance?

Cognitive dissonance is the *unavoidable* third stage of all habit re-education: mental, physical and emotional. It's unavoidable because the limbic system (feeling part of your brain) always lags behind the neocortex (thinking part of your brain) in the re-education process.

Cognitive dissonance is when you know how to do the correct or best thing, but you feel wrong when you do it. In fact, you feel as if you should be doing just the opposite thing. Your best or most correct behavior then feels like your worst or most incorrect behavior.

---

* The concept of cognitive dissonance used in rational self-counseling is more precisely defined and restricted in its use than the concept used in most introductory psychology courses. For the time being, just forget your psych 101. It won't help you get an emotional re-education.

My experience in Japan with driver re-education will give you a clear insight into cognitive dissonance. After I had been in Japan for three months, I bought a Japanese car.

I had had three months to thoroughly understand (get intellectual insight into) Japanese cars and Japanese-style driving. I understood that Japanese cars and traffic are the opposite to ours. I knew the steering wheel, etc., is on the right side of the car, and in Japan you drive on the left side of the road. But when I got my car, I still had a problem. In spite of my vivid mental map for Japanese driving, I didn't feel right doing it. That meant I didn't have emotional insight (the correct normal, natural emotional feeling) for doing it.

For several weeks, every time I drove my car, the thinking part of my brain (my neocortex) correctly directed me to drive on the left side of the road. But the feeling part of my brain (my limbic system) made me feel as if I was wrong. So I had a constant strong urge (gut feeling) to go back to right sided driving. And the moment I'd stop thinking about it, I'd find myself on the right (*but wrong*) side of the road.

I was in the third stage (cognitive dissonance) of driver re-education. My limbic system was lagging behind my neocortex. That made them work against each other. And it put me in the uncomfortable spot of thinking right, but feeling wrong. In other words, I understood how to drive a car in Japan, but I hadn't thoroughly learned to do it yet. But that didn't mean I couldn't learn to drive in Japan. Because I realized that fact, I *didn't* give up trying to learn Japanese driving.

My learning problem in driver re-education was more complex than my learning problem was when I first learned to drive. Then, I merely had to learn correct driving habits. In Japan, I *not only* had to learn new correct driving habits, I had to replace my old ones with the new ones.

Old habits don't just roll over and die. Instead, they actively compete with the new habits you are trying to learn. That makes you feel uncomfortable and get confused. When you are in driver re-education, that confusion can cause you to become a traffic hazard. And you can accumulate traffic points against your license so fast, you won't believe it. That's what happened to me in Japan.

The obvious solution to my driving problem was just more practice. But for me in Japan that wasn't quite as simple as it sounds. Japan had strict traffic laws, a high accident rate and polite but rigid cops. Within two weeks, I had three quick traffic tickets and no more traffic points to lose. Either I would learn to drive Japanese-style fast, or I'd be walking. That's when I remembered my high school driving class and mental practice on emotive imagery.

Every day for the next three weeks I followed this rigid schedule. Every two hours for ten minutes I did emotive imagery on driving wrong, which actually meant *correct driving* for Japan. I pictured myself going to my car on the left side of the street, opening the *RIGHT* door, getting behind the *RIGHT*-sided steering wheel, looking back over my *RIGHT* shoulder for traffic coming from behind me on my *RIGHT* side, etc. And most important, while doing emotive imagery, I made myself feel perfectly natural, normal and *RIGHT*.

By combining daily mental practice (emotive imagery) with just one or two hours per week of actual driving practice, I eliminated my cognitive dissonance fast. In fact, the change was so fast I could have kicked myself for my three tickets and lost traffic points. But I didn't get any more tickets, so I was none the worse for them.

At some time in their lives, most people replace an old habit of doing something with a new one. So most people understand the problem I had in learning to drive in Japan. But most people *mistakenly* believe that emotional habits are different from physical habits. Consequently, they refuse to work as hard, or as long at changing bad emotional habits as they work at changing bad physical habits.

With their emotional habits, most people make one or two sincere trials at changing them, experience cognitive dissonance and give up. Then they make the worst mistake of all; they *incorrectly* decide that:

(A) they can't change; or
(B) they can't change without expensive, long-term psychotherapy.

Jeffrey (the bridge player in Chapter 2) was a good example of what happens when people believe they can't change. During the third lesson of his first trial at learning bridge, Jeffrey made an obvious goof and got so angry at himself, he wanted to quit playing right then. But the game had just started. The other three players wanted to go on playing, so they talked Jeffrey into staying. They said: "Man, you take this game too seriously. It's just a game; so don't be so hard on yourself. You're supposed to enjoy it; have fun. Okay?"

Jeffrey stayed, but he didn't play seriously. In fact, he began to make stupid plays on purpose and joke about it. The other three guys didn't like that either. One said: "Look man, being a beginner is one thing, but being a stupid beginner is ridiculous. If that's your game, man, let's just quit. To hell with you, buddy."

By that time the others had lost interest too; so they quit. Jeffrey felt bad about that. He said: "Look you guys, I'm really sorry. I know I made an ass of myself. But don't give up on me. Look, I promise, next week I'll play it straight. When I make a stupid mistake, it'll really be because I'm stupid. And I won't joke about it either. Okay?"

"Yeah, but I'd just as soon see you joke about it as see you get so mad you want to break up the game."

"Okay, okay, okay! I won't get mad. I promise. I won't get mad! Even if it kills me I'll smile, but I won't joke. That's a promise. Okay?"

"Okay, man, that's cool; come on, let's go get a beer or something."

The next week Jeffrey did everything he said. He played seriously. He made honest mistakes. But he *didn't* joke nor throw a temper tantrum about them. He just passed them off with: "Oh well, it's just a game. It's not like it's the end of the world. Don't give up, old buddy. We'll get even with this hand."

That's what he said. But inside, his gut was churning. He was just as uptight and mad as ever. That was *cognitive dissonance*. He knew it was wrong, even stupid to feel so miserable. He really didn't want to be angry. But he was; and deep down he felt right — like he damn well ought to have been mad. So he called himself a phony for not showing what he really felt: "madder 'en Hell!"

The other three players felt good about Jeffrey's behavior, and they told him so. "Man, you are really getting with it. We knew you could do it. In no time, you'll be playing better than any of us. Come on, let's get a beer."

So, in spite of his churning gut, Jeffrey decided to give bridge one more try. But the next time was as bad as before. That's when Jeffrey decided: "Bridge just isn't my game. I can't do it."

Fortunately, Jeffrey was wrong. Most people can replace almost any bad physical or emotional habit with a better one. But, they must:

- (A) have average intelligence;
- (B) follow the directions in Section II of this book; and
- (C) work at least as hard as I did to learn to drive in Japan.

In the end Jeffrey proved that point.

How Long Will It Take?

Right after people get started in emotional re-education, they want to know: "How long will I have to practice?" The most accurate, honest answer always is: "You'll have to practice as long as it takes for you to get the result you want."

At first, most people think I'm just trying to be funny when I tell them that. To get them to see that I'm sincere and that it's really helpful to keep that answer in mind, I give them this advice. Think of the thinking part of your brain (your neocortex) as being a rider; and think of the feeling part of your brain (your limbic system) as being a horse.

When you start emotional re-education, your neocortex is like a rider who has ridden his horse up and down the same straight road to work for ten years. Until now, he could trust the horse to take him to and from work with little or no direct control. But recently the rider moved to another part of town. Instead of a straight road to work, he now has to make one right turn on the way out and a left turn on the way back.

From the very first day after the move, the rider (the neocortex) remembers and makes the correct turns without mistakes. But the horse (the limbic system) doesn't. Instead, it has a strong urge to go straight down the road, just as it has for the past ten years. The horse will require time and lots of practice in being guided around the correct turns, before it learns to make them without being directed.

How long will it take before the horse learns to make the correct turns automatically? No one can say beforehand. Every horse differs in its ability to learn. Every rider differs in ability and willingness to teach his horse. The rider who gives his horse the most practice will teach his horse to make the correct turns without direction in the shortest time possible.

The same logic applies to people who are giving themselves a rational emotional re-education. Those who consistently practice the rational self-counseling method of emotional re-education will emotionally re-educate themselves in the shortest time possible. But *it will still take as long as it takes.*

Summary

Whether you're doing physical re-education or emotional re-education, you use your brain in the same way. But in emotional *re-ed*ucation you have one more step to master than you have in emotional *ed*ucation. The five steps in emotional *re-ed*ucation are:

> first, intellectual insight with a mental map;
> second, correct practice;
> third, cognitive dissonance;
> fourth, emotional insight;
> fifth, emotional insight plus consistent practice causing you to form a relatively permanent personality trait.

Remember that cognitive dissonance is the *unavoidable* third stage in all habit re-education. Unless you resolve it in favor of new emotional insight, you will never re-educate yourself emotionally. To resolve cognitive dissonance fastest in favor of rational emotional insight, you must consistently practice the rational self-counseling techniques: rational self-analysis (next, Chapter 5) and rational emotive imagery (Chapter 7).

Emphasis Questions

(1) Your brain works in the same way whether you are learning new physical habits or new _____ habits. (P-43)

(2) New learning occurs in _____ stages: name at least three of them.   (P-43)

(3) The first stage of new learning is _____ insight.   (P-43)

(4) Intellectual insight means understanding what you are to learn.   True   False   (P-43)

(5) The second stage in your new learning is when your _____ uses your mental _____ to direct you in the correct practice of the new action.   (P-43)

(6) The third stage in new learning is when your neocortex causes your limbic system to give you _____ insight.   (P-43)

(7) Emotional insight means having the correct emotional feeling for what you are learning.
True   False   (P-43)

(8) You can develop emotional insight two ways: _____ practice, or _____ practice. (P-44)

(9) Another term for the use of mental practicing is _____ _____. (P-44)

(10) Your brain works differently when it replaces old emotional habits with new ones than when it replaces old physical habits with new ones.   True   False   (P-46)

(11) There are _____ stages in habit re-education. (P-46)

(12) The third stage in emotional re-education is _____ _____. (P-46)

(13) Cognitive dissonance is unavoidable because the limbic system always lags behind the neocortex in the re-education process.   True   False   (P-46)

(14) Cognitive dissonance is caused by the fact that in re-education your _____ _____ always lags behind your _____. (P-46)

(15) Cognitive dissonance is a fun experience; people usually like it.   True   False   (P-46)

(16) In your own words, briefly define cognitive dissonance. (P-46)

(17) Most people give up trying to replace an undesirable emotional habit when they are in _____ _____. (P-48)

(18) Then they _____ decide that they _____ change their emotional habits. (P-48)

(19) Everybody can replace almost any bad emotional habit with a better one, if: (A) they have _____ _____; (B) they follow _____; (C) they work _____. (P-50)

(20) How long does it take for emotional re-education? _____ (P-50, 51)

SECTION II

EMOTIONAL RE-EDUCATION THROUGH RATIONAL SELF-COUNSELING

Overview:

Rational emotional re-education through rational self-counseling occurs in three major phases:

(A) *First, you get rational intellectual insight. (Chapter 5)*

(B) *Second, you understand and avoid the "phony-fear." (Chapter 6)*

(C) *Third, you do rational emotional imagery, REI, (Chapter 7).*

CHAPTER 5

RATIONAL SELF-ANALYSIS (RSA)* or
The ABC's of Stopping Unhappiness Fast

Rational self-analysis (RSA) is exactly that. It's your rational analysis of how you directed your brain to control your emotional reactions to facts or events. Because RSA analyzes your emotions, the RSA format is based on the three parts of your complete emotions — your perception of specific facts or events, your evaluating thoughts or rating of those facts or events, and your "gut" feelings about them. Once you master RSA of complete emotions, the usually confusing, abbreviated emotions become easy to understand and deal with rationally. Then you can systematically get rid of old habits of useless anger, guilt and depression, and self-defeating fears, jealousies, etc.

Because you have to sit down and write out your own RSA, you can cheat, take irrational shortcuts, and distort or deny objective facts. But you will be cheating only yourself. And your attempts at RSA's will not help you. Still, they won't make you any worse than you would have been without attempting them. That's because you really won't be doing anything new, you will merely be using your brain in your usual way.

Doing RSA's whenever you're more unhappy than you want or need to be, is the first step toward rational emotional re-education. The two ways to benefit most from RSA's in least time are: (1) thoroughly learn each of their six parts and (2) always write them in the ABC order shown.

RSA Format

"A"	"Da"
Facts and Events	Camera Check of "A"

---

*My clinical research on RSA was published in *Psychotherapy: Theory, Research and Practice*, 1971, 8(3) 195–198.

"B" Self-Talk	"Db" Rational Debate of "B"
1.	1.
2.	2.
3. etc.	3.

"C" Emotional Consequences of "B" (Emotive response or feelings)	"E" Emotional Goal for Future "A's"

THE FIVE RULES FOR RATIONAL THINKING:

1. Based on objective reality
2. Protects your life
3. Gets you your goals
4. Keeps you out of trouble with others
5. Eliminates significant emotional conflict

Write each part in your own everyday language, but do the exercise as soon as possible after you begin to get upset. The longer you delay, the more you forget, and the less immediate help you will be able to give yourself with RSA.

"A" — The Facts and Events

Under this heading *WRITE* simple statements of the facts or events as you saw them. *DO IT RIGHT AWAY,* or as soon as possible.

If you absolutely *can't* write the RSA immediately, try to do it in your head. But *ALWAYS* write it out later *as soon as possible.* Wait until you have done at least fifty well done RSA's on paper before you try to do them in your head without later writing them down.

"B" — Your Self-Talk or Evaluating Thoughts

Here, write all of your thoughts, attitudes and beliefs about "A." Number each statement in order (1, 2, 3, etc.). Typical "B" section statements are: "It's not fair. He shouldn't have done that. I'm trapped in my marriage. Why don't they pay attention to me? How could they have done such a thing?"

This is an important point. REMEMBER it. The two thousand year old scientific fact about human emotions is: It's *not* facts or events that upset you. Your thoughts about the facts and events do it. That means you will feel good, bad or neutral, only if you believe thoughts that imply ". . . and it's good, bad or neutral for me."

To show yourself how your individual thoughts determine your specific positive, negative or neutral moods and specific emotions, classify each B — Self-Talk sentence. Write the one word — "good," "bad" or "neutral" — that best describes your feeling about that statement.

For example, if you say: "I'm trapped in my marriage, (bad);" that shows that you perceive yourself as being trapped in marriage and that you believe it's a bad thing. That combination forces you to feel bad at "C."

"C" — The Emotional Consequence of "B"

Under this heading write simple statements of how you felt. For example: "I felt anger towards my wife. I was depressed. I was upset about failing the test," etc. Be as specific as you can about how you felt; don't put opinions about who or what made you feel that way. Don't write: "My wife made me angry." That's a mistaken opinion. You alone control your emotions. Only you can make yourself angry. So correct such statements to read: "I got angry," or "I made myself angry about what my wife did." Also correct statements like, "I depressed myself because I made an ass of myself," to simply, "I depressed myself." The belief or thought, "I made an ass of myself," belongs in your "B" section.

Next, add up and compare the total "goods" to thē "bads" and "neutrals" in your "B" section. Then you'll see how your sincere beliefs alone determined how you felt at "C."

Immediately under the "C" section, write the Five Rules for Rational Thinking. Refer to them each time you debate a sentence in your "B" section or you try to come up with a more rational thought than that one for your "D" sections.

The "D" section is divided into "Da" and "Db." Write it only after you have written the ABC sections and the Five Rules for Rational Thinking. Then reread the "A" Section and apply the camera rule of thumb. Ask yourself: "If I had taken a moving picture of what I said happened, would I see and hear more or less than what I'm calling facts?" Look for opinions that are often mistaken for facts. A typical example is: "She put me down."

"Da" — Your Camera Check of "A"

Here you correct opinions like: "My wife put me down," to statements of fact such as: "She didn't put me down; she didn't even touch me. I felt put down; but I created that feeling. It was a silly way to feel though, because I was standing up the whole time."

Many people argue that I'm making too much of the statement "She put me down." They say: "He didn't mean that; he knows she didn't really put him down. He meant he resented what she said, and he felt insulted."

My response is: "That's a beautiful insight. If it's really true, it reveals two real causes of his problem with his wife. First, rather than calmly dealing objectively with what his wife actually said, this husband chose to resent it and feel insulted. Second, in an attempt to get her to accept blame for what he had done himself, he accused her of something she didn't do — put him down. There is no reason to believe that a wife (or anyone) can control what her husband (or anyone else) may choose to resent and feel insulted about.

"I don't believe that husband would accuse the race horses of driving him to the poor house just because he chooses to gamble away his money at the races. If he would refuse to blame the race horses, then there is hope for him. By starting to react as logically about what his wife does (versus what he does to himself) as he would about losing money at the races, he'd stop feeling useless resentment and insult. I'd bet he'd also stop having some of his problems with his wife. Doing correct RSA's is one of the fastest ways this husband could learn that kind of logical emotional control. That's why the camera check of his perceptions would be helpful to him."

The camera rule of thumb applies *only* to external events. However, simple statements of fact like: "My wife left me, and I felt depressed," can stay in the "A" section without correction. Granted, you can't do a camera check on an emotional feeling. But if the statement: "I felt depressed," is true, it would be a fact. So it *can be* (but doesn't *have* to be) put in the "A" section. In either case though, you always put statements like "I felt depressed," in the "C" section.

A well done "Da" section helps you see the difference between objective facts and your subjective opinions and false accusations. Habitually recognizing that difference is essential for rational emotional control.

Am I trying to say that subjective opinions are necessarily bad or irrational? No, of course not. I'm merely saying that your opinion often differs from the facts; and if you are doing rational self-counseling, you will base your reactions on the facts first and your opinions second, if at all.

"Db" — Your Rational Debate of "B"

After you write your "Da" statements, read the B-1 statement and see if it obeys at least three of the five rules for rational thinking. Actually ask and answer questions like: "Is that statement based on objective facts? If I act on that thought will I protect or endanger my life? Will that action help me achieve my goals," etc. Continue in this way until you go through the five rules. If your B-1 sentence obeys at least three of the rational rules, write: "That thought is rational" and then challenge B-2. But if your B-1 sentence does not obey at least three of the five rules for rational thinking, think of another *personally acceptable* thought for B-1 that does obey at least three of the rules: The more rational rules your new thought obeys, the better for you. Then write your more rational way of thinking at Db-1, under "Db" — Rational Debates of "B" Section. Next, challenge B-2, B-3, etc., in the same way.

Sometimes a "B" section statement will be *irrelevant* for one or more of the five rules for rational thinking. If so, skip those rules and decide if the statement obeys a majority of the relevant rational rules. Usually, an idea is not worth thinking if it is neither relevant for, nor obeys three of the five rational rules.

What to do about "B" section statements that you decide aren't worth thinking? Simply write in the corresponding "Db" section: "That idea is not worth thinking; so I'll stop thinking it now." Then either refuse to think that idea any more, or react indifferently to it if it happens to pop into your mind.

"E" — Your Emotional Goal for Future "A's"

Here describe the emotions you want to feel in similar future situations, instead of the one you actually felt. For the most rational results, make your emotional goals logical for your "Db" section. For example: Suppose you are angry at yourself and depressed because poor work or poor study kept you from being promoted. Under "E" you'd probably put: "I want to feel just enough rational irritation and dislike for my failure to cause me to improve my work and avoid further failure." It probably *wouldn't* be rational to want to feel again the useless self-anger and depression felt at "C." and it probably *wouldn't* be rational to want to feel happy about failure. Feeling good about your failure might cause you to want to fail again.

This is important. *Remember* it. Physically healthy, conscious people *always* have some type of emotional reaction to their thoughts. Feeling calm or neutral is just as much a real emotion as love or hate. So "E" sections that read: "I want to have no feelings at all," or "No emotion" are inappropriate. They don't describe rational emotional goals.

I want to emphasize that point because many people are thoroughly confused about negative emotions. They believe that if they stop feeling miserable, they will stop feeling *altogether,* i.e. have no emotions at all. They are wrong. As long as your brain and nervous system are physically healthy, you will *always* have some type of emotional reaction to your thoughts. Becoming more rational in your emotional control *cannot* rob you of your ability to feel. You will just feel more of the emotions you want to feel and fewer of those emotions you *don't* want to feel.

After One Well Done RSA

Don't expect a miracle. You *cannot* completely get rid of a life-long emotional habit in a flash. RSA is just the first step in rational self-counseling. But, it does let you start to feel better fast if:

(A) your "Db" section is rational;

(B) you believe that your "Db" section is the best way for you to think about your "A" or your "Da" situation; and

(C) you habitually think and act on your "Db" thoughts every time you think of, or you are in that "A" or "Da" situation.

To think and react to your "Db" thoughts once or twice, then go back to your old "B" section thoughts and reactions is a waste of time People who do that usually:

(A) are confused by cognitive dissonance; or

(B) are trying to trick themselves into feeling better without really thinking and reacting better.

You *have to think and react better first,* and *keep doing it,* to habitually feel better.

Example RSA

As I said in Chapter 2, Jeffrey (the card player) enrolled in a class in rational self-counseling. When he started doing RSA's, the first thing he analyzed was his decision to stop card lessons.

Jeffrey's First RSA

"A"
Facts and Events

I wanted to learn to play bridge and my friends tried to teach me. But the lessons made me feel so bad that I quit trying to learn.

"Da"
Camera Check of "A"

The first statement is fact. But the second one is only half fact and half irrational opinion. Yeah, I quit the lessons; that's fact. But the lessons didn't make me feel bad. I did that, and I irrationally blamed the lessons for it.

"B"
Self-Talk

(1) I was always making stupid mistakes. (bad)

(2) I'm so stupid that I couldn't think ahead; so I made mistakes that I shouldn't have made. (bad)

"Db"
Rational Challenge of "B"

1. That's a lie. My friends said I was really good, considering that I was just starting. Actually, I didn't make very many mistakes; I was mostly mad because I wasn't winning much. I thought I should have been an expert, just because I had learned all the rules of the game.

2. Those are stupid statements. If I really couldn't think ahead, then there was no way for me to avoid the mistakes that I said I shouldn't have made. The fact is, I could have thought ahead, if I had already learned enough good game strategy to know what to have thought about. But I hadn't been playing long enough for that. I wasn't stupid. I was just inexperienced. But, because those were the objective facts, I *should* have made every mistake I did make.

(3) I'm just a dumb ass who can play a little football — an All American dumb jock. (bad)

3. That statement is just irrational crap. I'm not a dumb ass. An "ass" is a small horse. I'm a fallible human being. Sure, I play football, and I'm damn good at it because I work at it. But I'm also as good a student as most. Calling myself a "dumb jock" is a dumb thing to do. So I'm going to stop doing that crap right now.

(4) My friends must really think I'm a prize idiot. (bad)

4. Even if my friends think I'm an idiot, I know that I'm not. So I have no reason to get upset about their mistaken opinion. Their thinking I'm an idiot won't make it so. No matter what they think, it probably isn't as bad as what I have been thinking and believing about myself. I felt as if I really was dumb. But that was a dumb thing to do because I have no objective facts or reasons to believe that. So I'll stop it right now.

(5) I can't learn to play bridge. (bad)

5. That's just an irrational cop-out. I can learn, if I stop making myself feel so bad about mistakes. If I had spent half as much time and energy practicing as I have making myself miserable, I'd have been playing decent bridge by now. I think I'll start playing again just to prove my point.

"C"
Emotional Consequences
of "B"

"E"
Emotional Goals for Future
"A's"

Anger, self-hate, depression. Five "bad's"; no "good's" or "neutral's." With that type thinking, it's only logical that I was hating bridge.

(1) feel rationally calm about making mistakes at playing bridge.
(2) feel good about starting to play bridge again.
(3) stop feeling dumb and inferior.
(4) feel good when I know I played my best.

FIVE RULES FOR RATIONAL THINKING:
1. Based on objective reality
2. Protects your life
3. Gets you your goals
4. Keeps you out of trouble with others
5. Eliminates significant emotional conflict

This was a well done RSA. The week after Jeffrey did it, he started his bridge lessons again. But no miracle took place. He still got angry at himself when he made mistakes. But there was one big difference now. When he'd start to get angry, he'd remember and think the rational thoughts he had written in the "Db" section of his RSA. So, he didn't get as angry as he used to. Also, when he got home, he still rethought his mistakes. But this time he didn't depress himself about them. If he started to feel depressed, he'd reread his RSA over and over until he felt indifferent about his mistakes. Then he'd calmly rethink each mistake one time. As he rethought it, he'd make notes on what would have been better to do than what he did. He'd then memorize his notes and go to bed feeling calm.

When Jeffrey went to his bridge lessons the second, third and even tenth week, he still got somewhat upset when he made mistakes. But, each time he got *less* upset than he did the week before.

In spite of his obvious progress in the first three weeks, Jeffrey wasn't satisfied. He began to wonder if his old way might not have been the right way for him after all.

It *wasn't* that he liked to feel miserable; he was confused by cognitive dissonance. The experience of feeling better at the times he usually felt worse seemed strange to him — almost unreal. He also wondered why he still felt some of the old feelings even though he was thinking rationally. He reasoned: "If I really can choose how I feel, and I choose not to be angry and depressed, why then do I still get angry and depressed?" He couldn't think of a logical answer. So he made a very common mistake; for a little while, he stopped thinking with his brain and started thinking with his gut. He thought: "I still get angry and depressed; so that must mean that I'm supposed to feel that way. If so, then this rational stuff is for the birds. It's not real; it's just a game. It's phony, and if I do it, I'll be a phony. I hate phonies. Right or wrong, I have got to be me — the real me — not some rotten phony."

Those are typical examples of the believable but irrational reasons people who are confused by cognitive dissonance give themselves for going back to their old emotional habits. Their real problem is *not* the possibility of becoming a phony. It's just that they have the "phony-fear." Fortunately, during this time of emotional confusion Jeffrey had progressed to the class reading assignment, "The Phony-Fear" (the next chapter). So he was able to understand his confusion, get rid of it fast, and continue his emotional re-education.

A Useful but Often Overlooked Insight

RSA is as useful in helping you increase your skill in having happy times as it is in increasing your skill in eliminating unhappy times. When you have unusual happiness or success, *DON'T* say: "Boy, I sure was lucky," when in fact your own actions produced the results. Instead, objectively point out to yourself: "Boy, I really handled myself and that situation rationally." Then do an RSA of the event to fix firmly in your mind how you did it. That way you will be more likely to do it again when you want those same results.

Summary of RSA

Always write up your RSA's completely in the format below, using your everyday language, in this order: A, B, C, five rules, then Da, Db, and E.

"A" Facts and Events	"Da" Camera Check of "A"
"B" Self-Talk (Evaluating Thoughts)	"Db" Rational Debate of "B"
1.	1.
2.	2.
3. etc.	3.

"C"	"E"
Emotional Consequences of "B" (Emotive response or feelings)	Emotional Goal for Future "A's"

THE FIVE RULES FOR RATIONAL THINKING:
1. Based on objective reality
2. Protects your life
3. Gets you your goals
4. Keeps you out of trouble with others
5. Eliminates significant emotional conflict

Do your RSA as soon as possible after you experience the facts or events listed in "A."

Emphasis Questions

(1) Rational self-analysis has _____ parts.   (P-55)

(2) RSA is based on the _____ parts of an _____.   (P-55)

(3) List the five rules for rational thinking.   (P-56)

(4) Under "A" (_____ & _____), you are to write statements of the facts of a situation as you saw them.   (P-56)

(5) You should do an RSA as soon as possible after you become upset because the longer you delay, the more you forget.   True   False   (P-56)

(6) Under "B" (_____ - _____), you are to write your _____, _____ and beliefs about "A." (P-56)

(7) Under "C" (_____ _____ of "B"), you are to write simple statements of how you _____.   (P-57)

(8) _____ and _____ alone control your emotions. (P-57)

(9) "Da" and "Db" sections are based on the _____ rules of rational thinking.   (P-59)

(10) You apply the camera rule of thumb to the _____ section.   (P-57, 58)

(11) A well done "Da" section helps you see the important differences between _____ facts and _____ opinions. (P-58)

(12) When doing "Da" and "Db" sections, the more rational rules your new way of thinking meets, the better for you. True   False   (P-59)

(13) All "B" sections statements are irrational. True   False   (P-59)

(14) Under "E" (_____ _____ for _____ "A's"), describe the emotions you'd rather feel instead of the ones you actually felt. (P-59)

(15) Your "E" section is usually the same as your "C" section. True   False   (P-59, 60)

(16) A physically healthy person always has some type of _____. (P-60)

(17) Rational emotional control robs you of your ability to feel.   True   False   (P-60)

(18) You have to think better, and keep doing it, to feel better.   True   False   (P-60)

(19) When people are in cognitive dissonance and they don't understand it, they are likely to call themselves a _____. (P-64)

(20) People who are trapped by the "phony-fear" do not understand cognitive dissonance.   True   False (P-64)

CHAPTER 6

THE PHONY-FEAR   or
The Neurotic Fear of Being a Phony*

Introduction

The neurotic fear of being a phony (the phony-fear) is a common pitfall in emotional re-education. If you don't understand it, it may cause you to give up emotional re-education and go back to being miserable. But as the following case history shows, once you understand it, you can quickly get rid of it.

Mrs. Wilder, a young housewife, sincerely wanted to stay married; but she told her lawyers to file for divorce. Fortunately, her lawyers, a relatively new breed called "counseling lawyers," advised Mrs. Wilder to try rational self-counseling for three months. Then, if she still wanted a divorce, they'd get it for her. Because of their heavy case load, they referred Mrs. Wilder to me for training in rational self-counseling. The following are excerpts from her third training session.

MRS. W: Dr. Maultsby, I'm sorry but I just feel that rational self-counseling is not for me. I don't feel it'll work for me.

DR. M: Oh! Why is that?

MRS. W: I don't know. It's just that when I tell myself that it is not terrible that my husband refuses to spend less time with his work and more time with me, that it's only socially inconvenient like you said, and that it doesn't mean that I'm a worthless person, and all that; I just don't believe it.

DR. M: Why don't you believe it?

MRS. W: Well, I get this feeling in the pit of my stomach which says, "You're lying to yourself."

DR. M: You're confusing your thoughts and beliefs with your feelings. It's your sincere belief that you're worthless and

---

*A shortened version of this chapter was published in the *Journal of Corrective Psychiatry*, 18 (4), 1972.

inferior that causes your sunken "gut" feeling, every time you think you have proof that you are worthless. And as long as you believe that you are worthless, the thought that you are *not*, will seem just as untrue as the thought that you're standing up when you know that you're sitting down.

MRS. W: Well, isn't it logical to feel worthless when you have proof that you are?

DR. M: Yes, it would be logical, if you really had proof; but you don't have any. All you have is an irrational assumption about yourself, that you mistakenly believe your husband's behavior proves to be fact.

MRS. W: I don't understand what you mean.

DR. M: I think you have the irrational assumption that if you were *not* worthless and inferior then your husband wouldn't break dates with you. Your husband does break dates with you, so you call that proof that you are worthless and inferior, and you feel miserable about your *so-called* proof. You then mislabel your miserable feelings, "feeling worthless and inferior." With your sincere but irrational assumption, plus your *fake* proof and real, intense miserable feelings, it's only logical and natural for you to call yourself a liar when you think "I'm not worthless." Objectively though, the only thing you have proof of is that you have miserable gut feelings when you give yourself *fake* evidence that your irrational assumption is fact. I call that gut thinking as opposed to brain thinking.

MRS. W: But if I don't follow my feelings, I feel like such a phony. I hate phonies. I don't want to be something that I hate.

Author's Note #1

People who repeatedly use "I feel" when "I think" or "I believe" would be more accurate are likely to be gut thinkers. When Mrs. Wilder said, "I don't feel that rational self-counseling is the solution to my problems," she meant, "I think or believe that rational self-counseling is not the solution to my problems; and I react to my beliefs with the urge or desire to give up rational self-counseling."

You may think I'm making a big fuss over nothing. After all, everybody uses "I feel" in that way. Why go to all the trouble to say it in the longer way? The following example will show how saying "I feel," when you mean "I think," can cause unnecessary emotional pain and why rational self-counseling teaches you to use the two words more accurately than most people do.

At a party one night I was talking to a stranger in a joking way about some *true* facts about how the language of some American Indian tribes influences their behavior. I never dreamed that the stranger was part American Indian; so I was flabbergasted when he got insulted and left the party in an angry huff. The next day I happened to see him, and I asked him about it. He said, "I felt that you were trying to make a fool out of me." I told him that he was wrong. I was merely describing in a joking way objective facts that fit the scientific theory of rational self-counseling — what people think and believe causes them to feel and act the way they do. I had in *no way meant* to appear insulting to him personally nor to American Indians. I further explained that had he asked the other two people in the conversation about it, he would have seen his mistake.

When I asked him why he hadn't asked the others about it before he left, he said, "It never occurred to me to ask anyone, because I really felt like you were trying to make a fool of me; so, I felt the best thing for me to do was to leave before I made a bigger fool of myself."

What he really meant was he had the negative belief that I was trying to make a fool of him. So, he reacted to his negative belief with negative feelings and blamed me for causing them. Since his negative feelings were real and intense, he assumed that they proved that his belief was correct. He reasoned that if I weren't trying to make a fool of him, he wouldn't feel like I was; therefore, I must have been doing it. That's typical of the irrational thinking people upset themselves with when they don't know that they control their own emotions.

Had that fellow known how his brain and emotions work, he would have thought: "I feel as if he's trying to make a fool of me *only* because I believe that's what he's doing." Then if he had been a brain thinker instead of a gut thinker, and he had analyzed the situation using the five rules for rational thinking, he would have thought: "My feeling is irrational because the only way he could turn me into a fool is by magic. But there is no rational reason to believe that magic exists. The objective reality is that I'm the same now as I was before I started talking to him — only a fallible human being, just like him. So even if he is trying to work magic on me and turn me into a fool, he's going to fail because it's not possible to do that in the first place.

But is that really what he's trying to do? I'll give it the old camera rule of thumb check and see. A moving picture of this situation would only show a guy telling objective facts that he thinks are funny, but facts just the same, about American Indians. It's just that I'm sensitive about what people say about Indians, maybe even too sensitive. After all, how can his opinions really hurt me or Indians? They can't. So even though I don't like what he's doing, and I certainly wouldn't joke about blacks or Jews, it's irrational of me to get so upset that I don't enjoy the party. I'll go talk to somebody who talks about things I like."

Rational Thinking Versus Gut Thinking

Rational thinking is objective or factual thinking. Gut thinking is the subtle form of magical thinking most normal people sometimes do, usually without realizing it. Because magical thinking is a naive or childish way to think, Mrs. Wilder (like most normal people) said, "No, don't be silly," when I asked her in her first session if she believed in magic. She was telling me the sincere truth as she saw it. It had never occurred to her that her gut reactions revealed her unnoticed belief in magic, or more specifically — her ignorance being mistaken for knowledge.

The phony-fear is caused by an unnoticed belief in magic. In rational self-counseling magic or magical thinking means trying to make something happen to someone or something separate from you, merely by thinking or wanting it or by doing something to yourself. For example, if you think that your wearing a certain color of socks will help your favorite basketball team win, that's magical thinking. Mrs. Wilder believed that if her husband were to change his work habits, his action would magically — there is no other way it could happen — transform her from a worthless, inferior person into a worthwhile, non-inferior person. The stranger at the party thought that a few words by me could and might make a fool out of him or somehow do harm to Indians. Again, ONLY by magic could that have happened.

Both that stranger and Mrs. Wilder were part-time magical thinkers without realizing it. But there was no point in telling her that here. She would have merely denied it again. To avoid possible argument and wasted time, I decided to keep my insight to myself. By getting Mrs. Wilder to think more clearly in general, I hoped to get her to make the insight for herself. Then she would be most likely to benefit from it.

DR. M: So, what you are saying is that you refuse to learn rational self-counseling because you really believe that if you use
it, you would stop being your real self and become a phony;
and you hate phonies even if it means hating yourself? Right?

MRS. W: Right. No matter what, I want to be the real me.
Unless you can show me a way to use rational self-counseling
without being a phony, I guess this will be my last session.
I have tried everything else, so I feel that maybe I should
just give up and try divorce.

DR. M: But, is it really true that you have tried everything?

MRS. W: I feel that I have. Before I came to see you, I had
already had three years of psychotherapy and one year of
marriage counseling and all I got for my trouble was two
big fat bills. I don't know what else I can do except try
divorce.

DR. M: You could try rational self-counseling. You haven't even
bothered to learn it yet, and you are ready to give up on
it. So you see, it's not true that you've tried everything.

MRS. W: It's not that I want to give up; it's just that I don't
feel that it's right for me. But if you can change my feelings,
I'll be willing to try it.

Author's Note #2

Only with magic could I change Mrs. Wilder's feelings without
drugs or electric shock. Yet she challenged me to change them.
Therefore her challenge was either more evidence that she had
an unnoticed belief in magic, or that she didn't really want to
change. I had *no valid reason* to believe that she was playing
games with me. But I still saw no point in bringing up the issue
of believing in magic at this time.

DR. M: Well, if I could change your feelings I would; but I
can't. Only you can do that. But, what I can do is teach
you why it would be rational for you to change your feelings,
and how to do it. But for me to do that, you will have to
refuse to go on being afraid of an impossibility.

MRS. W: What do you mean?

DR. M: You said that your fear of becoming a phony is the
only thing keeping you from using rational self-counseling.
Right?

MRS. W: Right.

DR. M: If I can describe objective facts that prove it's impossible for you or anyone else to ever become a phony, would you then give up your irrational fear and learn rational self-counseling?

MRS. W: Yes. If you can make me believe that, I will change my feelings.

Author's Note #3

By her last statement, Mrs. Wilder showed what most normal people know, but choose to ignore when they are upset: namely, all it takes to change personal feelings is a change in personal beliefs. You may wonder: "Well, if she knows that, and if she's so sincere, why did she challenge you to change her feelings for her? Why doesn't she do it herself and solve her problem?" She doesn't because she has the usual emotional confusion that most people have who don't know how their emotions work. But her statement may be a sign that she's willing to learn in spite of her confusion. If so, her willingness to learn is all she'll need to get rid of her phony-fear.

DR. M: All rational discussions begin and end with objective reality; so, describe a phony person for me in objective terms so that I will be able to recognize one if I see it.

MRS. W: Well, phonies are people who try to be what they aren't.

DR. M: I don't understand. Can you be more specific? Can you apply your definition to yourself?

MRS. W: Well, yes, I am being a phony when I think that I am not worthless and inferior when I know I am.

DR. M: How do you know that? What is the evidence for it?

MRS. W: My feelings; that's the way I feel.

DR. M: Have you ever felt that an idea was true and later learned that you were mistaken?

MRS. W: Why yes, hasn't everybody? Oh, I see what you are getting at. Now, you are going to ask me how can I be sure that I'm not mistaken this time.

DR. M: That's right. How can you be sure?

MRS. W: Well, I just feel.

DR. M: But where do your feelings come from?

MRS. W: Well, according to you, they come from what I think, but I'm not so sure that I believe that.

DR. M: I think it's obvious that you don't believe it; that's why you have the phony-fear.

MRS. W: Why do you say my fear is phony? It's real to me. I feel it.

DR. M: I'm not saying that your fear isn't real. I know that it is. But it's a real fear of something that can't happen in the real world of objective reality. So the word "phony-fear" is just the name used in rational self-counseling to label a real fear of nothing: nothing in the sense that there's really nothing to be afraid of. For example, if I wanted to, I could make myself afraid that I'm going to turn into a garbage can. But, in reality, there is no way that I know of that I could turn into a garbage can. In rational self-counseling, we call that kind of fear a phony-fear. In other words, terms like phony-fear and phony-person are just metaphors: they don't really say what you mean. That's why you get confused if you use them without knowing the big difference between the *useful* ones and the *useless* ones.

MRS. W: (Smiling) Now I'm really confused. Just what do you mean when you say metaphor?

DR. M: Okay; to me a metaphor is a way of saying what you *don't mean* and *meaning what you don't* say. For example, if you say to someone: "You SOB," you *don't* really mean, "You puppy; you male offspring of a female dog." You really mean, "I believe that you're a hateful person, and I hate you and want you to suffer because of it," or something like that. The fact makes "SOB" a meaningless metaphor.

MRS. W: Well to me a metaphor is just a fancy word for slang. Do you agree with that?

Author's Note #4

You may now wonder if Mrs. Wilder and I aren't getting way off the point. No, we aren't. This discussion of metaphors and slang is very important. You can't think about anything in a useful way without using words. Since that's true, the words you believe are your thoughts or beliefs. That means you really choose your emotions by your choice of words.

But, rational thinking means precise thinking — saying what you mean and meaning what you say. You can't do that unless you precisely choose your words. The only exception to that rule is when you use *useful* metaphors.

DR. M: Yes, I agree that a metaphor is a type of slang; but there's useful slang and useless slang. When you forget that fact, you often cause yourself unnecessary problems. But you can easily avoid such problems, if you'd remember how your emotions work on the one hand, and what the most rational use to make of words is on the other. What do you think is the most rational use of words?

MRS. W: I've never thought about it really, but I guess it has to do with communicating with other people.

DR. M: Only secondarily! The most rational use to make of words is to communicate with yourself. That's why you need to make your thoughts, or self-talk, as rational as you possibly can, so you can control your emotions and actions as rationally as you can. You see, when you are *neither* joking *nor* lying, your words are the thoughts that you believe. Since the thoughts that you believe cause you to have the emotional feelings and actions you have, you cannot have rational self-control unless you are *rationally* using words. That's why rational self-counseling is *not just* semantics, it's *all* semantics. To really impress that fact on your mind, for just twenty seconds try to have and hold a thought, any thought about anything, without using a word.

Author's Note #5

We stopped the session for twenty seconds while she tried to have a thought without using a word. I suggest that you try it too. It is possible to do it; but most people can't. Even those who can, *cannot* use that kind of thinking for solving their problems in everyday life. Mrs. Wilder failed too.

DR. M: Now do you see why I say you can't think rationally without rationally using words?

MRS. W: Yes, but how do you tie that in with using slang and metaphor?

DR. M: Easily! A useful metaphor or useful slang will trigger the same emotional feelings that saying what you really mean would trigger. For example, if you ask me, "How do you like your job?" and I say, "It's a snap; it's groovy; I really dig it, etc.," my metaphors or slang would be useful because they would trigger the same positive emotions in me that the following statements of objective facts would trigger! "I really like my job; for me it's more like fun than work." Still, the reality is, there's no such thing as a "snappy" or "groovy" job. And no matter how many pictures you take of me at work, you'll never see me holding a shovel or digging.

When you use slang or metaphors, you need to remember that you're not saying what you mean. To *really see* the importance of that insight, the next time you feel like calling someone a SOB, instead of saying that, shout: "You male offspring of a female dog, you!" and see what happens to your feeling. Do you think you'll stay as angry as you would if you say: "You SOB?"

MRS. W: (Laughing) No, but why isn't SOB a useful metaphor? I mean, there are people you hate and want to make suffer sometimes.

DR. M: That's right! But in rational self-counseling, you think first in terms of the best way for you to rationally control your emotions and actions. If you aren't joking when you call someone an SOB, you're really trying to justify your anger and in addition you usually get angrier. But the angrier you get, the worse you feel and the more likely you are to cause yourself more personal problems than you are to solve the original problem.

MRS. W: Are you saying it's bad to get angry? Don't you get angry sometimes?

Author's Note #6

Again you may wonder why I'm spending so much time on a point that may now appear to you (the reader) to be irrelevant. All of the points are relevant because Mrs. Wilder is trying to find a reason, any reason, to justify doubting the possible value of rational self-counseling to her. At this point Mrs. Wilder is showing the behavior that's typical of people who make up their minds without first having a valid reason for their opinions. They then try to hide that fact by attacking any contrary opinion. That's why it's essential that I effectively debate each of her objections, regardless of how irrelevant it may seem. If she appears to "win" any one of the debates, she will conclude, "Aha! I knew that rational self-counseling wasn't for me." The use of such irrational logic is the major cause of her phony-fear and feelings of inferiority. Since each of these debates is extremely important to the therapeutic outcome of this session, I ask the reader to be patient and follow each of them. You'll see that I bring her back to the point as soon as I think it's safe.

DR. M: No, I'm not saying anger is necessarily bad. Yes, I sometimes get angry, but I get rid of my anger as quickly as possible because I can get furious at the drop of a hat. And when

I get furious I get quite irrational. Anger is useful for me *only* when it's *just* moderate irritation or displeasure. That's all I need to motivate me to protect myself and stand up for my rights. Anything more than that, and I'm *not* effective, especially if other people are involved. Then I'm likely to want to fight. So I forget the original problem and get caught up in trying to figure out the best way to win the fight. That's why anger is definitely irrational for me all the time. But, we're getting off the point. Let's get back to your phony-fear.

MRS. W: Are you trying to tell me that there are no phony people in this world?

DR. M: No, I'm not saying that. There are lots of phony people in the world. You see them every day in department store windows; they're called mannequins, but they're *not* living human beings. That's the important insight you must make to eliminate your phony-fear. You're alive; therefore, you *can't ever* be a mannequin. Therefore, you *can never* be a phony person. Even when you die, you will just be a *real dead person.* So if you are really afraid of becoming a phony person, you can get rid of that fear in a hurry by just refusing to·be afraid of things that can't happen to you. This is not just a semantical difference. You'd feel a lot different if you said, "I'm a mannequin," every time you now have the urge to say, "I'm a phony." Right? Try it if you don't believe me.

MRS. W: (Laughing) But I'm not worried about being a mannequin, and there *are* people who pretend to be a way they're not, and who will fool you if you let them. That's what I hate.

DR. M: I know you don't worry about being a mannequin. But those are the only phony-people there are. That's why your use of the word keeps you from understanding your problem. And you are right; there are people who fool others. There are also people who fool themselves. That's what you're doing, fooling yourself. But people who fool others as well as you (who are fooling yourself) are all real people pretending and fooling others and yourselves. If you or those others don't fool yourselves or others *all* the time, the very worst thing you can accurately say about you all is that you are real people who sometimes fool yourselves or others by behaving differently from your usual or normal way.

MRS. W: But that's it. That's what I hate: people who behave differently than their normal way.

Author's Note #7

That's a beautiful example of the irrational emotional binds you can put yourself in when you irrationally use words. Mrs. Wilder said she hated people who behave differently than their normal or usual way. But her normal, usual way of behaving when her husband broke a date was to feel depressed, worthless and inferior. So, for her to be sincere in her statement: "I hate people who behave differently than their normal way," she'd have to hate herself if she stopped feeling depressed, worthless and inferior. Yet she came to therapy with sincere desire to stop feeling that way.

My job now was to get Mrs. Wilder to see that her irrational use of words was keeping her confused. Only then could she make progress in getting rid of her phony-fear.

DR. M: What's your usual or normal feeling when your husband refuses to spend as much time with you as you want?

MRS. W: Anger, depression.

DR. M·   And worthless, inferior, etc. Right?

MRS. W: Right, (smiling) but you make it sound so bad.

DR. M: (Laughing) I don't make it sound half as bad as you did in the first two sessions when you cried almost the whole time. Didn't you tell me that it was terrible, awful, unbearable, and you couldn't stand it anymore?

MRS. W: (Smiling) Yeah, and that's how I really felt.

DR. M: I believe you. That's why I'm trying to help you get rid of your phony-fear, so you can keep from ever feeling that way again. So, your usual reaction when your husband refuses you is to feel bad. Now, according to what you said a moment ago, if you stop behaving in your usual way, you will be a phony. Since you hate phonies, that means if you stop feeling depressed and worthless you'll have to hate yourself. The only choices you're giving yourself are to go on feeling depressed, worthless and inferior and not hate yourself, or to stop feeling depressed, worthless and inferior, but hate yourself. Since you don't want to hate yourself, you have to go on being miserable. The way you have it, being your real self means being real miserable. Right?

MRS. W: (Laughing) Wrong. I mean, I don't want to be misera-
          ble. And I know my husband is a good man, and I know
          it would be hard, if not impossible, to find another one like
          him.

DR. M: But if you think you would want another like him,
          why get rid of him?

MRS. W: Because he's a good man and I love him, but I can't
          get rid of this feeling . . .

DR. M: No, it's not that you "can't get rid of" it, it's just that
          your phony-fear makes you afraid to do what's necessary
          to get rid of the feeling.

MRS. W: Okay, then you tell me how I can get rid of the feeling
          that I'm a phony and I'll do it.

DR. M: Oh, telling you how to get rid of your miserable feeling
          is easy. What I want to know is if I tell you, would you
          be willing to try it for just one week?

MRS. W: I'll do anything if it'll help.

Author's Note #8

You may wonder: "If getting rid of the phony-fear is so easy,
why did you waste all this time before you told her?" Before
now, her sloppy use of words kept her so confused that she would
have either ignored my advice or rejected it. Most people in emotional distress have insights into and explanations for their
distress; but their insights and explanations are usually based
on *ignorance* of self, which they mislabel *knowledge* of self and
get confused.

Admitting ignorance is the first step toward useful knowledge. As long as Mrs. Wilder *knew not* that she *knew not*, trying
to tell her something useful would have been a waste of time.
Actually getting rid of the phony-fear is as easy as getting rid
of any other mistaken or illogical fear. All you have to do is
think and react rationally.

DR. M: Okay, rational thinking starts with a precise description
          of objective fact. Objectively, what you call being a phony
          is merely thinking and believing thoughts that would make
          it logical for you to feel and act one way when you actually
          feel like acting in a different way.

MRS. W: I don't see what you mean.

DR. M: What you and most people call being a phony is really
          cognitive dissonance. It's just your brain telling you it's ratio-

nal to believe and act on one idea, while your gut is telling you to act on a different idea. For example, suppose you begin to live alone in a new apartment in a new neighborhood. Now, let's say that as far as you know it's a safe area. In addition, you carefully lock all your doors and windows every night; but you're still afraid to go to sleep at night. Let's say it's your first time living alone in the city, and you're just plain scared.

MRS. W: It's funny that you should pick that example because that's exactly what happened to me before I got married; but I got over it in a few weeks.

DR. M: Good! I'll bet you I can tell you exactly how you got over it. Every night you'd rationally point out to yourself that you were securely locked in and no one could possibly get in without awakening you as well as the neighbors. Even so, at first you still felt a little scared when you went to bed. Right?

MRS. W: Right.

DR. M: That was cognitive dissonance. Your brain told you that you had nothing to be afraid of. But your gut told you that you did. You ignored your gut though, and proved that you believed your rational thought that you were safe, by calming yourself down and going to sleep every night. That means you acted as if you were not afraid even though you actually felt afraid. By doing that every night, your fear became less and less, and in a few weeks you got rid of it completely.

MRS. W: That's exactly what happened.

DR. M: More precisely, that's exactly what *you did*. But in order to do it, you had to keep thinking and believing that you were safely locked in and then act as if you were safely locked in by turning out the lights and going to sleep in spite of your fear. When you later started going to sleep without any fear, that meant that you had resolved your cognitive dissonance in favor of the rational use of your brain, rather than the *irrational abuse* of your gut. Now, do you see why I call your present fear a phony-fear? What you call being a phony is really . . .

MRS. W: Cognitive dissonance!

DR. M: Right! That's a beautiful insight. Your phony-fear has you trapped in a vicious emotional circle. Every time you get a new idea about yourself you veto that idea in favor of your old gut response to your old belief about yourself. Your phony-fear is forcing you to try to do the impossible: to try to *feel* better *without* first *thinking* better. Unfortunately, emotional re-education works the other way. First you have to start thinking and physically acting better and only second can you start having better emotional feelings. In short, you're going to have to be willing to behave *as* logically about the fear of becoming a phony person as you were about your apartment fear.

MRS. W: You make it sound so easy, but I'm so used to going by my feelings. I don't know if I can do it.

DR. M: Sure you can! You proved it with your apartment fear. It's as easy as one, two, three. One, give up the irrational belief that you or anyone can ever be a phony person. That will force you, in the second place, to give up the irrational idea that you are a worthless, inferior person. There's absolutely no *objective reason* to believe it. There is no rational way to rate a person as a human being. All humans are fallible. That fact makes them all equal. It's true that people are unequal in their various behaviors or roles. But all that means is some people show their fallibility less or more than others, but they are equally fallible. Since fallible human being is the most accurate and only unchangeable thing you can say about yourself, and since no rational people are willing to hate themselves for being fallible, you can safely give up your belief in worthless, inferior people. Third, prove to yourself that you have actually given up both of those irrational beliefs by refusing to feel depressed, worthless and inferior when your husband continues to work the way he always has.

MRS. W: Yes, but how do you refuse to feel that way?

DR. M: Easily! You are already an expert at it.

Author's Note #9

This is one of the most helpful insights that beginners in rational self-counseling can make. They already know how to do most of the things rational self-counseling gets them to see they need to do. It's extremely *rare* that rational self-counseling asks you to do something that you haven't already done at least a few times in your past.

In the next few exchanges I will try to get Mrs. Wilder to see that she is already an expert at refusing to feel miserable when she gets tired of suffering.

MRS. W: Me! An expert. Why do you say that?

DR. M: When you first saw me last week, you said that one of your main problems was frequent depression because of your belief that your husband doesn't care enough about you. Then you told me that your husband breaks two or three dates a month with you because of unexpected business appointments. You also said that after the angry fights about it (which you always lose) you feel worthless, inferior and depressed and stay that way for four or five days. Then, you said that you snap out of it by telling yourself, "Well, I've suffered enough. I refuse to be upset about it anymore. I'll just forget the whole damn thing." Right?

MRS. W: Right.

DR. M: And you immediately get undepressed, right?

MRS. W: Well, not right away. I really have to work at it.

DR. M: That's irrelevant. The fact is that when you decide that you have suffered enough, you stop depressing yourself by refusing to think about the matter, right?

MRS. W: Right.

DR. M: Beautiful. Now, all I'm suggesting is that you stop depressing yourself the very first second that you start. You can do that by focusing immediately on the objective reality that it is not really terrible that you don't get everything you want from your husband when you want it. That's an objective fact. Right?

MRS. W: Well (pause) I guess so.

DR. M: So if it isn't really terrible, then you don't really have to get terribly upset. Right? I mean, it really is true that you don't have to get terribly upset just because you don't get what you want, when you want it. Right? Mildly irritated, somewhat disappointed, yes. But not terribly upset, right?

MRS. W: Well I don't know. One thing keeps bothering me . . .

DR. M: No, that's not quite accurate. The accurate choice of words would be: "One thing that I keep bothering myself about is . . ."

MRS. W: (Smiling) Okay. I keep bothering myself about the fact that if I can't go by my feelings, how will I know when I really believe something?

DR. M: That's a very good question. You tell me. How do you now know for sure whether or not you believe an idea?

MRS. W: When I feel it.

DR. M: Is there any other way?

MRS. W: Well, let me think for a minute. (Pause) No, I believe something when I feel it. If I don't feel it, I can't accept it.

DR. M: You can't or you refuse to accept it?

MRS. W: Well, I guess I refuse.

Author's Note #10

Saying "I can't" when you mean "I refuse" or "I'm afraid" or "I don't want to" is one of the most common copouts people use for demanding pills or some other magical solutions to their emotional problems. They say, "Doctor, you've just got to give me something for my nerves; I can't stand it without my pills."

DR. M: Okay, think this thought: "There is a bomb in this room, and I'd better get out of here in a hurry, because I don't want to die." (pause) Did you think the thought?

MRS. W: Yes.

DR. M: Do you believe yourself?

MRS. W: No.

DR. M: How do you know that you don't believe yourself?

MRS. W: I don't feel afraid, and I'm still in the room.

DR. M: Beautiful. Suppose that you had calmly hurried from the room. Would that have proved that you had believed yourself, assuming that you weren't trying to fool me?

MRS. W: Well, I guess so, but I'm not sure that I see what you are getting at.

DR. M: Just stay with me; I think you will get it. Why do you wait for the light to say "Walk" before you cross the busy street?

MRS. W: It'd be dangerous; I'm afraid of getting hurt.

DR. M: Okay. Now, while you are standing at the corner waiting for the light to change, do you feel afraid? Are you trembling with fear, etc.?

MRS. W: Of course not. That would be silly.

DR. M: Beautiful! That proves that you don't have to actually feel afraid in order to believe and act as if you are in danger. Merely by thinking, "I'm in danger," and then calmly doing what's necessary to protect yourself, you prove to yourself that you believe your thoughts. So, you would have known you believed the idea "There is a bomb in this room," if you had felt afraid *and/or* if you had acted physically as if you were afraid. That *and/or* is very important. It's what causes you to have cognitive dissonance. But it's also what lets you resolve cognitive dissonance in favor of your brain, instead of your gut.

All you need to do to prove that you believe an idea is just keep thinking it and physically acting on it. That'll force you to ignore your gut and get rid of the phony-fear at the same time. Understand?

MRS. W: Yeah, I think so. But it sure sounds difficult.

Author's Note #11

As with any new mental activity, once you make rational self-counseling a habit, you see that it is *no more* difficult to do than your old irrational self-counseling. That fact proves that when you say rational self-counseling sounds difficult, before you have diligently tried it for at least a month, you really mean: "too difficult for me to do." That's an important insight because the belief that rational self-counseling is too difficult for you to do, kills your self-motivation to learn it. But if you could benefit from rational self-counseling, then it's irrational to believe it's difficult before you've even tried to learn it. To help people avoid that pitfall, I teach them the objective use of the idea of difficulty.

When you are using the idea of difficulty objectively you apply it only to tasks requiring primarily physical activity and *never* to tasks requiring primarily mental activity. The following examples will show why this habit increases your self-motivation for new learning.

No matter how well you learn to carry ten gallon buckets three miles, if the reward is the same and you have the choice, you will always choose to carry an empty bucket instead of a full one. The difficulty in carrying a full bucket versus an empty bucket has such a negative effect on your self-motivation that you'd never choose a full bucket.

If you don't know the Spanish alphabet, and you have the choice of saying it or the English alphabet for the same reward if you don't make mistakes, you will probably always choose English. But you'd be choosing on the basis of increased likelihood of success and *not* on the basis of objective difficulty.

Now suppose you pointed out to yourself that saying the Spanish alphabet is never objectively more difficult than saying the English alphabet. Then you'd be much more self-motivated to learn the Spanish one than you would be if you believed that no matter how much you practiced, the Spanish alphabet would always be much more difficult to say than the English alphabet.

But, if you actually learn the Spanish alphabet as well as you know the English one, if you then liked the two languages equally, you'd be as likely to choose Spanish to recite as English. Similarly, once you learn rational self-counseling as well as you know the irrational kind, you'll choose rational self-counseling more often because it gives greater personal rewards.

After I explained those facts to Mrs. Wilder, I ended with:

DR. M: It's *only* as difficult as it is, but it is definitely *not* impossible. If you meant it when you said, "I can't stand my marriage anymore," you've already decided that going on like you have been is impossible.

MRS. W: , Well, I've tried the impossible and don't like it. So I may as well give the difficult a whirl.

Once Mrs. Wilder accepted and began to act on the rational insights gained in this session, she was on her way to eliminating her phony-fear and saving her marriage. All she had to do to complete the process quickly was to start doing daily rational emotive imagery (next chapter).

Emphasis Questions

(1) The neurotic fear of being a phony is a common pitfall in emotional re-education.   True   False   (P-67)

(2) If you don't understand the phony-fear, you may give up trying to get rid of undesirable emotional habits.
True   False   (P-67)

(3) People who repeatedly say "I _____" instead of "I think" or "I believe" are usually gut thinkers.   (P-68)

(4) It doesn't really make any difference if you say "I feel," when you really mean "I think."
True   False   (P-68, 69)

(5) The gut thinker reasons like this: "What I say I feel must be true, otherwise I wouldn't _____ it?"   (P-69)

(6) Gut thinking lets you mistake _____ for knowledge.   (P-70)

(7) Rational self-counseling means thinking, believing and acting on rational thoughts.   True   False   (P-70)

(8) Magical thinking is a useful way to think.
True   False   (P-70)

(9) No human being can be a phony except through magic.
True   False   (P-70)

(10) Magical thinking means making things happen to someone or something separate from you merely by
_____ or _____ it.   (P-70)

(11) "It, he, she, or they drive me up the wall," is a common
example of _____ thinking.   (P-70)

(12) People who have the phony-fear don't really feel afraid.
True   False   (P-73)

(13) The phony-fear is a real fear of something that
_____ happen.   (P-73)

(14) "Metaphor" is just a fancy word for slang.
True   False   (P-73, 74)

(15) The most rational use of words is to _____ with
_____.   (P-74)

(16) The words you use are your _____.   (P-74)

(17) The thoughts you believe control your _____.
(P-74)

(18) Rational emotional control requires you to _____
choose your _____.   (P-74)

(19) Rational self-counseling will rarely cause you to do something that you haven't already done at least a few times
in your past.   True   False   (P-80)

(20) Saying "I can't" when you mean "I refuse" or "I'm
afraid" is one of the most common copouts people use
for demanding pills or some other magical solutions to
their emotional problems.   True   False   (P-82)

CHAPTER 7

RATIONAL EMOTIVE IMAGERY* (REI) AND BEYOND or Reprogramming Your Brain and Rational Self-Control

Part I
REI

Introduction

Emotional insight is the last active stage of learning in both new learning and in re-education.† It shows that your new behavior is now normal and natural for you. It feels right. That's because your perceptions, thoughts, feelings, and reactions are all logical for each other and support each other. After I had gained emotional insight into driving in Japan, left-sided driving felt as normal and natural to me as right-sided driving does here in America.

Emotional insight in emotional re-education comes about in the same way that emotional insight comes about in driver re-education. Mrs. Wilder had emotional insight into *rational self-acceptance* when she began to feel neutral to mildly disappointed (instead of inferior and worthless) when her husband broke dates with her. Then she not only felt satisfied with herself when her husband worked, she also felt as normal and natural doing it as she did when she used to feel angry and depressed.

That radical change in her emotional habits *did not* magically happen just because she gained more rational insight and self-understanding. She had to put those insights and self-understanding into daily practice.

---

*A version of this chapter was published in *Rational Living*, 1971, 6(1), 24–26.
†The final stage (emotional insight plus practice) mentioned in Chapter 5, *isn't* active learning; it's merely converting a new habit into an old one.

Now you're probably wondering, "Since Mrs. Wilder only had two or three broken dates per month, how could she have daily practice in accepting them?" The answer is: she did daily Rational Emotive Imagery (REI).

You learned about emotive imagery in Chapter 4 when I described my driver education and re-education experiences. It's merely mental rehearsal of the habits you are trying to learn. Emotive imagery is rational when it obeys at least three of the five rules for rational self-counseling. (Chapter 1).

By using rational emotive imagery (REI) you make your emotional re-education both *safe* and *private*. Yet, REI gives you the same fast results that real life experiences give you.

To understand why REI is such an effective self-teaching technique, you must remember that your brain works like a camera (Chapter 2). You *don't* see and react to "what's right before your eyes"; you see and react to the image of it your brain makes in your neocortex. Remember, your brain does not automatically distinguish between images it makes of a real external event and images it makes from your imagination or memory of old events. If you let it, your brain will cause you to react to your memory of an event in the same way you react to the real external event.

Mrs. Wilder is an excellent example of what people can do with REI. Immediately after she decided to give up her phony-fear, she quickly did four good RSA's (Rational Self-Analyses) of her reactions to her most recent broken dates. Then she started doing daily REI on each of her RSA's.

For at least ten minutes before falling asleep at night, Mrs. Wilder recreated in her mind all of the events of broken date number one. She kept everything exactly as it was *EXCEPT* for herself. Now, she refused to see herself thinking her *irrational* ("B" Section) thoughts and she refused to see herself feeling inferior, worthless, angry and depressed. Instead, she saw herself thinking *only* her *rational* ("Da" and "Db" Sections) thoughts and feeling the rational self-acceptance she described in the "E" Section (Her Emotional Goals for Future Broken Dates). At least ten minutes before getting up each morning and before lunch and supper she repeated REI on one of her other three RSA's.

Rational Emotive Imagery Versus Irrational Emotive Imagery

Rational Emotive Imagery (REI) is practicing the habit you want to learn. Irrational Emotive Imagery is practicing the habit you want to get rid of. That is a very important point. Remember it well; otherwise, you will end up like Jeffrey — practicing your irrational habits.

After Jeffrey's friends got angry at him for willfully playing cards stupidly that one time (Chapter 4), Jeffrey made a sincere commitment to get rid of his undesirable temper and improve his playing skill as fast as possible. But when he sat in his room trying to rethink and correct his errors, he naively but effectively continued to practice his undesirable temper. The longer he thought about his errors, the angrier he got, just as he had done at the card game.

Jeffrey's emotive imagery was *irrational* because he had *not* changed any of his irrational attitudes and beliefs about his making mistakes. So, instead of *rationally* improving his skill at bridge, he was irrationally improving his skill at angrily downgrading himself as a person.

Like most people who fail at emotional re-education, Jeffrey had arbitrarily decided to make his emotional reactions more rational, but without first *thinking* more rationally. That's an impossible feat, and naturally Jeffrey failed to do it.

Later, in his rational self-counseling class, Jeffrey began to do RSA's on his irrational anger. Only then did he challenge and get rid of his irrational beliefs about himself and making mistakes. By using those RSA's as the basis of his emotive imagery, Jeffrey made his emotive imagery rational. Then, both his desire and skill at playing bridge quickly increased.

How to Do Rational Emotive Imagery (REI)

First you must keep in mind that *REI IS NOT A GAME.* REI is an effective training and retraining exercise for your brain. Because REI is "as-if" practice, or mental rehearsal, of the rational habit you are trying to learn, it has almost all of the advantages of real life practice, with *none* of the hazards. That makes REI one of the safest and fastest ways to learn any new habit. In addition, by doing daily REI, you gain four other important advantages: (1) You correct past mistakes; (2) You get practice in handling old real life situations with much more rational skill and many *fewer* mistakes in the future; (3) Your emotional re-education progresses many times faster with REI than it would otherwise; and (4) You begin to feel more rational self-confidence in your ability to cope with new life experiences.

Before beginning REI, reread *only* the "A", "Da", "Db" and "E" sections of your well done rational self-analysis (RSA). Then get comfortable either lying or sitting down. Next, quickly calm yourself by doing the instant better feeling exercise described below

For Instant Better Feelings

(A) In one slow but continuous motion, take in a deep breath and force it all out. As you are breathing out, think just one word: "Relax."

(B) At the end of breathing out, hold your breath for at least ten seconds, then repeat steps A and B. To estimate the seconds count: "One thousand one, one thousand two, one thousand three," etc. It takes about a second to say one thousand one.

(C) Keep repeating steps A and B for two or three minutes or *as long as it takes for you* to feel calm.

When you are calm, picture in your mind the *corrected* "A" situation (i.e., your old "A" plus the camera corrections in "Da") of your RSA. See everything exactly as a video or movie camera would have shown it, *EXCEPT FOR YOU*. See yourself thinking or saying *ONLY* your rational "Db" Section thoughts; and most important, *make* yourself feel only the feelings you described in your "E" Section. Repeat the scenes over and over for ten minutes.

What if You Start Getting Upset?

Immediately stop the imagery. Calm yourself with the slow breathing exercise and begin your mental images again. If you start getting upset again, immediately stop the imagery and calm yourself again. Then reread your "A", "Da", "Db" and "E" Sections. Look for errors in applying the five rules for rational thinking; if you find any, correct them. Whether you find any errors to correct or not, ask yourself if you are sincerely convinced that your "Db" and "E" Sections meet three or more of the five rules for rational thinking. *MOST IMPORTANT,* honestly answer this next question: Do you really believe that this new way of thinking, feeling, and acting is both in your best interest and acceptable to you as a new personality trait? If your answer to this important question is "No" or "I'm not sure," rewrite your "Db" and "E" Sections more to your *rational* satisfaction. Then, do daily rational emotive imagery (REI) on that.

Don't, I repeat, *DON'T* do REI using thoughts that you recognize as rational *BUT* you are not convinced are best for you to adopt. If you do you'll just end up like Jeffrey — practicing your old irrational habits. You probably *won't* be any worse off; but you won't be helping yourself either.

When you are convinced that your "D" and "E" Sections are rational and acceptable to you, try rational emotive imagery again with greater relaxation and concentration.

Remember, all re-education takes time and repetition. Don't demand perfect REI's of yourself the first trial — or even the first several trials. Just keep doing them as directed and you can rationally expect steady progress toward your emotional goals at "E."

Problems with REI and Their Solutions

My extensive research and clinical use of REI have revealed only two problems in using it correctly: (1) having vague, unclear images and (2) having distracting thoughts. I'll discuss each in that order.

People vary greatly in their ability to evoke vivid mental images. Some people do it so effortlessly, I call them image thinkers (Part II of this chapter). Other people (like myself) do it so poorly, in spite of intense concentration, I call them concept, idea, or word thinkers.

The ability (or lack of ability) to evoke images is probably an inherited trait, like any other talent. If so, you *can't* do much to change it. Fortunately however, the ability to evoke vivid images at will is merely helpful; it's *NOT* essential for efficient emotional re-education.

The brains of concept thinkers process concepts with the same ultimate thorough learning that results when the brains of image thinkers process images. It just takes concept thinkers a bit longer on the average to achieve the same level of immediate desirable results.

That fact *does not* mean that image thinkers are necessarily more fortunate than concept thinkers. As a rule, concept thinkers tend to be much less irrationally sensitive, changeable, moody and phobic than image thinkers. Consequently, concept thinkers usually have fewer intense emotional hang-ups that need REI. So the extra effort concept thinkers must put forth tends to be balanced by their having fewer problems to solve in the first place. On the average, therefore, concept thinkers and image thinkers end up requiring about the same total time to achieve relatively comprehensive emotional re-education. In summary then, if you don't evoke clear-cut vivid images when you try to do REI's on your RSA's, *DON'T WORRY ABOUT IT!* Just rethink your "Da", "Db" and "E" Sections with as intense mental and emotional concentration as possible for at least ten minutes, four times per day.

The more often than four times per day you do REI, the more efficient your emotional re-education will be. But only four times a day every day gives a satisfactory rate of rational change for most people.

Usually just ignoring distracting thoughts during REI is the best way to handle them. Sometimes though, people have the same persistent thoughts so often that REI is temporarily impossible. Whether they realize it or not, such people usually are having those thoughts as a subtle form of civilized voodoo, to magically prevent some feared event from happening. In short, these people are usually afraid not to have their distracting thoughts. Part II of this chapter tells you how to deal with that irrational habit as well as the habit of procrastinating.

In my experience, all the other complaints patients have had about REI have disappeared rapidly when they diligently do it strictly as directed. That means excluding all, I repeat, *ALL*, personal short-cuts or interesting but *untested* personal variations on REI, as it is described here.

Is REI Just Pretending?

No, it's not. It is simply one of the best ways to use your brain to learn anything. "But," many people ask, "can't people just use REI to pretend to be working on their problems, while in fact they are avoiding working on them?" Yes and no. Yes, people can avoid working on their problems. But no, those people will *not* be using REI. They will be merely practicing their old habit of trying to trick themselves into feeling better without having first begun to think better. Since they will be thinking and reacting in their usual ways, they will get their usual results.

No one can stop people from pretending or playing games with themselves. The people who play games with rational self-counseling would also play games if they were receiving professional psychotherapy and counseling. I have never been able to prevent nor make such people stop playing their little games, nor have I ever heard of any other mental health professional who could. Of course, for people who are so crippled by emotional problems as to be unable to function or to control their daily lives, neither REI nor RSA is an adequate substitute for professional help (although both may make receiving professional help easier and more efficient). It's normal people who can get along in life — even if not to their complete satisfaction — that rational self-counseling (i.e., RSA's and REI's) alone can help to improve their emotional health. But whether people are receiving help from a professional or trying to help themselves, no benefit is likely unless those people sincerely want to improve themselves, are honest with themselves, and are willing to work diligently as instructed.

How to Tell Pretending from Practicing

Pretending to become more rational is like pretending to learn to play the guitar. When you are pretending to learn to play, you don't follow instructions, you change the suggested fingering technique, and you don't make music — you just make musical noise. Even if you often pretend to be learning, your ability to play the guitar doesn't increase.

When you are practicing learning to play the guitar, you follow instructions and you use the suggested fingering technique. You still make a lot of musical noise, but you also begin to make some music. And most important, your ability to play the guitar gradually increases. But, you wouldn't stop practicing the guitar after one or two weeks and expect to maintain or increase your skill in playing. Instead, you would logically expect to lose rapidly whatever skill you have gained. The same logic applies to practicing rational self-counseling and its self-help techniques.

Rational self-counseling, RSA and REI are skills. If you don't use them, you quickly lose them. Fortunately, you won't be any worse off for having lost them than you were before you started. In fact, if you later decide to relearn them, you will usually do it must faster than you did the first time.

Isn't Real Life Experience More Important than REI?

Usually not. Experience is a good teacher. But by itself experience is usually neither the fastest nor the best teacher. Most people learn best by combining a lot of "as-if" experiences with appropriate real life experiences. Only if you refuse to do REI, will real life experiences become more important than REI for your re-education. That's true whether you are doing emotional re-education or any other type — for example, pilot re-education.

When pilots want to learn to fly a new type of airplane, they don't immediately start flying the new plane. They first go to ground school. There they act "as-if" they were flying the new plane. They sit in false pilot seats, look at fake instruments, and learn the technique and feel of flying the new plane — all while sitting in an electrical rocking machine that's bolted to the floor. This "as-if" practice is the safest and fastest way to learn to fly the real plane.

I described the beginning process of pilot re-education because most people can easily see the logic and value in it. But for some reason, most people either forget or ignore that the principles of learning are the same for pilot re-education and for emotional re-education.

It would be *illogical* for student pilots to wait until they go up in a new type of plane before they try to learn to fly it. And it's illogical for you to wait until the *next time* you have a problem before you try to learn to use rational self-counseling. RSA plus REI starts you practicing the rational solution to your most recent problems before you have had time to have them again.

Remembering the student pilot example is especially helpful for people who have the phony-fear. Student pilots know that their fake machines in ground school are not real airplanes. Yet they don't wonder if they're just pretending to be pilots, nor do they call themselves phony pilots. They *know* for *sure* that they are *practicing* being real pilots.

By using their brains as if they were actually flying, student pilots give themselves excellent mental maps for correct flying. Those "as-if" mental maps give the students the correct emotional feeling of correct flying. Consequently, when they go up in the real planes, these student pilots have little or no cognitive dissonance or phony-fear to confuse them.

Summary

Rational emotive imagery or REI means practicing correct thinking, feeling, and acting. As you imagine the events in the "A" Section — (Facts and Events) — of your RSA, you now picture yourself having only the rational thoughts and actions described in the "Da" and "Db" Sections of the RSA and feeling only the desired rational feelings described in Section "E" — Emotional Goals.

REI's should be done regularly, for ten minutes at least four times a day. Think of it (REI) as being your emotional ground school. Use it well and it'll give you the same four benefits flying ground school gives student pilots:

(1) You will learn in the safest way possible. (Your mistakes won't hurt you nor anyone else.)
(2) You will correct mistakes fast without shame or fear.
(3) You will greatly increase your chances for feeling and doing exactly what you want to about the next real life problem.
(4) You will decrease the chances of having the same problem again.

Part II
BEYOND REI, RATIONAL SELF-CONTROL

Introduction

If you are physically and mentally healthy, and awake, you are always in control of you. The common irrational excuses for continuing irrational habits: "I can't get myself to . . .; I can't stop myself from . . .; I just have to" . . . etc., are all just that: *IRRATIONAL EXCUSES*. If you are physically and mentally normal and you are willing to rationally control yourself, you can get yourself to learn almost any habit other normal people have learned.

Why is it then that so many normal people fail to get rid of their personally undesirable emotional and other bad habits? They don't understand self-motivation. They don't know what it is, nor how to bring it about at will.

What Self-Motivation Is and the Two Kinds

Self-motivation consists of two different forms of the emotion: *DESIRE*. Everything you do is motivated *either* by your *desire* to get something you want, or by your *desire* to avoid something you don't want. The something you desire may be social acceptance, approval, love, power, money, fame; or you may desire to avoid poverty, pain, humiliation, neglect, hatred.

Of course, no one merely has one desire. We all have a great hodgepodge of them: hopefully many useful ones, some that are in conflict with others and usually a few that are frankly harmful to us. That's why rational self-counseling keeps forcing people to balance and weigh their desires against each other. The man who desires money *and* social approval will not be able to rob a bank or become a slum landlord, nor will he be able to become a poor social worker or a penniless monk. The person who sits in an all electric home and dreams about a camping trip into the Yukon to satisfy a desire for frontier adventures needs to take into account his habitually strong desire for instant automated comfort.

Most of us make these adjustments with relative ease and control our varying desires in almost robot-like fashion on the basis of well learned habits. If you desire to get to work on time and avoid a ticket for speeding, you usually motivate yourself to get up early enough to drive to work within the speed limit. Usually you've formed these habits with so little conscious thought that it's hard to understand why everyone doesn't naturally have them. That's the usual result of having rational desires that fit together logically. And when people who have desires like that decide they could benefit from rational self-counseling, they have little trouble motivating themselves to do diligent RSA's and REI's.

There are, however, some other quite normal but unhappy people who have never learned the skill of putting their desires in cooperative order. Without realizing it, they have rational desires paired with irrational ones. Consequently, they act like bank robbers who want to be applauded in the newspapers, or losers who believe they still deserve the prize for winning. When these people decide they could benefit from rational self-counseling, at least in the beginning, they try to get its benefits *without* doing the rational self-counseling. In my experience, this is the most common type of irrational desire that prevents rational emotional re-education. People who have this type of irrational self-motivation will religiously come to psychotherapy and pay for it for years, but refuse to change their irrational behavior one iota. Their most common irrational excuses for refusing to change are: "Oh, I tried that and it didn't work;" or "But doctor, that's too hard."

Even if the therapist can get these people to stop making irrational excuses and start practicing rational self-counseling, they usually do it for only a week or so. Then they quit, in spite of having made real progress. Their most common excuse is: "I thought I should have gotten rid of that problem by now." Or, they angrily ask, "Why do I have to keep working at it so long?" Obviously, they will not be able to re-educate themselves emotionally until they replace their irrational self-motivation with the rational kind.

The next most common type of self-motivation (desire) that prevents emotional re-education is the irrational desire (self-motivation) for guaranteed success before attempting to make self-changes. Because there is no such objective guarantee, this irrational desire motivates people to start practicing the civilized form of voodoo that is better known as worry, and usually confused with rational concern.

Rational concern is just enough desire to avoid an undesirable event, to motivate you to take the most efficient and effective action possible, with the least amount of emotional discomfort. Worry is emotional upset about events that are beyond your control. Because the events are beyond your control, your emotional upset is merely a magical attempt to help yourself without being able to help yourself. And in addition to being useless, worry most often prevents you from doing well, what you can do about aspects of undesirable events you can control.

Fortunately, the things most chronic worriers worry about most rarely happen anyway. Unfortunately though, chronic worriers get confused by that fact and end up believing that their worry somehow prevents the events they worry about from happening. That irrational belief forces chronic worriers to be *afraid not to worry.*

Ms. Betty Green* was a typical example of chronic (magical) worriers. She was a 20-year-old college student referred to me for psychiatric evaluation as a possible suicide risk. Several hours prior to her evaluation, she had been found by her roommate, comatose, on the floor of their apartment. It turned out that she had not tried to kill herself. She was just trying to get to sleep as fast as possible by drinking Mickey Finns (Bloody Mary's spiked with chloral hydrate). She did that often because she was "scared to death" when she didn't have someone to talk to at night. She explained: "Whenever my roommates are out of the apartment at night or asleep, I begin to think, 'I'm all alone with no one to talk to! What if something terrible happened to me and I couldn't handle it? That would be awful! What would I do? Someone might break in. Oh! I'm afraid. Something is going to happen! I just know it!' Then I get panicky and either visit or telephone someone."

"If it's too late at night to visit or telephone someone I write letters, thinking at the time I'll mail them; but I never do. I

---

*Tape recordings of her rational behavior therapy are available as emotional self-help aids for people learning rational emotional self-control. For information about obtaining these and similar tapes, write the author at, Department of Psychiatry, UKMC, Lexington, Kentucky, 40506.

started drinking Mickey Finns about six months ago because my roommates threatened to move out of the apartment. I was keeping them awake every night because I couldn't go to sleep. Every time I'd close my eyes I'd see, I mean I'd imagine that someone was in the room. Then I'd jump up and turn on the light. After doing that fifteen or twenty times a night, my roommates usually got mad. But now, after two or three MF's, (Mickey Finn's) I drop off to sleep like a rock."

To understand why I say Betty's worry was magical nonsense, you must keep in mind that nothing objectively dangerous had ever happened to her, nor to anyone else in her neighborhood. So all of her worry was about possible but unlikely fearful events. Yet she was afraid not to worry about them. She was convinced that the night she refused to worry would be the night the terrible things she was afraid of would happen.

Betty was an excellent example of severe emotional distress due to ignorance of how the human brain works. Betty was largely an image thinker. That is most of her thoughts were accompanied by clear visual images. For example, if you were to say to her: "There was a six car accident on the freeway," Betty would have a vivid image of six cars in an accident, complete with bodies and blood scattered all over the highway. Her images would be formed from her imagination and memory of other accidents. But, she would react emotionally to her images as if she were there looking at the real accident.

Even though her emotional reaction would be much too intense for the neutral statement: "There was a six car accident on the freeway," her reaction would be quite appropriate for her mental images.

Remember, it's your brain's mental image that controls your emotional and physical reactions. With that insight you can more easily understand Betty's problem.

When Betty was alone, she'd get the thought: "What if someone broke in and tried to rob, rape or kill me!" Then she'd immediately get vivid mental images of a robbery, rape or murder scenes and frighten herself out of her wits. Because her emotional feelings were so intensely real, she believed they meant there must be some (yet unknown) realistic reason to be afraid.

With typical "gut" thinking logic, Betty reasoned: "If I really didn't have something to be afraid of, I don't feel I'd be afraid. So I don't feel I can relax because I'm afraid if I relax something might happen." When I first challenged that irrational logic, she told me an interesting story.

When Betty was thirteen she dreamed she was in England visiting her grandparents. On the day she was to leave, her grandfather begged her to stay with him. She saw herself laughing, telling him not to worry, everything would be fine. She didn't think any more about her dream until two weeks later when her grandfather actually died in a fishing accident. She then blamed herself for the accident because she believed that if she had been more concerned (worried in her dream) about her grandfather, she might have prevented the accident, even though she was over a thousand miles away. From that time on Betty became more and more of what she called a "worry wart." "I know it sounds silly," she said, "but the things I worry about could and sometimes do happen."

I had to agree with her on that point. But I quickly added that her worrying was *not* a guarantee against fearful things happening. And since her worry *didn't* protect her, it had always been merely a painful waste of her time and emotional energy. And now, it was causing her to abuse alcohol and have problems with her roommates.

Because Betty was bright (usually, image thinkers seem to be bright) I was quickly able to show her that emotionally healthy living is based on what is likely or probably going to happen. Because it was impossible for her to guarantee that *no possible* harm could ever come to her, it was useless to use worry as a form of insurance. In addition, I pointed out that her worry led to her drinking herself to unconsciousness, so even if a burglar did break in, she would be least likely to protect herself. That fact made her worry disobey four of the five rules for rational emotional control: (1) It ignored objective reality: the fact that she lived in a relatively safe neighborhood; (2) It *didn't* cause her to protect herself; it caused her to get defenselessly drunk; (3) It caused her trouble with her roommates and (4) It made her feel miserable.

Once Betty agreed to make her thoughts and images about being alone always obey at least three of the five rules for rational thinking, she was ready to do REI. Specifically, four times per day for ten minutes, she would vividly recreate in her mind the details of her nighttime routine with these two important exceptions: Instead of thinking about it, using her habitual, fearful thoughts and images, she pictured herself calmly sitting alone in her locked apartment thinking, feeling and acting as any other non-phobic coed would act. Next, she'd picture herself calmly dressing for bed, then calmly lying in bed sleeping peacefully.

The first couple of nights she did REI, she controlled herself beautifully as long as she was doing REI. But the moment she tried to study or actually fall asleep she'd immediately have her old images, thoughts and fear. So she ended up drinking herself to sleep anyway.

Her problem then was *not* fear of being alone. Instead, her problem was *FEAR* of *not being afraid of* being alone. She still wanted that pseudo-extra protection that she believed worry gave her. In short, she had a conflict in habits of self-motivation. She wanted the benefit of rational thinking and of the pseudo-magic of worry.

To help people quickly resolve such conflicts as well as help them get rid of related problems of irrational goofing off and procrastination, I suggest some form of self-administered aversive conditioning.

Self-Administered Aversive Conditioning

Self-administered aversive conditioning is based on the insight that there are *only* two basic self-motivating desires: (1) the desire to get something and (2) the desire to avoid something. The idea is to get people to make their desire to avoid one event lead them to satisfying their desire for another event. In Betty's case, I wanted her desire to avoid sleep-disturbing thoughts and images to lead her to the satisfying desire for peaceful, *sober* sleep. To achieve that goal, I put her on my no-drug, sleep routine.

Because I wanted being in bed to become an effective cue for sleep, I advised her to do nothing in bed other than sleep. Reading, talking, planning, eating, watching TV, etc., were all prohibited. Once in bed the rules to follow were: Continuously do the slow breathing routine recommended for beginning REI. But now, with each expiration, calmly think "relax," and have *only* images that your normally associate with "tranquilized" relaxation. In other words, remember the drowsy feeling you get after a couple of tranquilizers or three quick stiff cocktails. With each expiration create that tranquilized feeling more and more. After it seems that 20 minutes or more have passed, glance at a conveniently placed clock. If 20 or more minutes have passed, get out of bed and do at least 15 (25 for men) male-type push-ups. If immediately prior to getting out of bed you have been thinking any thoughts that are not related to relaxation and sleep, force yourself to think those same thoughts when you begin the push-ups. That causes you to pair your sleep-preventing thoughts with your self-administered aversive stimuli — in this case, push-ups.

Having completed 15 push-ups (25 for men), return to bed immediately and repeat the initial 20 minute attempt to go to sleep. If you are unsuccessful again, get up immediately and add 20 additional push-ups to your original number and return to bed immediately. With each subsequent failure to fall asleep in 20 minutes, repeat the whole routine, adding 20 more push-ups to the prior number.

Like most patients, Betty complained that she *couldn't* do more than five or six push-ups at a time. As usual, I told her to rest as much as she wanted to, as long as she did it on the floor. Again like most patients, she awakened two or three mornings on the floor. But that was okay; she had had an undrugged sleep. That was the main goal.

I have never had a patient to require more than six sets of push-ups (one hour and 20 minutes) in order to get to sleep, either on the floor or in bed. Also, within one week, a diligent person is almost always sleeping "like a lamb" without drugs. After the third or fourth night, the mere thought of push-ups is enough to inhibit sleep-disturbing thoughts. The effect is almost auto-hypnotic.

These results are achieved *only* by patients who doggedly follow through as instructed. Betty was diligent. Three nights of push-ups and she began dropping off to sleep "like a rock", almost as soon as she got in bed.

Haphazard or inconsistent use of auto-aversive conditioning can result in making your insomnia *appear* to get worse. Therefore, I tell patients that if, for any reason, they are not willing to follow the instructions exactly, *don't* attempt self-administered aversive conditioning. Persistent REI alone will ultimately solve the insomnia problem.

Aversive conditioning is not a substitute for either Rational Self-Analysis (RSA) or rational emotive imagery (REI). It merely makes both of them more efficient. I advised Betty to use male push-ups as her aversive conditioning maneuver. However, any moderately uncomfortable, quickly tiring physical activity is just as effective. Some people prefer sit-ups. If you do sit-ups, I recommend starting with thirty and doubling them each time you have to repeat them during the same night. Running in place is also good. I recommend starting with ten minutes of it, and adding an additional five minutes each time you have to repeat it in the same night. Needless to say, if you have any physical ailment or disability that physical exercise may make worse, don't do self-administered aversive conditioning. You can still overcome your insomnia with just RSA and REI alone.

Non-Physical Aversive Conditioning

For people who are more thought than muscle motivated, I advise a personal contingency management form of self-administered aversive conditioning. This means selecting an activity that you are most likely to do every day; then re-refusing to do it until you have done your rationally chosen new task. For example, when people "can't find time" to do RSA's or REI, I suggest that they refuse to eat or watch TV until they have done their RSA or REI's. Some people penalize themselves for procrastinating by fining themselves $50.00 for each day of procrastination. Then they send the $50.00 as a gift to support their most hated organization. That's like the Birch Society penalizing backsliding members by requiring them to contribute to the Communist Party.

Needless to say, there is no magic in self-administered aversive conditioning. It is *only* as effective for self-motivation as people are willing to be diligent in following through exactly as directed.

Rational Insight

Self-help is available *ONLY* to those who honestly believe they are worth their efforts to help themselves.

Emphasis Questions

(1) _____ _____ is the last active stage of learning in emotional re-education.   (P-87)

(2) Emotional insight means that you have become used to your new habit.   True   False   (P-87)

(3) Emotional insight in emotional re-education comes about in the same way as it does in driver re-education. True   False   (P-87)

(4) Mrs. Wilder made rational changes in her emotional habits by putting her rational insights into daily _____.   (P-88)

(5) Emotive imagery is rational when it obeys _____ of the _____ rules for rational behavior. (P-88)

(6) By doing _____ _____ _____ you make emotional _____ both safe and _____. (P-88)

(7) Rational emotive imagery (REI) is an effective self-teaching technique. True   False   (P-88)

(8) Because your brain works like a _____ REI is effective. (P-88)

(9) REI means practicing the emotional _____ you want to learn. (P-88)

(10) Irrational emotive imagery means practicing the emotional habit you _____ to get _____ of. (P-88)

(11) The first step in effective REI is to keep in mind that REI is *not* a _____. (P-89)

(12) If you plan to do REI, you don't need to do RSA. True   False   (P-89)

(13) Before doing REI, it is a good idea to _____ yourself down with _____ better _____ exercise. (P-90)

(14) If you start to feel upset doing REI _____ immediately. (P-90)

(15) It doesn't matter if you do REI using thoughts that you don't really believe. True   False   (P-90, 91)

(16) The two most common problems in doing REI are having _____ _____ images and having _____ thoughts. (P-91)

(17) REI is pretending to be rational when you know you really aren't. True   False   (P-92, 93)

(18) You can't tell for sure if you are pretending or practicing. True   False   (P-93)

(19) Real life experience is usually a better teacher than REI. True   False   (P-93)

(20) REI is really your _____ ground _____. (P-93, 94)

SECTION III

EMOTIONAL SELF-TEACHING THROUGH "AS-IF" LEARNING FROM OTHERS

As you read this section, keep these two things in mind. First, normal people raised in the same culture usually have the same rational as well as irrational beliefs. Second, you almost never see yourself as others see you, but often see elements of your own personality in others. In fact, the most impressive things to you about other people usually are the positive or negative traits that you have, have had, or wish to have. So expect to get many views of your own personality as you read the case histories. In addition, the case histories that you identify with most will usually give you many rational insights that you can use to help yourself.

CHAPTER 8

"AS-IF" RATIONAL SELF-ANALYSIS (RSA)*
(The Self-Hassled Mother)

Introduction

You can learn all about swimming by reading books. But if you don't get in the water and use your knowledge, you won't learn how to swim. So if you are interested in swimming for physical exercise, you will have to do more than just read about it.

The same is true of RSA's. You can learn all about them by reading this book. But unless you actually work through RSA's yourself, you still won't learn how to do them. Ultimately, you'll "have to get into the water." Just reading about RSA's won't solve many problems for you; for that, you'll have to start doing RSA's.

That seems rational, and obvious enough. But many emotionally distressed people balk at this idea of actually working to solve their emotional problems. These people agree that they have to do RSA's before RSA's can help them. But, they nevertheless come up with sincere but irrational excuses for *not* actually doing RSA's. The three excuses I hear most often are:

    (A) I'm waiting until I have another problem to analyze.
    (B) I'm afraid I won't do the RSA's right.
    (C) I just can't find the time to do RSA's.

Those excuses may appear to be quite rational; but if you accept any one of them you put yourself in an irrational bind. And, you won't learn to solve your problems rationally, until you get out of that bind by refusing to make those excuses.

When people who have been waiting to have another problem to analyze finally get one, they usually think: "I know I should try to do an RSA to solve this problem, but I'm too upset now. I'll wait until I calm down, then I'll do it." But when they

---

*The "as-if" RSA was perfected as an aid to emotional growth by the Association for Rational Thinking (ART) in its group rational growth activities. If you want more practice in using "AS-IF" RSA's, you can purchase them from the National Headquarters of ART (See Introduction and Appendix A).

calm down, they say: "Well, the problem is gone now. Why stir up old stuff? Let sleeping dogs lie. But, the next time I have a problem, I'm really going to try that RSA thing."

Their irrational bind is: they're forever waiting for new problems to solve rationally without ever having learned the skill of rational problem solving.

The people who are afraid of doing RSA's wrong are like students who want to be given an "A" for a course before they sign up for it. They say: "I don't want to waste time trying to learn something if I'm going to fail at it." They correctly see that the chance to succeed in helping themselves with RSA's also means the chance to fail in helping themselves. But they ignore the insight that they are unlikely to fail in trying to use RSA's if they do what is necessary to succeed.

Their irrational bind is: While they wait for guaranteed success, they *fail* to learn how to solve their problems rationally.

People who can't find time to do RSA's usually have two irrational beliefs:

(A) They believe minutes and hours are concrete objects — like wild berries to be looked for and found.
(B) They believe they *have* to do all the things they usually do.

The belief that minutes and hours are concrete objects causes these people to make a logical but self-defeating oversight. They ignore that every minute of every hour of every day is always there. That makes them *unaware* that every hour of *their* day is already filled with their habitual activities.

Because they sincerely believe that they have to do everything they usually do, they don't bother to decide which of their daily habits are important and which are not. Consequently, they religiously force themselves to do unimportant things with the same diligence they do important things. When faced with a new activity like RSA, they never schedule time for doing it. That would mean giving up an *old* activity. Just the thought of doing that makes these people feel anxious. To avoid that anxiety, they stubbornly maintain that they have to continue all of their old daily habits. But, because they sincerely want to do and benefit from the new activity, they start a diligent search for a twenty-fifth hour for doing RSA. But, because there is no twenty-fifth hour, they never find one.

Their irrational bind is having to find something that *isn't* there, before they can help themselves.

Occasionally, valid insight into an irrational bind is enough to make people give up the irrational excuse that causes it; but sometimes insight is not enough. When it isn't, people can ease themselves into doing RSA's by using practice or "as-if" RSA's.

"As-If" RSA's

"As-If" RSA's are practice exercises using someone else's problem. They are designed to insure that you gain understanding, skill, and confidence in using the RSA technique and the five rules for rational behavior, even if you don't now have personal problems.

In this and the next chapter, you will read rational self-analyses done by a real person with real problems. You are to imagine that you are the person who wrote them. Then, try to solve these problems rationally, "as-if" they were your own. It doesn't matter if you've never had a problem similar to those in the "as-if" RSA's. The "as-if" RSA's are used mainly to increase your skill in thinking in the RSA format and in using the five rules for rational thinking to think of rational debates to any irrational idea.

Part one of the "as-if" RSA's consists of the A, B, C and E sections of the real person's emotional problem. In the space under the "C" section, fill in the five rules for rational thinking and use them to give the "A" section a camera check and to fill in the "D" section the way you believe would enable you to replace the old emotional habit at "C" with the new one at "E."

Part two of an "as-if" RSA consists of what the real person and the therapist actually said about those A, B, and C sections. Check your answers against theirs.

By following those steps, the "as-if" RSA will give you a fast, easy and safe way to learn rational self-analysis. So even if you don't have a personal problem now, you won't have to wait until you get one to learn RSA. And even if you do have a personal problem now, the "as-if" RSA will be the safest way to learn rational self-analysis before you attack your own problem.

Think of doing "as-if" RSA's as being like learning to drive using someone else's new car. That way you won't have to worry about damaging your own. But once you learn to drive, you can safely drive your own or anyone else's car.

Remember! Don't expect all of your answers to be exactly the same as the therapist's or the other person's. What's rational for one person, even about the same problem, may not be rational for you. The "as-if" RSA *does not* try to give you a pat formula to be applied blindly. Rather, "as-if" RSA's are like being in an emotional ground school, similar to the ground school of student pilots. Remember! The main goal of "as-if" RSA's is to give you practice in using the technique of rational self-analysis (RSA). "As-if" RSA's *DON'T* analyze you. You will do that when you do RSA's on your own problems.

"AS-IF" RSA #1
(The Self-Hassled Mother)

Mrs. Roman was an average, normally concerned mother. She wanted to do right by both herself and her children. Yet she felt trapped in a situation where she didn't seem to be doing right by either. Although the problem in this RSA seemed trivial — she couldn't get her daughter to voice lessons on time — the hassles about this kept getting worse and worse. Mrs. Roman saw that clearly; but she failed to see (before RSA) that her hassles were really not so much with her tarrying daughter as they were with herself.

This is Mrs. Roman's first RSA of the problem. But you are to imagine that Mrs. Roman is you; her A B C and E sections are your perceptions and thoughts. Read the "ABC and E" sections through and fill in the five rules for rational thinking in the space under the "C" section. Then come back to this page and fill in the spaces under "Da" and "Db" using the five rules for rational thinking. Finally, compare your responses to those Mrs. Roman and I gave, starting at the top of page 114. Don't be surprised or discouraged if your responses are different from ours. It takes time and practice to think according to the five rules for rational thought. If it were really easy, everybody would be doing it already.

"A" *Facts and Events*	"Da" *Reader's Camera Check of Her "A"*
A–1 My daughter is taking voice lessons twice a week, but she is always late. She just stalls and piddles around and never seems eager to go.	Da–1

Her lessons last half an hour, and she has to go to the other side of town to get to them, and I have to drive her, usually through rush hour traffic. Even though I arrange her lesson time to avoid the rush hour traffic, I still can't get her in the car in time. Consequently, her teacher takes other students ahead of her and I end up catching the heavy traffic anyway.

A–2 One day I waited over two hours for my daughter to take a half hour lesson. Her teacher took every child who arrived before she took my daughter.   Da–2

A–3 Even when the teacher schedules my daughter last, she still manages to dilly-dally around so much that she often keeps her teacher and the piano accompanist waiting for half an hour or more.   Da–3

A–4 Last week I decided to stop the lessons. I told the teacher that I needed three weeks to cool off. But if my daughter changed her attitude and asked to take lessons again, I would agree.   Da–4

A–5 While I want to provide opportunities for my children to develop their talents and to enjoy cultural activities, I don't like having to hassle and bawl my daughter out in the process of getting her there.   Da–5

A–6 Her teacher said I should overlook all this and should somehow manage to   Da–6 make my daughter develop her talent because later on she will be sorry I didn't make her persist. I wish she had kept her damn mouth shut. Instead of helping me, she just made me feel more confused, guilty, angry and depressed.

"B" *Self-Talk*	"Db" *Your Debate of Her "B"*
B-1 It just doesn't seem that my daughter really has any consideration or respect for me, her teacher, or the accompanist. (bad)	Db-1
B-2 I seem more eager for her to take lessons than she does. (bad)	Db-2
B-3 She should have more consideration for me, her teacher, and the accompanist. (bad)	Db-3
B-4 It is so cold waiting in the car during the wintertime and hectic at times keeping the two younger ones occupied. (bad)	Db-4
B-5 She won't even let me come in to hear her lessons, and I think that is just snotty behavior on her part. (bad)	Db-5
B-6 She acts like she's doing me a damn favor by taking voice lessons. (bad)	Db-6
B-7 It isn't fair to me to be making all the efforts and taking so much wear and tear. (bad)	Db-7
B-8 I really don't mind making the effort or the money if she'd just care enough to do her part by being on time. (good)	Db-8

B-9 Her teacher is just trying to make me feel guilty about stopping the lessons. (bad)	Db-9
B-10 I'm damned tired of putting up with all this rushing around and all this damned waiting. (bad) It's so hard on the two younger ones to wait so long. (bad)	Db-10
B-11 If the lessons were important to her then she'd make every effort and be more eager about getting there on time. (neutral)	Db-11
B-12 She just sulks around and tunes me out. If I say anything to her she doesn't respond. She just acts as though everything is just fine. (bad)	Db-12
B-13 I want to be a good mother. I am trying to help my daughter, but she has just got to take more initiative on her own behalf. (good)	Db-13
B-14 If she doesn't care enough about her lessons to get to them on time, then I'll stop the whole damn thing. To hell with it. (good)	Db-14

"C" Mrs. Roman's Actual Emotions	"E" Her Future Emotional Goal for "A"
Anger at my daughter and her teacher; frustration and guilt. I had three good's, one neutral and eleven bad's.	Less anger and guilt and more patience.

FIVE RULES FOR RATIONAL THINKING:

1. Based on objective reality
2. Preserves my life

3. Achieves my goals
4. Keeps me out of
   significant trouble with
   others
5. Prevents significant
   personal emotional conflict

Mrs. Roman's Camera Check of "A"

(Refer to pages 110–112 for her "A")

Da–1   "Statement of facts."

My Comments

I doubt that "always" and "never" are correct. If they aren't, then you are likely to overreact if you say them. "Stalls and piddles around," what's that? You're much more likely to solve a problem if you describe it accurately. Say exactly what your daughter does and what you want her to do. That's the first step to solving your problem.

Da–2   "Statement of facts."

My Comments

O.K.

Da–3   "Statement of facts."

My Comments

My remarks in Da–1 about "stalls and piddles" apply here to your use of "dilly-dally."

Da–4   "Statement of facts."

My Comments

"Cool off" implies that time, rather than you, controls your emotions. All time does is pass. Unless you refuse to think about the matter, you will not "cool off" even after three years. Even if you do "cool off" by refusing to think about the matter, unless you also change your present beliefs about it, you will surely "heat up" again when you think about it again or when your daughter starts lessons again.

Da–5   "Statement of facts."

My Comments

"Hassle and bawl" are more negative subjective opinions about what you do, and *not* neutral objective descriptions of what you do. Also, you *don't* "have to" do what you do with your daughter. You choose to do it. Were you to remind yourself of that, you would stop blaming your daughter for things that you choose to do.

Da-6 "Statement of facts."

My Comments

The teacher merely said what she thought, and she's probably right. However, you are mistaken in accusing the teacher of making you feel more confused, guilty, angry and depressed. You did that to yourself.

Mrs. Roman's Rational Debate of Her "B"

B-1 "It just doesn't seem that she really has any consideration or respect for me, her teacher, or the accompanist."

Db-1 "This statement is an exaggeration."

My Comments

It's not only an exaggeration, it's an irrational opinion that causes you needless pain. You haven't described any evidence that she doesn't respect you. All you said is that your daughter is not as concerned as you are about getting to voice lessons on time. Then you decided that her lack of concern means or proves lack of respect. In reality, it proves *only* lack of concern. It may also mean that she doesn't respect you. But, she could respect you and still be less concerned about promptness than you are. The only "evidence" you have for your belief is your belief. But your belief may well be wrong.

B-2 "I seem more eager for her to take voice lessons than she does."

Db-2 "I don't understand how to challenge this."

My Comments

If your statement is true, then it is a simple statement of fact. However, just because a situation seems to be a certain way, that doesn't prove that the situation really is the way it seems to be. But let's assume that you are more eager than she is; you don't have to upset yourself about it. There's no law requiring your daughter to be as eager as you are for her to learn to sing.

B-3 "She should have more consideration for me, her teacher and the accompanist."

Db–3 "It is irrational to believe that my daughter should be different from the way she is."

My Comments

You are right; everything is always exactly the way it should be under its circumstances. So, your daughter behaves exactly the way she should behave. That is the only way she has been taught and apparently it's the only way she has been required to learn to behave in this case. She hasn't learned yet the same value that you place on being prompt. Therefore, she should be as late as she is. By saying that she shouldn't behave the way she does, you are trying to justify being upset merely because your daughter disagrees with your idea about promptness. You probably realize that your behavior is a bit childish. So you are trying to cover over that fact by irrationally using "should."

You haven't given any valid evidence for believing that your daughter doesn't have consideration for you. She probably does have some. It's just that she apparently has more concern for her own desires than she has for yours or those of her teacher.

B–4 "It's cold waiting in the car during the wintertime, and hectic at times keeping the two younger ones occupied."

Db–4 "I am feeling sorry for myself."

My Comments

If your "B" statements are true, they are statements of fact. Merely saying that you are feeling sorry for yourself doesn't help you solve your problem. You need to use the five rules for rational thinking and acting to see if your thoughts and actions are rational.

You probably thought something like: "This is awful and unfair." Then you made yourself depressed and angry about that thought. That possibility needs to be considered because people *rarely* feel sorry for themselves about things they do to themselves. Only if people convince themselves that someone else or the world is "mistreating" them will they dive in the pool of self-pity. In your case though, no one seems to be mistreating you.

A more personally helpful rational debate of your Db–4 would be to say: "My B–4 statement is a fact that I can either calmly put up with, or calmly refuse to put up with." Then based on your strongest personal desire, you could make a rational decision about what to do.

B-5   "She won't even let me come in to hear her lessons, and I think that's just snotty behavior on her part."

Db-5   "I don't understand how to challenge this either."

My Comments

I doubt that she forces you to stay out when she has her lessons. Define "snotty" and see if your definition makes rational sense. A definition that makes rational sense would apply to almost anyone in similar circumstances. If your definition does *not* make rational sense, it probably indicates that you're angry at your daughter merely because she is not giving you what you want, when and how you want it. If that's true, it's not very rational behavior by you.

B-6   "She acts like she's doing me some kind of damn favor by taking voice lessons."

Db-6   "I don't understand how to challenge this one."

My Comments

Your B-6 is your subjective opinion. You haven't given any evidence that your opinion is fact. But let's assume that your opinion is fact, why get upset about it? If your daughter is doing you a favor, why not enjoy it? Favors are usually acts of love, kindness and respect — all the things you seem to want from your daughter, but claim you *are not* getting.

B-7   "It isn't fair for me to be making all the efforts and taking so much wear and tear."

Db-7   "I don't understand how to challenge this."

My Comments

To speak rationally of fairness, you must first have an agreement. Not once have you said that your daughter agreed to be prompt. Also, you keep ignoring the fact that you chose to carry her to her lessons. If the personal rewards for your efforts were not enough for your satisfaction, you could have calmly chosen to stop the lessons long before you angrily chose to stop them. Your use of "wear and tear" was meaningless noise that kept you from thinking rationally about the problem. You weren't worn and torn, so it didn't make rational sense to say it. But believing that you were worn and torn gave you a *logical* but irrational reason to be angry and stop the lessons.

B-8 "I really don't mind the effort or the money if she'd just care enough to do her part in being on time."

Db-8 "This must be some form of the irrational attitude that if a person has a talent, they should "live up to their potential."

My Comments

Not necessarily. It is perfectly rational to resist putting yourself to needless inconvenience. However, the fact that you angrily persisted in putting yourself to inconvenience probably means that you do have a bit of that irrational attitude with reference to your daughter. If so, it would be well to get rid of it.

B-9 "Her teacher is just trying to make me feel guilty about stopping the lessons."

Db-9 "No one can make me feel guilty unless I choose to feel guilty and I refuse to do it any more."

My Comments

As stated, your challenge is quite rational. The only thing I would add is that you were attempting to read the teacher's thoughts and determine her motives. In reality, all you did was read your own mind or opinion and make yourself feel guilty about it. It was therefore irrational of you to blame the teacher for what you did to yourself.

B-10 "I'm damned tired of putting up with all this rushing around and all this damned waiting. It's so hard on the two younger ones to wait so long."

Db-10 "Maybe the teacher really doesn't care if my daughter is late, so I really ought not get so upset over being late."

My Comments

Your challenge may be true, but it's irrelevant to your B-10 statement. Irrelevant statements confuse rather than clarify issues. However, you made a logical conclusion about the teacher — maybe she doesn't care about your daughter being late. But, your conclusion about the teacher has no logical relationship to how you ought to feel. Even if the teacher drove herself out of her mind about your daughter being late, that wouldn't be a rational reason for you to get upset.

How tired is "damned tired?" Is it more tired than "very tired" or "too tired to do it again?" When you are "damned tired" you are also likely to be "damned mad." If you are *only* too tired to keep carrying your daughter to her lessons, you are not likely to waste emotional energy being angry at her. You'll just calmly stop carrying her.

B-11   " If the lessons were important to her, then she would make every effort and be eager about getting there."
Db-11   "I don't understand how to challenge this."

My Comments

In light of the fact that your daughter is already getting to her lessons, your B-11 statement does not make sense. I see no rational reason for her to put forth any more effort to get to her lessons than is necessary to get her there. She's now getting there, so she probably sees no reason to make any more effort than she now makes. I don't see any reason for her to do it either.

B-12   "She just sulks around and tunes me out. If I say anything to her she doesn't respond. She just acts as though everything is fine."
Db-12   "My daughter seems to be denying reality, specifically me."

My Comments

Objectively speaking, your first B-12 thought is just a meaningless metaphor rather than a statement of fact. Your second statement is false. Your daughter does respond to you. Ignoring you is a response. Your last statement is another of your futile attempts at mind reading. Your attempts to read your daughter's mind won't help you, so I advise you to stop them.

B-13   "I want to be a good mother. I am trying to help my daughter, but she has just got to take more initiative on her own behalf."
Db-13   "Statement of facts."

My Comments

I accept your first B-13 statement as a statement of fact. If you would first state what you think a good mother does, you would probably be less frustrated and more successful in trying to live that role. When you decide what you think a good mother does, use specific terms that can be put into specific action. For example, don't say things like "Is loving, understanding and has respectful children."

I have no idea what you mean by your use of initiative in B–13. I doubt that your daughter has an idea either. If you had said, "She will have to be in the car, ready to go to her lesson at 4:00 p.m., if she wants me to take her," then, I and your daughter would know what you expect her to do. That type of clearcut self-talk (personal thought) would help you too.

B–14 "If she doesn't care enough about her lessons to get to them on time, then I'll stop the whole damn thing. To hell with it."

Db–14 "I am setting goals for her that she resents."

My Comments

Your Db–14 statement is irrelevant to your B–14 statement. Maybe you are setting goals for your daughter that she resents. That *doesn't* have to be bad for your daughter, *nor* wrong of you. Your daughter's resentment may well be irrational. This is especially likely, if your daughter is too young or naive to set rational goals for herself. Later when she's more mature, she may well be glad you set these goals for her. Getting angry at your daughter for possible immaturity won't help the situation. It would be better for you and for your daughter, if you would try to get her to see why you think it's in her best interest to accept the goals that you are setting for her.

Your B–14 statement would have been more helpful to you and your daughter if you had added: "So from now on, if she's not in the car ready to go at 4:00 p.m., she'll just have to get herself to her lesson or miss it."

Mrs. Roman's Emotional Goal for Future "A's"

E — "Less anger and guilt and more patience."

My Comments

Your emotional goals seem rational. If you were to change your "Db" debates more toward the ones just suggested, you'd probably begin to make progress toward your goals.

This was a good first trial at RSA. But like most first trials, your "A" section was too complex. Each of the paragraphs in

"A" is a topic for a separate RSA. This RSA was really a summary of six separate RSA's. I suggest that you go back and do an RSA on each "A" section paragraph.

In spite of its shortcomings, this RSA did two important things:

> (A) It pointed up your main irrational habits of thinking.
> (B) It pointed up your main emotional conflict.

Your main irrational habit of thinking is that you often confuse your exaggerated opinions and meaningless metaphors with objective facts. That habit makes your emotional reactions exaggerated and often inappropriate for the objective reality.

Your main emotional conflict seems to consist of a sincere desire to give your children the best growing-up experience that you can, and an interfering irrational fear of failing to be a good mother. To eliminate your conflict fastest, you must do these two things:

> (A) Using the five rules for rational thinking, examine each of your beliefs about what a mother has to do to be a good mother. If (as I think you will) you find beliefs that cause you to make irrational demands on yourself, get rid of those beliefs.
> (B) Systematic RSA's and REI's to eliminate your irrational fear should be done.

Emphasis Questions

(1) You are much more likely to solve your problems if you describe them accurately.   True   False   (P-114)

(2) Time does not control your emotions. All time does is _____.   (P-114)

(3) Using words like always and never sometimes causes you to overreact.   True   False   (P-114)

(4) "Hassle and bawl" are objective descriptions of facts. True   False   (P-114)

(5) Just by "cooling off", your problems disappear. True   False   (P-114)

(6) The teacher really did make Mrs. Roman feel guilty and depressed.   True   False   (P-115)

(7) It had to be a fact that the daughter didn't have any consideration for her mother or teacher. True   False   (P-115)

(8) If you sincerely believe that you're not getting respect, you have a rational reason to be angry.
True   False   (P-115)

(9) People feel sorry for themselves because they believe someone or the world is mistreating them.
True   False   (P-116)

(10) Feeling sorry for yourself usually just causes you to feel bad.   True   False   (P-116)

(11) People often accuse others, using meaningless phrases like "being snotty", and then react with real angry feelings.
True   False   (P-117)

(12) Unfair is what you agree is unfair.
True   False   (P-117)

(13) It *doesn't* make any difference whether you say, "My job is wearing me out and tearing me up," or "I've been putting in more hours at work than I want to."
True   False   (P-117)

(14) Mrs. Roman really did have to rush around and be anxious about her daughter being late for lessons.
True   False   (P-117)

(15) Who is most likely to be angry, (a) the person who is "damned tired" or (b) the person who is merely too tired to do anymore?   a,   b   (circle one)   (P-119)

(16) When someone ignores you, they are not responding to you.   True   False   (P-119)

(17) Trying to read someone's mind is a good way to know what they are thinking.   True   False   (P-119)

(18) Mrs. Roman was usually very specific in her expectations of her daughter.   True   False   (P-120)

(19) Mrs. Roman's emotional goals were irrational.
True   False   (P-120)

(20) Because Mrs. Roman's RSA was not perfect, she just wasted her time doing it.   True   False   (P-121)

CHAPTER 9

"AS-IF" RSA #2
(Not So Self-Hassled Mother)

Mrs. Roman was determined to give rational self-counseling an honest trial. She took my advice and did a separate RSA on each of the six paragraphs in her first "A" section. When she did the RSA on paragraph #6 (where she accused the music teacher of making her more angry and frustrated) she faced up to her fear of failing as a mother and started to deal with it rationally.

Some weeks later, her younger daughter's teacher told her that little Suzie had a poor self-image. Mrs. Roman was hurt, but she handled the event much more rationally than she would have in the past. When she got home, she did this RSA of the event.

Again, fill in the blank spaces as previously directed.

Her "A" Section *Facts and Events*	"Da" *Your Camera Check of "A"*
A–1 Suzie's teacher told me that Suzie has a bad self-image and that she seems scared to death of making mistakes. She asked me how Suzie responded to criticism at home. I felt sick, like someone had kicked me in the pit of my stomach. Even so, I managed to keep a straight face, and by the time we finished talking, I was feeling somewhat better. But I thought I could use a better look at myself, so I did this RSA.	Da–1

Author's Note #1

When people diligently work at doing RSA's and REI's for two or three weeks, they automatically begin to handle emotional upsets better. As you read the "B" section below notice the improvement in Mrs. Roman's thinking. After her first three, completely irrational thoughts, her thinking became *much less irrational*. That's why she was feeling somewhat better toward the end of her talk with Suzie's teacher.

Her "B" Section Self-Talk	Your Debate of Her "B"
B-1 She must think I'm a terrible mother. (bad)	Db-1
B-2 Oh no! What have I done to my little girl? Why did I have to criticize her so much? (bad)	Db-2
B-3 I should have been more patient. Oh, this is awful. She must hate me. (bad)	Db-3
B-4 What am I saying. I'm not that bad. Maybe I did make a few mistakes, but there's no point in acting stupid about it now. (bad)	Db-4
B-5 Who's she to talk; I had her daughter in Brownies, and she was so shy, she was afraid of her own shadow. I didn't accuse her of being a bad mother. (good)	Db-5
B-6 But she's not accusing me of being a bad mother. She's really trying to sympathize with me. Why else would she say that she knows how I feel? (neutral)	Db-6
B-7 She looks like she's more uncomfortable talking about it than I am. Poor thing. (neutral)	Db-7

B–8   Well, that's her problem. I wonder why Suzie's so sensitive? I don't criticize her any more than I do Emma. There's nothing wrong with her self-image, dilly-dallying around making everyone wait on her hand and foot just so she wouldn't miss her voice lesson. Well, I put a stop to that. She hasn't been late but twice since I started making her take the bus, if she's not in the car by 4:00. It's absolutely amazing what two cross-town bus rides with two transfers in freezing weather did for her sense of time. (good)

Db–8

B–9   She's right. Suzie does have a bad self-image. I wonder what I can do to help her get over it? I think I'll try to teach her to think more rationally about herself. Dr. Maultsby says that children have the same ability to learn rational thinking that they have to learn irrational thinking. (good)

Db–9

B–10   Poor Mrs. Carpenter looked so bewildered when I thanked her for telling me about Suzie's problem and assured her that I would start to work on it right away. (good)

Db–10

"C"
Her Actual Emotions

I felt sick, embarrassed, then guilty; then somewhat relieved.
   I had four bad's, two neutral's and four good's. Not

"E"
Her Emotional Goal for Future "A's"

To be calm from beginning to end.

bad at all; in fact, I'd say
that's pretty good for me.

FIVE CRITERIA FOR
RATIONAL THINKING:
(Fill them in and then go back
and do "Da" and "Db"
sections.)
1.
2.
3.
4.
5.

Mrs. Roman's Camera Check of "A"

A–1 "That's exactly what
happened."

My Comments

Okay. I'll accept that as an objective description of the situation.

Author's Note #2

Some people may wonder about her putting the statement about her feelings in the "A" section. A camera could neither record nor check her feelings. Still, it was a fact that Mrs. Roman felt the way she felt. Simple statements of fact about how you feel are okay in the "A" section.

If Mrs. Roman had said: "Suzie's teacher really kicked me in the stomach and made me feel sick," that wouldn't have been a fact. It would have been subjective nonsense that she would need to challenge in "Da" like this: "That's not true. No one kicked me. I made myself feel as if I had been kicked. But since no one did kick me, my feeling was irrational."

Mrs. Roman's Rational Debates to Her "B"

B–1 "She must think I'm a terrible mother."

Db–1 "I don't know what she thinks. But if she thinks I'm a terrible mother, she's mistaken. I know I'm not a terrible mother. So, I refuse to feel guilty and upset about her mistake. I do the best I know how for my children. That's all anybody can do. So I take full responsibility, but no blame, for my best effort even though it may not be everything I hoped for."

My Comments

That seems rational to me. I'm glad you are finally seeing the difference between self-blame, which requires you to feel angry or otherwise upset, and merely being responsible, which requires you only to accept the consequences of your actions rationally. As I've said many times before, rational acceptance means remaining calm, but doing all that you are willing and able to do about the consequences of your past actions. All you need to do now is make yourself act in light of that difference all the time.

B–2   "Oh no! What have I done to my little girl? Why did I have to criticize her so much?"

Db–2   "What have I done? Only the best I know how. But it's apparent that it wasn't enough. So I'll see if I can learn to do better. Why did I have to criticize her? I didn't have to do it; I chose to do it. I honestly thought she needed to be corrected, and I still do. It probably would have been better for her though, if I had made it clear that I was criticizing her behavior and not her as a person. I'll really make that point clear next time. But when her behavior is wrong, it's wrong and needs to be corrected. I'd be negligent as a mother if I didn't correct her when she needs it."

My Comments

A very good application of the five rules of rational thinking to child rearing problems.

B–3   "I should have been more patient. Oh, this is awful! She must hate me."

Db–3   "I should have done exactly what I did do. That's all I could have done and still follow my own mind. Since I couldn't follow anybody else's mind, I had no choice but to do as I did. Being more patient probably is *not* the answer. It doesn't seem very rational to stand around and patiently watch a child practice inappropriate behavior. I just need to get her to see that *it's* her *wrong behavior* and *not her* that I'm criticizing. Nothing is awful. I was just catastrophizing. That was irrational of me; so I'll stop it right now. Suzie doesn't hate me. No child could hate anyone and talk and act as lovingly as she does to me, day in and day out. And even if she does hate me, it will have to be because of childish misinterpretations of my actions. I'm definitely *not* a hateful mother. So, if she hates me now, when she's older and sees her mistake, she'll stop hating me, just like I stopped hating my mother."

My Comments

I don't see anything I can add to that except, *ACT* on it every day.

B-4 "What am I saying? I'm not that bad. Maybe I did make a few mistakes, but that's no reason to act stupid about it now."

Db-4 "I think that's pretty rational."

My Comments

I agree.

Author's Note #3

Even in first trials at RSA, some of the "B" section sentences may be rational. And as you begin to do daily RSA's and REI (rational emotive imagery) you can expect more and more of your self-talk sentences to be rational. The ultimate aim of RSA and REI is to make your self-talk rational in all situations.

With her B-4 thoughts, Mrs. Roman began to think more rationally while still talking to Suzie's teacher. As soon as she began to think more rationally, she began to get rid of that kicked feeling in her stomach.

B-5 "Who's she to talk? I had her daughter in Brownies, and she was so shy, she was afraid of her own shadow. I didn't accuse her of being a bad mother."

Db-5 "She is who she is to talk. It's irrelevant how shy her daughter was and still is. So what if I didn't accuse her of being a bad mother? I had no right to do so anyway. I'm just upset because I thought she was accusing me of being a bad mother. But that's just my subjective nonsense, as my therapist would say."

My Comments

I agree.

B-6 "But she's not accusing me of being a bad mother. She's really trying to sympathize with me. Why else would she say that she knows how I must feel?"

Db-6" "I think my thoughts were rational."

My Comments
I agree.

B–7   "She looks like she's more uncomfortable talking about it than I am. Poor thing."
Db–7   "That's just a statement of fact as I saw it. But I think it's relevant for the situation.

My Comments
I agree. However, I question the appropriateness of calling her a "poor thing." She's just a fallible human being who felt badly; you did too earlier. But neither you nor she is a "poor thing."

Author's Note #4
Often your "B" section thoughts will be simple statements of facts. When they are, simply say so. But always decide if the facts are relevant or not. Often, distressed people get as confused by cluttering their minds with irrelevant facts as they do by thinking irrational ideas. Suppose Mrs. Roman had thought: "If she had spent more time paying attention to her husband, he wouldn't be such a drunkard." Even if that statement had been a fact, it would have been irrelevant for this situation. So it would have been better *not* to clutter up her mind with it.

B–8   "Well, that's her problem. I wonder why Suzie's so sensitive. I don't criticize her any more than I do Emma. There's nothing wrong with her self-image, dilly-dallying around, making everyone wait on her hand and foot just so she wouldn't miss her voice lesson. I put a stop to that. She hasn't been late but twice since I started making her take the bus, if she's not in the car by 4:00. It's absolutely amazing what two cross-town bus rides with two transfers in freezing weather did for her sense of time."
Db–8   "The first part of that seems factual. In the last part, I started exaggerating and using meaningless metaphors. But I stopped doing that, and the rest were just facts. Maybe they weren't so relevant, but I think it's good to remind myself that I really am making some progress with my kids."

My Comments
Very good. I agree.

B–9   "She's right, Suzie does have a bad self-image. I wonder what I can do to help her get over it? I think I'll try to teach her to think more rationally about herself. Dr. Maultsby says that children have the same ability to learn rational thinking that they have to learn irrational thinking."

Db–9   "I think that's rational."

My Comments

I agree.

B–10   "Poor Mrs. Carpenter looked so bewildered when I thanked her for telling me about Suzie's problem and assured her that I would start to work on it right away."

Db–10   "That just seems factual to me."

My Comments

I agree except for the "poor Mrs. Carpenter" bit. My comment on your Db–7 applies here. This was an excellent RSA. To get the most from it fastest, all you need to do is daily REI's on the event, using *only* your rational thoughts. Then, follow through with action on those REI's every day.

Mrs. Roman followed my advice. She also continued to do new RSA's and REI's until she had become as satisfied with herself as a mother as she desired. A big step in that direction was when she began to teach Suzie the rational view of making mistakes. That is: "All fallible human beings make mistakes. Since you are a human being, and *all* human beings are fallible, you will always make mistakes. When you feel badly for any reason, you are *more* likely to make more mistakes. That fact makes it *irrational* to feel bad about your mistakes. You will be far better off if you calmly accept your mistakes and correct them as fast as you can."

Every time Suzie made a mistake, Mrs. Roman repeated the rational view of making mistakes to her. Next, she had Suzie to repeat it. Then she calmly showed Suzie how to correct her mistakes fast, *without* feeling badly at all. Gradually Suzie began to get rid of her budding irrational fear of making mistakes. When last heard from, Mrs. Roman and all her children were doing quite well.

Emphasis Questions

(1) The fact that Mrs. Roman felt hurt when her daughter's teacher told her Suzie had a poor self-image proves that rational self-counseling had not helped her.
True   False   (P-123)

(2) Because Mrs. Roman had honestly been trying to teach herself to think more rationally, she was able to start feeling better while still talking to her daughter's teacher.
True   False   (P-124)

(3) When you are making simple statements of fact about your feelings, it's okay to put them in the "A" section of your RSA.   True   False   (P-126)

(4) The teacher really did hurt Mrs. Roman's feelings.
True   False   (P-126)

(5) Mrs. Roman really was a terrible mother, otherwise she wouldn't have felt guilty about what the teacher said.
True   False   (P-126, 127)

(6) When you take full responsibility for your actions (but no blame) you're *less* likely to feel upset.
True   False   (P-127)

(7) It's *not* enough to just have rational thoughts; you have to act on them to get results.   True   False
(P-127, 128)

(8) Parents should never criticize (i.e. correct) their children's behavior.   True   False   (P-127)

(9) It's okay to criticize children's behavior, but you need to make sure they know you're *not* criticizing them as people.   True   False   (P-127)

(10) Even though Suzie had a beginning inferiority complex, Mrs. Roman should have done exactly what she did.
True   False   (P-127)

(11) Even though you do RSA's daily, your "B" section will always be irrational.   True   False   (P-128)

(12) Any factual statements will always be helpful in solving problems.   True   False   (P-129)

(13) The final goal in doing RSA's is to make your "B" section rational.   True   False   (P-128)

(14) In emotional distress, sometimes filling your mind with
_____ facts can be as bad as filling it with
_____ ideas.   (P-129)

(15) Children usually have as much ability to learn rational
thinking as they have to learn irrational thinking.
True   False   (P-130)

(16) If children hate their parents, that proves the parents are
hateful.   True   False   (P-127, 128)

(17) If children hate their parents, they will always hate them.
True   False   (P-128)

(18) Because the teacher's daughter was shy, she had no business
telling Mrs. Roman about Suzie.
True   False   (P-128)

(19) It was cruel to make Suzie take the bus to her lessons.
True   False   (P-129)

(20) When you make stupid mistakes, you just have to feel
bad.   True   False   (P-127)

CHAPTER 10

WHAT MAKES YOU YOUR OWN ENEMY?
(Irrational Attitudes Hidden Behind Your Thoughts)

Sometimes people find themselves doing repeated RSA's about the same or related events. Or they keep having the same irrational emotions even though they can quickly get rid of them. This case history explains why that happens and what to do about it.

After six weeks of using RSA and REI to overcome his irrational fear of rejection by women, Tony Mallat had achieved a great deal of success. He was dating regularly for the first time in his life, and in general was enjoying himself more than ever before. But he still had a mild panic when he'd first see a pretty woman he'd like to meet. Most of the time though, by thinking through his ABC's or irrational fear, he'd quickly calm down and meet her anyway. Even so, while Tony was thinking away his irrational fear, the woman would sometimes get away. Naturally, Tony was irritated about that and he was curious about why he was not yet over his fear. In this rational behavior therapy session he learned the answer.

TONY: I thought I'd be over my fear of rejection by now. I mean, RSA's and REI's have helped me a lot; but after all that work, I still get uptight when I see a new girl I want to meet. Why is that?

DR. M: Well, let's take a quick look at your latest RSA on your fear and see what we can see. Okay. The format's right; your "A" is factual; you know the five rules for rational thinking. Oh, here's your problem. You're getting hung up on your irrational attitudes hidden behind your "B" and "D" section thoughts.

TONY: What attitudes? I didn't see any hidden attitudes.

DR. M: No, I'm sure you don't. By the time you were ten or twelve years old you had learned these irrational ideas so thoroughly that you stopped noticing them even though they kept triggering your emotional fear of being rejected.

TONY: But you said it was my thoughts about my perceptions that triggered my emotions.

DR. M: That's true. But you're forgetting that an attitude is really nothing more than a thought and perception that you have put together and acted on over and over, for so many months that you now do it automatically. For example, when you see a snake you don't have to think 1. There is a snake; 2. A snake is dangerous; 3. Dangerous things can hurt me; and 4. I should be afraid. You just see a snake, or even think you might see one, and (if you are like most people) you automatically feel afraid. Now, all that your actual self-talk about snakes does is either keep your automatic fear going or stop it. Don't you remember reading about that in those articles about human emotions that I gave you? (Chapter 3 in this book)

TONY: Well, you see, Doc, I lost some of that stuff before I had a chance to read it.

DR. M: You lost it?

TONY: Yeah, I meant to ask for another set.

DR. M: Never mind; I'll give you another set before you leave. I think I can quickly show you what I mean with this RSA. Let's look at your self-talk; the clues for your hidden attitudes are always there, if your "B" section is honest.

TONY: Mine's honest, all right.

DR. M: I agree, that's why we should be able to solve your problem relatively easily starting right here with your B–1 sentence.

His B–1 Statement and D–1 Rational Debate

"B" Self-Talk	"D" Rational Debate of "B"
1. If I ask her for a date and she refuses, that will prove what a fool I am for wanting her.	1. Maybe she won't refuse me; after all, she did tell me to call her sometime. I may not have anything to worry about this time. I think I'll call her.

DR. M: Your B-1 thoughts seem to be hiding (that is, they imply) these irrational attitudes:

(1) that you are, or could be, a fool;

(2) that it would be terrible if something proved you to be a fool;

(3) that being refused a date will prove it.

Can you see that too, or am I just imagining things?

TONY: No, now that you mention it, I see it. I mean, if I had really given up the idea that I'm a fool or could be a fool, then I would not be afraid that I could be proven to be one.

DR. M: Right! If I were to tell you that I'm going to examine you to see if you are a girl, would you be afraid that my examination would prove you to be a girl?

TONY: No, of course not.

DR. M: Right. You know you have nothing to be afraid of, even if I do examine you. But when you see an attractive new girl, your automatic fear makes it seem as if you really do have something to be afraid of.

TONY: But Doc, if there really isn't anything to be afraid of, what makes me *feel* afraid?

DR. M: Your old irrational attitudes, the three we just found hiding in your self-talk. Now that you have learned how to debate your thoughts, you can quickly talk yourself out of your fears, but *only* temporarily.

TONY: Why?

DR. M: Because you aren't challenging and getting rid of the attitudes that keep triggering your fear. In fact, your self-talk here either reinforces your irrational attitudes or leaves them unchallenged. Look here. You wrote: "I may not have anything to worry about this time." That implies that you may well be a fool, that being rejected would prove it, and that being proven to be a fool is a frightening thing that you may not have to worry about this time, but that you certainly will have to worry about the next time! Can you see that too, or am I just fooling myself?

TONY: Yeah, I didn't see it before, but I do now.

DR. M: This is a good example of having a rational thought for irrational reasons.

TONY: I don't understand.

DR. M: It was perfectly rational for you to point out to yourself that you didn't have anything to worry about because that really was a true statement; but not for the reasons you gave yourself. You decided that you didn't need to worry about being made a fool of because she probably would *not* reject you that time. That was an irrational way to decide that you had nothing to worry about. The rational reason to use to make that decision is: It was then and still is impossible for you to be objectively proven to be a fool. So, you arrived at the rational conclusion that you *needn't* worry, and you went ahead and asked for a date. But, you did it for an irrational reason; and you left unchanged your irrational attitude that being refused a date could prove you to be a fool and is, therefore, an objectively dangerous thing that you sometimes need to worry about. And that's the irrational attitude hidden behind both your "B" and "D" section thoughts. That's also the reason you are still afraid when you first see a new desirable girl. Do you follow that?

TONY: I think so.

DR. M: Explain it to me.

TONY: Well, take the snake example. If I'm about to cross a ditch, and I see a snake sunning himself on a rock, I would probably think things like, this snake doesn't look like any poisonous snake I've ever seen; anyway, I won't get very close to him, and even if it wakes up, most snakes will run from you if they can. So, I'd probably go on across the ditch without being afraid.

DR. M: Okay, that sounds rational. But why wouldn't you kill it?

TONY: Well, I just don't like the idea of killing things that can't defend themselves.

DR. M: I see. Well, what if it had been a little lizard sunning on the rock — would you feel afraid?

TONY: No, I wouldn't give it a second thought, because lizards can't hurt you.

DR. M: Right. But why wouldn't you give yourself a rational debate about a lizard?

TONY: It wouldn't be necessary.

DR. M: Right! It wouldn't be necessary because neither your attitude nor your belief about lizards trigger fear. And to stand there and debate the matter would make it seem that even if this lizard is safe, maybe the next one won't be. But since your attitude is that no lizard is dangerous, you neither feel afraid nor need to debate anything. When you are willing to be as logical about asking for dates as you are about lizards, you'll solve your problem.

Let's see if you can find the irrational beliefs or attitudes hidden by this "B" statement from one of my patient's RSA's on pre-exam anxiety. She wrote, "I have to get the highest grade on this test because I have to prove to myself that I'm better than they are; otherwise, I can't accept myself."

TONY: Well, one irrational belief there is, that as a person, one fallible human being can be better or superior to another fallible human being.

DR. M: Good! You're right! That irrational belief is based on the equally irrational idea that if people act better in certain roles than other people, their actions magically turn them into something more than *only* a fallible human being. In reality though, no matter how well you act, you will always remain *only* a fallible human being. Can you find another irrational belief hidden in there?

TONY: Yeah, I see two more. One is the irrational belief that getting the highest grade will prove that she's a better human being than she would be if she got the lowest grade.

DR. M: Good! What's the other one?

TONY: I sure wouldn't miss that one; I was hung up on it for so long myself; it's the crazy idea that it's possible to reject yourself. You can't reject yourself because everywhere you go, you're always there. So the only thing you can do is reject the things you did in the past, by not doing them anymore. But no matter what you do, you have to accept yourself as a person. The only choice you have is whether you are going to accept yourself calmly, miserably, or happily. Right?

DR. M: Right, that is, if you are going to stay sane. But if you really flip out and become psychotic, you can convince yourself that you don't exist; then it would appear to you that you are refusing to accept yourself. The most common examples of that nonsense are when psychotic people convince themselves that they are someone else, like Henry VIII or the emperor of the United States. Objectively, though, they are still themselves, denying the reality of themselves. But that's psychotic behavior, and neither you nor she is psychotic; so let's check out her "D" section debate to that "B" sentence. She wrote, "Objectively, I really haven't studied much for this course because I really wasn't interested in it. So even if I don't get the highest grade, it won't prove that I'm inferior." What do you think of that?

TONY: Well, at first she sounds almost rational; but if you really think about it, you see that she's saying this exam doesn't count merely because she didn't study for it. But she also seems to be saying that if she had studied for it, then she'd have to get the highest grade in order to accept herself.

DR. M: Exactly! So, even though her "D" section debate helped her to stop worrying about that particular exam, because it left untouched the irrational beliefs and attitudes hidden in her "B" section, at her next exam. . .

TONY: She'll be as uptight as ever.

DR. M: Right! Who and what does that remind you of?

TONY: Me! I'm good at talking myself out of my fear of meeting girls, but when I first pick out a new one, I'm as uptight as ever.

DR. M: That's because you are not using your RSA's to find and get rid of your old irrational beliefs and attitudes hidden by your everyday thoughts. The best way to get at them is do your RSA's as usual, then go back over each statement asking yourself: "What hidden belief or attitude does this thought imply?" If you find one, check it out against the five rules for rational thinking. If it doesn't meet at least three of them, replace it with a more rational thought. After you act on the new thoughts long enough, you'll turn them into rational attitudes and beliefs. Well, I see the time is up. I'll get that article for you. It'll give you more specific details about attitudes and beliefs.

TONY: Yeah — but I think I see my problem now.

DR. M: But I think you still could benefit from rereading these articles several times to make sure that you really understand how your conscious thoughts can and do hide irrational attitudes; and most important, to make sure that you can put those ideas into your own words, so that you will be able to use them in real life practice. (The reader may also benefit from rereading Chapter 3.)

TONY: Oh, I agree, and I'm gonna read it this time for sure.

Tony did three more weeks of intensive REI's using rational challenges to his hidden attitudes. By the end of that time, he had stopped having any noticeable fear when he approached a new girl.

Emphasis Questions

(1) RSA's give you all the help you need in finding your hidden enemies.   True   False   (P-133)

(2) By acting on the same perceptions and thoughts year after year, you transform them into attitudes and beliefs. True   False   (P-134)

(3) By the time Tony was a teenager he so thoroughly converted his fearful thoughts about being rejected into fearful attitudes that now, he no longer needed to actually think those thoughts in order to feel afraid at the sight of a new girl.   True   False   (P-134)

(4) When your attitude triggers your emotions, it seems that you don't really control your own emotions. True   False   (P-134)

(5) Attitudes and beliefs are merely well learned pairs of old perceptions and thoughts.   True   False   (P-134)

(6) You can arrive at rational conclusions for irrational reasons.   True   False   (P-135)

(7) Irrational attitudes can keep triggering an old irrational feeling even though you have learned to quickly get rid of it.   True   False   (P-135)

(8) "Sometimes I make an ass of myself," can be a rational statement.   True   False   (P-135)

(9) It's rational to believe that some people are superior to others as people.   True   False   (P-137)

(10) Tony demonstrated that it's often easier to pick out the rational attitudes and beliefs hidden behind someone else's thoughts than it is to find your own. True   False   (P-138)

(11) Students who consistently make A's are really superior human beings to people who flunk. True   False   (P-137)

(12) Attitudes and beliefs consist of habitually paired_____ and_____.   (P-134)

(13) When attitudes trigger your emotions, it seems that external events instead of you are controlling your feelings. True   False   (P-134)

(14) To change that illusion you must reacquaint yourself with your long forgotten_____or self-_____.
(P-134)

(15) Tony's irrational attitudes were even hidden by some of his rational challenges.   True   False   (P-135)

(16) Sometimes people arrive at rational_____
for_____reasons. (P-135)

(17) It's only rational for a fellow to be afraid that the woman he asks for a date may refuse him and prove what a fool he is.   True   False   (P-136)

(18) Consistent good behavior can turn you into a better person.   True   False   (P-137)

(19) Tony was still afraid because he was *not* using his RSA's to_____and_____rid of his fearful_____
and beliefs about being refused dates. (P-138)

(20) To root out the attitudes and beliefs hidden behind your thoughts, just ask yourself what_____or belief would lead logically to that thought. Your answer to that question usually reveals the attitude or_____you may need to_____.   (P-138)

SECTION IV
RATIONAL SELF-COUNSELING CURES ALCOHOL AND DRUG ABUSE

The quandary about chronic alcohol and other drug abuse is an excellent example of the obvious being the most difficult to discover. People abuse alcohol and other drugs for the same two reasons they do virtually everything else:

    1.) They *hope* to get something they *want.*

    2.) They are *afraid* of getting something they don't *want.*

When people have frequent severe conflicts between their hopes, fears and wants, they often turn to alcohol or other drugs for relief. Their habitual use of addictive agents causes their bodies to start craving them. Such people almost never have a rational self-understanding. Therefore they don't see that their strong craving is merely a learned habit; that's why they *don't see* they *can eliminate* that habit *as readily as* any other one, providing they can go about it rationally.

Chapter 11 Irrational Feelings Drive People to Drink

Chapter 12 RSA's Drive People to Sobriety

Chapter 13 The Rational Approach to Drug and Alcohol Abuse

Chapter 14 Doug In the Five Stages of Rational Drinking Re-education

Those chapters show and explain all the above facts in the case history of a young executive in the early stages of chronic alcohol abuse.

Because alcohol is an addictive drug, the basic mechanism of the alcohol habit is the same as that of the hard drug habit. Therefore, once people are out of the withdrawal phase of the hard drug habit, all they need to stay free of their old hard drug habit are the rational self-counseling techniques described in the next four chapters.

Because hard drugs are so much more addictive than alcohol, I don't believe that anyone can ever use hard drugs socially. With hard drugs, I believe that complete abstinence is the only rational solution.

CHAPTER 11

IRRATIONAL FEELINGS DRIVE PEOPLE TO DRINK

The emotions you feel, like love, hate, or fear, are real. Furthermore, they are always logical, correct and appropriate — but only for what you think and believe. If you believe sharks make the ocean a dangerous place, it's logical to be afraid of it, even though three hundred people are splashing merrily in the waves, and it's an objective fact that a shark hasn't been within miles of that beach for years. Your fear will still be logical, correct and appropriate for your belief but *not* for that beach.

Why don't phobic but otherwise intelligent people see that? They are confused about who does what to whom. They mistakenly believe that external people or situations control their emotional feelings. So when they feel afraid (for example) they logically assume that they must be in a dangerous situation. "I'm not crazy," they reason; "I wouldn't go around being afraid of nothing. My feelings tell me there's danger there, even though there's no evidence of it." And that's why they insist that the external situation frightens them. Actually, though, *only* their fearful beliefs about the situation can make them afraid.

The same thing is true when Bill gets angry at Frank. Like most people, Bill doesn't know that *it's* his own belief about Frank that is making him angry, so he naturally concludes that Frank is doing it. Because anger is a painful feeling, Bill wants relief fast. Since he believes Frank is causing his painful anger, it is quite logical for Bill to want to make Frank stop it. But the reality is, Bill is causing his own anger with his angry attitudes or beliefs about Frank; therefore, only *Bill* can stop it. By demanding that Frank stop Bill's angry feelings, Bill puts himself in an irrational bind.

If Frank changes his behavior, Bill probably will change his belief and angry feelings about Frank. Fine — Bill's anger will be gone, even though Frank wasn't causing it in the first place. Bill, however, will probably believe that that proved Frank really was guilty all along.

You (the reader) may say: "So what? If Bill feels better, and if Frank were none the worse for having changed what he was doing, what's wrong with that?" Of course, the answer is: Nothing's wrong. But what if Frank or someone else refuses to change the next time? To feel better then, Bill will have to do one of four things: (a) change his beliefs (He probably won't do that unless he learns about rational self-counseling). (b) forget the whole thing (He'll probably do that temporarily; but he will be likely to get angry again in a similar situation, or if he rethinks the old situation.) (c) stay angry indefinitely, and start down the road to nervous tension, chronic hostility, and maybe even ulcers or high blood pressure, or (d) dull his painful emotions with drugs or alcohol. That's how irrational emotions drive people to drugs and drink.

The following case history shows you this process clearly. It also shows how painfully foolish it is to believe that you are not what you most certainly are, especially if you then try to prove that you are, what you are convinced you are not. This is one of the most common, but cruel tricks people play on themselves when they masquerade their ignorance as knowledge.

Doug Maxwell was a conscientious young business executive. He liked his work, worked hard, and got along well with his fellow workers. When he was promoted to office manager, all of the ten people he was to supervise felt good about the promotion. Six months later, they were still happy, but Doug was miserable.

Instead of his old coffee breaks, Doug now took beer breaks. Instead of his usual two sandwiches and milk for lunch, he had two or three martinis and six to eight cigarettes. In spite of this, Doug still maintained his high work output and good work relations. A few office people began to suspect something was different about Doug, but they couldn't put their fingers on it. Only his wife was convinced that he was in deep trouble. And out of sincere rational love, she told him she would not patiently watch him drink himself to death. He had to get professional help that week or she was leaving him.

Psychiatric evaluation revealed a basically normal, intelligent young man who habitually made above-average demands on himself for success. But he rarely enjoyed the happiness and self-satisfaction success like his normally causes. Instead, the more objective basis for personal satisfaction he created, the more miserable he felt. Since his psychiatric evaluation failed to show any significant mental disturbance, Doug was an ideal candidate for short-term rational behavior therapy. Below are excerpts from his first therapy session.

DR. M: (Smiling) Well, Doug, the worst thing that I can say about you is that you are a bright, normal, all American neurotic male.

DOUG: (Laughing) Is that good or bad?

DR. M: (Smiling) Neither, it's just a fact. For six months or more, you seem to have been diligently teaching yourself to be more and more irrationally anxious and depressed. Because you didn't realize what you were doing, you didn't know what to do to feel better except drink too much.

DOUG: I don't understand. I'm the same guy now I've always been. There's a little more job pressure maybe, but I think I can handle it. If I could just shake my morning blues and tension I'd be okay. Or better yet, if I could start my day at 2 p.m. I'd be fine. I must be a night person, because from 2 p.m. 'til midnight I'm a ball of fire. It even takes three to four stiff nightcaps to slow me down enough to go to sleep.

DR. M: I have a different explanation. I think that you're just a person, day and night, who has a few life-long irrational attitudes and beliefs that you are reacting to more strongly now than ever before. If I'm right, then your so called "job pressure" is really "Doug pressure."

DOUG: What irrational attitudes and beliefs?

DR. M: I'm not sure; but I expect you to show them to both of us when we go over your rational self-analysis. Did you read the articles I gave you last week on human emotions and rational self-analysis?

DOUG: Yeah, I even tried to do one this morning, but it didn't do anything for me.

DR. M: Did you bring it with you?

DOUG: Like I said, it didn't do anything for me, so I didn't think you'd be interested in it.

DR. M: Well, you were mistaken. I'm especially interested in RSA's that you don't find helpful. Let's go through it anyway. You tell me what happened this morning, and I'll write it up in the ABC format for you. Okay?

DOUG: Well . . . I woke up this morning feeling this black hole in the pit of my stomach. I felt chained to the bed — like it would take all my energy just to move. The longer I laid there the more I felt I should just roll over and go back to sleep. But I wasn't sleepy and I couldn't go to sleep. I forced myself to get up, but still felt tense and weighted down, like I was being pulled in eighteen different directions at once. Then Candy, my wife, told me I was ten minutes behind schedule. So I took a quick cold shower and shave and dashed off to work.

DR. M: Well, when did you try to write the RSA?

DOUG: Well, you see, I didn't actually write anything down. I mean, I tried to think what I would write if I had had the time to write one. But I couldn't think of anything. Like I said, I just felt depressed, tense and anxious. There was none of that self-talk that you talked about in your articles. I just felt weighted down and pressured. And no sooner than I got to the office, I had three calls to make. I was late to my 8:30 staff meeting. I had a pile of letters to answer a mile high, and my old treadmill feeling just swallowed me up. But I toughed it out until 2 o'clock or so, then I began to feel half way human.

Author's Note #1

You have just seen a perfect example of why RSA's don't help some people — they don't do them. All Doug did was give a fleeting thought to doing an RSA. Because a miracle didn't immediately occur, he concluded that the RSA didn't do anything for him. That makes no more rational sense than thinking today about calling a taxi to take you to work tomorrow, but not actually calling it, then getting angry because the taxi doesn't show up the next morning.

That gave me a useful insight into at least part of Doug's problem: he was very careless about objective facts when they related to his emotions. As the session progresses, notice how he distorts the facts and confuses himself with his popular, but sloppy language.

DR. M: No wonder your RSA didn't do anything for you. It couldn't have because you didn't do it. RSA's can help you *only* if you actually do them. Thinking about the one you would do if you took the time to do it is not enough. You have to actually do them to benefit from them.

DOUG: Okay, okay, I know I should have. But I couldn't think of anything to write, and anyway there wasn't any time.

DR. M: There is never time for anything; you always have to take the time to do everything you do.

DOUG: Yeah Doc, I know and I'll do it. Don't give up on me. I'll do it. I'm really not that bad.

DR. M: It's not a matter of me giving up on you. It's merely a matter of your *refusing to stop* giving up on yourself. Okay, let's look at the RSA you would have done this morning if you had been as concerned about yourself as you were about your work. First, you would have written your "A" section just as you described it. Because you woke up with negative feelings and you weren't aware of any self-talk, you would have just left blank space for your "B" section. Then you would have written your "C" section and the five rules for rational thinking.

Now, we know that your emotional feelings can be caused either by your conscious perceptions and thoughts or by your unnoticed attitudes or unspoken beliefs. In an RSA, you can make your unnoticed attitudes or unspoken beliefs obvious by filling in the "B" section with the answers to these questions: "By feeling depressed, tense and anxious this morning I was reacting 'as if' I was thinking and believing what?" Now you tell me, what were you reacting "as if" you believed?

DOUG: Well, when I'm depressed I'm feeling as if I believe that I can't do the job. It's too much. The more I do, the more I have to do. Everybody's just waiting for me to fall flat on my face so they can pounce on me. Then I wonder how long I can stand the rat race. Then I feel I'm going off in eighteen different directions at once, and I can't quit. I feel I've just got to prove to myself that I'm as good as they think I am. But at the same time I feel I can't. Then I wish I could just take off and just go. But I am trapped.

DR. M: Now we've got something we can work with. It sounds to me like you see the world as a threatening place, full of people just waiting to pounce on you the moment you're not looking.

DOUG: I've always had that feeling.

DR. M: Why do you think that is?

DOUG: I have this feeling that I don't really deserve my success because I've just been fooling everyone, and one day they'll catch me with my pants down. That's why I've always felt

I had to be kind of a loner. I mean, I've always had a lot of friends, but I never let anyone get too close; you know, to really get to know me. Not even my wife really knows me. She thinks she does, but she really doesn't.

DR. M: Why is that?

DOUG: I'm a phony. Like I said, I've always had the feeling that the happy, successful guy everybody sees is not the real me. The real me is a frightened little kid, and I can't let them see that.

DR. M: But you're not a frightened kid. You are a thirty year old successful businessman. Why do you ignore that fact and call yourself a kid?

DOUG: That's what I feel. How can I tell myself I'm a man when my gut tells me every morning that I'm a frightened kid? What you see is not the real me. My feelings are real, so what I feel must be the real me. That's why I don't see how writing down my thoughts can help me. I don't have any problem with my thinking. It's my feelings that I can't handle.

DR. M: Well, where do you think your feelings come from?

DOUG: They come from me — from the fact that I'm a phony, scared to death of being found out.

DR. M: Did you read the article I gave you about human emotions and how they work?

DOUG: Yeah, I skimmed over it. But you see, that doesn't apply to me, because there are no perceptions and thoughts involved in my feelings. I just wake up feeling depressed and tense. So when I saw your ABC model of emotions, I figured that I must be different from the people you were writing about. So I just skipped over that article and went to the one about rational self-analysis. Now *that* one I spent some time on because the other article said rational self-analysis was the main self-help tool used in rational behavior therapy. It was very interesting, too. But like I said, I must be different from the people you've been seeing because I wasn't thinking anything. I just felt bad, and that was all there was to it. So I didn't see any point in wasting time on something that wasn't going to help me.

Author's Note #2

Doug is typical of people who want to solve their emotional problems without first learning about their emotions. Yet they wouldn't think of trying to tune their car engine without first learning about motors. It's only when people are willing to act as logically toward themselves as they do toward their cars, TV's, lawn mowers, etc., that they can really help themselves emotionally without alcohol or other drugs.

One of Doug's biggest problems was his sloppy use of words. He said "I feel"when he really meant "I believe." That kept him confused about what was real versus what he mistakenly believed was real. Written RSA's are one of the easiest ways to clear up such confusion fast. But Doug refused to try even one.

My task now was to get Doug to do two things: (a) stop thinking that his emotions were unique, and (b) start rationally using, "I think," or "I believe" and "I feel."

DR. M: Your biggest mistake is assuming that your emotions are unique. In reality, your emotions work the same as mine and everyone else's. Another mistake you often make is labeling "feelings" what frequently are not feelings at all. Instead, they are a mixture of irrational attitudes hidden by logical emotional feelings.

DOUG: You know, in some strange way, I really feel that what you're saying could help me if I could understand it; but I honestly don't see what you are trying to tell me.

DR. M: There — you just did it again! You don't "feel" that what I'm saying could help you. You have the *thought*, opinion, or belief that what I'm saying could help you. And that belief triggers a positive feeling. If you are healthy and undrugged, you cannot have an emotional feeling unless you first have an appropriate attitude, belief, or *thought* to trigger it. Feelings and thoughts are two separate things, but you are lumping the two together, calling them both a feeling and keeping yourself confused.

DOUG: But I feel what I feel; so how can I change that?

DR. M: By changing your thoughts. There is no way that I know of to change the way you feel without drugs, alcohol, or electric shock, unless you change the way you think. But I don't advise the use of alcohol or drugs because they don't solve your problems. They merely add to them. And you certainly don't need electric shock; so, I recommend that you examine and change some of your thoughts. But first, let me give you a concrete example of how your thoughts trigger your feelings. Suppose a noise wakes you up at night and you think someone is in your house. How would you feel?

DOUG: Scared.

DR. M: Why?

DOUG: I'd feel my wife and I might be in danger of being killed.

DR. M: Nope, you wouldn't feel that; you'd think or believe that. In terms of what human emotions are made of, you would have:

(A) *perceived a noise;*

(B) *thought* it was a burglar and believed you were in danger; *THEN* and *ONLY* then would you have

(C) reacted with fear.

Let's suppose that you got up and investigated the noise and found that it was just a venetian blind flapping in the wind and hitting the window. How would you feel then?

DOUG: Probably relieved.

Dr. M: Now, explain how your feelings could go from extreme fear to relief even though the noise is the same.

DOUG: Well, at first I thought it was a burglar, and you'd have to be crazy not to be afraid in that case. But after I saw it was just a harmless venetian blind banging against the window, I'd have to be crazy not to feel relieved.

DR. M: That's exactly right. But you wouldn't have *felt* there was a burglar there, and you wouldn't have *felt* it was just a harmless venetian blind. You would have first *thought* those things, THEN felt a logical emotional reaction for your thoughts. You would have gotten rid of your fear by changing your thoughts about the noise. Do you understand and believe what I've just said?

DOUG: Yes, but I don't understand what that has to do with my morning depression. There is no noise then to think about, but I still feel depressed.

DR. M: It has everything to do with your depression. All human emotions work the same way. If you can understand how to analyze any one of your emotions, you then understand how to analyze all of them.

Author's Note #3

I had put Doug's statements about his morning depression in the ABCD format. The next thing we did was run the camera check on what he was calling feelings without perceptions or thoughts.

DR. M: Now for your "A" section, you would have written: "I woke up this morning feeling a black hole in the pit of my stomach. I felt chained to the bed — like it would take all my energy to move." Now, if I had taken a picture of what you described, would I have seen a hole in your stomach or chains on you?

DOUG: No, of course not. That's just a manner of speaking.

DR. M: When you are having emotional problems, it's a very confusing manner of speaking to yourself because you feel and act as if it were true. Now, from a rational point of view, since there was no hole in your stomach and no chain on you, was it logical to have felt as if what wasn't, really was, especially since you hated the feeling and could have easily changed it without alcohol or drugs?

DOUG: Well, it wasn't logical, but how can you change a feeling like that?

DR. M: The same way you would have changed your feeling of fear when you saw there was no burglar. Remember, to get rid of your morning depression you're going to have to start using your brain just as logically then, as you would have used it in the burglar example. The objective reality was, there was no hole in your stomach nor chains on you. Yet you mislabeled your feeling and confused yourself. If you had accurately labeled that feeling in your gut, what would you have said?

DOUG: I would have said I feel tense, nervous and scared.

DR. M: Beautiful! Now, the key to rational emotional control is remembering that all emotional feelings are logical, correct and appropriate for what you believe, but *not necessarily* for objective reality. That's why correct RSA's require you to check your perceptions against the first rule for rational thinking — objective reality. So, the "hole" was really a feeling of fear. That feeling was logical, correct and appropriate for some of the beliefs you stated a few minutes ago. You said: "Everybody's just waiting for me to fall flat on my face so they can pounce on me. I'm a frightened kid, and I can't let them see that." Now as long as you hold those fearful beliefs, you're going to wake up afraid.

DOUG: But that's how I felt.

DR. M: No, no, no! That's what you *believed*, and those beliefs caused you to feel scared. I want you to see how logical and understandable your emotions become when you use words correctly. You didn't wake up with this "black hole" as you said. You woke up feeling afraid, and in your imagination, *as if* you had a black hole. But since you have never had a black hole in your stomach, and you don't have the foggiest notion how one would feel, it would have been less confusing had you said what you really meant. Now let's go on to your "feeling chained to the bed." I'd say that came· from your belief that you're trapped.

DOUG: Right! That's how I feel — I mean, how I *see* myself.

DR. M: Okay, now we've got the perception part of your morning fear and depression. So it's not true that there was no perception involved in your depression. We now see that you perceive yourself as being trapped. Right?

DOUG: Yeah, I see what you mean.

DR. M: Okay. If you had done an RSA this morning, in your "Da" section you would have rewritten your "A" section something like this: "I woke up this morning feeling depressed and afraid. I lay there awhile, then got up feeling tense and anxious. My wife told me I was ten minutes behind schedule, so I took a quick shower, shaved, and left for the office."

DOUG: If you're only supposed to put in the "A" part what a camera would take a picture of, why did you write about my feeling tense and anxious? A camera can't take a picture of a feeling.

DR. M: That's right. The camera rule applies only to external events. But you always have some emotional feeling, even if it's only indifference. The camera rule helps you decide if the feelings you describe are appropriate to what's actually happening to you. For example, the camera rule would have told you that you were not objectively chained nor trapped. Therefore, your feeling as if you were had to be coming from your subjective opinion or belief about your situation. Also, your feelings are real; they're facts. You really feel what you feel. Any fact can be put in the "A" section. But when the fact is a feeling, you also put it in the "C" section. Understand?

DOUG: Yeah.

DR. M: Okay. Everything else you called facts was really hidden attitude or unspoken belief. They need to be rewritten in your "B" section as the thoughts they would have been had you thought them. You said: "The longer I lay there, the more I felt I should just roll over and go back to sleep." That would be rewritten as simply, "I thought that I should just roll over and go back to sleep, but I wasn't sleepy." In your "Db" section you would have used the five rules for rational thinking to debate that thought with something like: "It's merely because I incorrectly see myself as trapped and threatened that I want to escape back into sleep. But my perception *is not* based on objective reality. Also, going back to sleep *won't* get me my goals, and it might get me in trouble at work. That's three reasons why going back to sleep is an irrational idea. I need to stop thinking it and get up and go to work." Tell me now, wouldn't that have been a much more logical and mentally healthy way to think than the way you thought? I mean, is there any sane reason why you'd object to replacing your old way of thinking with this way of thinking?

DOUG:. No, when I look at it that way, my old way seems silly.

DR. M: That's a useful insight because it shows you that you have been reacting with logically correct feelings to silly beliefs. But you didn't know about your silly beliefs before now because you kept yourself confused with your sloppy habit of calling your attitudes, beliefs and thoughts your feelings. Emotional feelings are internal physiological states. They have simple one or two word labels like "anger", "happiness", "love", "hate", etc. The moment you say: "I feel that. . .", or "I felt as if. . .", or "I feel he (she or it) is. . .", etc., you are probably talking about a mixture of beliefs plus your emotional feeling about beliefs. It's very important to remember that, because the only way you can change your feelings is to change the beliefs hidden behind them. If you don't know there is a belief involved, or if you are not willing to admit it, the feeling may drive you to alcohol and further needless suffering, as yours did you. Do you now understand better what I have been trying to tell you?

DOUG: Yes, and I see that I also need to review the articles you gave me about emotions.

DR. M: That's a useful insight. I see our time is up. I want you to reread the articles I gave you and then actually do the RSA that you thought about doing but didn't do this morning.

DOUG: Okay, I'll do it tonight.

DR. M: Good, then I'll have my secretary call you if I have a cancellation before your next regular session. I'd like to get you actually working on eliminating your morning fear and depression as soon as possible.

Emphasis Questions

(1) You either feel an emotion or you don't.
True   False   (P-143)

(2) Your emotions are always real, logical, correct and appropriate for what you _____.   (P-143)

(3) If you have a real emotional feeling toward someone, that person is making you feel that way.
True   False   (P-143, 144)

(4) Accusing others of making you love or hate them puts both you and them in an irrational bind.
True   False   (P-143)

(5) It's irrational feelings that drive people to drink.
True   False   (P-144)

(6) Since Doug had been teaching himself to be miserable for six months, that must mean that he really wanted to be miserable.   True   False   (P-144)

(7) Doug was telling an emotional white lie when he said he tried to do an RSA.   True   False   (P-146)

(8) One reason Doug had the problems he had was his habit of _____ facts and _____ himself.   (P-146)

(9) Doug's first RSA didn't help him because he _____ do it.   (P-146)

(10) Because Doug was unaware of his self-talk, Dr. Maultsby left the "B" section blank at first.
True   False   (P-147)

(11) Emotional feelings are caused by conscious _____ and _____ or unnoticed _____ and _____.
(P-147)

(12) Written RSA's are a good way to tell the difference between what is _____ versus what you mistakenly believe is _____.   (P-149)

(13) You cannot have an _____ unless you have an attitude or _____ to trigger it.   (P-149, 150)

(14) You can't change your emotions except with alcohol or drugs, unless you change your _____.   (P-149)

(15) Alcohol and drugs do not solve problems; they merely _____ to them.   (P-149)

(16) Your emotions always involve perceptions and thoughts
     or _____ or _____.   (P-149)

(17) The key to rational emotional control is remembering
     that all emotional feelings are logical, correct and appro-
     priate for what you believe. . .   True   False
     (P-151)

(18) Even though your feelings are correct, logical and appro-
     priate for your beliefs, your feelings still can be inappro-
     priate for your external situation.   True   False
     (P-151)

(19) Some people want to solve their emotional problems with-
     out first _____ about their _____.   (P-148–149)

(20) Doug's biggest mistake about his emotions was assuming
     that his emotions _____ work like other people's.
     (P-149)

CHAPTER 12
RSA'S DRIVE PEOPLE TO SOBRIETY

Three days later Doug returned with his first real attempt at rational self-analysis. The "A" section was the same simple statement of facts that we had agreed on in the last session. So we just picked up where we had left off in the "B" section three days earlier.

DOUG: It was like you said in your article, I've practiced my present emotional habits so long I had stopped noticing the perceptions and thoughts and was just focusing on my feelings.

DR. M: So, you now see the difference between an unnoticed fact and an absent fact?

DOUG: Right! I see now that most of my emotions are controlled by the thought-shorthand of my attitudes that you talked about. That's why my "B" section here is the same as what we talked about the last time. It's all "as if" thoughts because all I really noticed were the feelings. So for B-1, I wrote: "By waking up feeling depressed and scared, I'm reacting as if I were thinking and believing that I can't do this job."

DR. M: Now read me your Db-1 rational debate of that.

DOUG: "That's an irrational idea. I'm doing the job, and my boss says I'm doing it better than anyone has ever done it before. So I need to stop thinking that idea."

DR. M: Very good debate.

DOUG: "B-2 — It's too much; the more I do, the more I have to do." My rational debate of that was: "It's not too much. I'm just hassling myself too much about it. It's true that the more I do the more there is to do, and I hope it goes on being that way; otherwise, I won't have a job. Your work is endless if you are both creative and productive. There was work in that job before I took it and after I retire there will still be work to do in the job. The rational thing for me to do is decide if my present objective job performance is enough to satisfy me, and let me enjoy my life the way I want to. I know that my boss and my staff are satisfied. I'm the only one who is upset. That's irrational, so I'll stop it."

DR. M: Excellent! I couldn't have debated that one any better myself.

DOUG: "B-3 — Everybody's just waiting for me to fall flat on my face so they can pounce on me." My debate is: "Horse-shit! In the first place, unless I trip and fall, I won't fall on my face. And even if I did, I don't think anyone would pounce on me. What I meant was that everyone seems to be just waiting for me to make a mistake so they can show me up for the phony I am. But that's crap too, because I've made several big mistakes and everybody, including some of the old timers on my staff, was as sympathetic and helpful as could be in correcting my mistakes. I'm being uptight about nothing."

DR. M: Very good!

DOUG: "B-4 — How long can I stand this rat race?" My debate was: "I don't seem to have anything to worry about. I'm winning the race."

DR. M: That's not rational. It doesn't obey the first rule for rational thinking, and it leaves untouched your irrational idea that you are in a rat race. It's true that you don't have anything to worry about, but the reason you gave for that fact is really nonsense. It sounds more like positive thinking than rational thinking.

DOUG: Are you saying that positive thinking is bad?

DR. M: No, not necessarily. I just want you to realize the dif-ference between the two. Positive thinking, in my opinion, is merely saying something that sounds good in an attempt to trick yourself into feeling better without actually thinking better. Rational thinking is based on objective reality. Some-times it justifies feeling good, sometimes it does not; but it's always the most objective type thinking under the cir-cumstances. You're not in a rat race, so you can't win it or lose it. Plus, there is nothing for you to "stand." Those are the rational reasons you have for not worrying. If you stop worrying just because you think you're winning the rat race, you'll still be behaving rationally, but because of an irrational idea that's not worth thinking. Nonsensical thinking is okay, only if you keep in mind that it really is nonsense and *not* appropriate for personal problem solving.

DOUG: Yeah, I see your point. I have this guy on my staff who's a real good worker, but, damn it, he tells even more stupid jokes in staff meeting than he does at parties. At a party he's great, but at my staff meeting he's a royal pain in the ass. Is that rational?

Author's Note #1

An important insight about rational thinking: It's not enough that your thinking is factual and obeys at least three of the five rules; to be rational, thinking must also be relevant and useful for solving or avoiding some problem. If you ignore or forget that insight while trying to solve problems, you will often confuse yourself with irrelevant or useless facts. To help Doug avoid that fate, I used his question about his joking staff member to introduce this new insight about rational thinking.

DR. M: Not really, but if you'd say that you react to him in staff meeting "as if" he were a pain in your ass, the statement would probably be a statement of fact. But just because a statement is factual, that alone doesn't make it rational. To be rational, your statement has to be relevant to the solution of a specific problem. In this case, it would be rational to say: "It's irrational of me to react as strongly as I do to his jokes; so I'll stop. But, because his jokes disrupt my staff meetings, I'll also ask him to stop the joking." Okay, what's your B-5?

DOUG: "I feel I'm going off in eighteen different directions at once." My debate is: "I have never gone off in eighteen directions at once, so I can't know if I'm feeling that way or not. The most accurate thing I can say here is I think I feel that way. But the objective reality is I can only go in one direction at a time. So it's stupid to keep feeling like I'm going off in eighteen different directions. That's like going on being afraid after I see that the noise that woke me up was merely the harmless venetian blind hitting the windowsill."

DR. M: Excellent! That's what I mean about being as logical about all of your emotions as you are about any one of them.

DOUG: Actually, it really gets to be easy to stop feeling a certain way when your objective analysis shows how illogical you are being. My B-6 was, "I feel I can't quit." My debate is:

"There's no such emotional feeling." What I mean is, when I think of quitting I get so scared that I refuse to think about it.

DR. M: Now that's a beautiful insight. What do you get scared of?

DOUG: I'm scared that I'll prove that I really couldn't hack it, and that I really am a phony. That leads me logically to my B-7 and B-8 which are: "I feel I've got to prove to myself that I'm as good as they think I am. But I feel I can't."

DR. M: Okay, how did you debate them?

DOUG: Well, all I said was that there are no such feelings. There are just these thoughts plus my fear and frustration because I think that this might be the one time when I *don't* prove to myself that I'm as good as they think. So, in spite of all your rational insights about my feelings, I still feel scared. So I can't say they are doing me any good.

Author's Note #2

That was a beautiful example of how quickly emotionally distressed people are willing to give up just because a miracle doesn't occur after they've had five or six relatively rational thoughts. With his phrase, ". . . in spite of all *your rational insights,*" Doug demonstrated that he hasn't given up his belief in his irrational use of "feel." He is also showing that he still sees rational thinking as something that's *mine instead of his.* However, it's *not* what you think that controls your emotions; it's what you *think and believe.* Like most people at this early stage of emotional re-education, Doug wanted to feel better before being willing to commit himself to thinking and believing better. But that just can't happen. So my job was still to get him to see that only by thinking and believing better first and continuing to do it can he feel better without alcohol or other drugs.

DR. M: I agree. My insights haven't helped you yet because you haven't yet begun to make them your beliefs by acting on them. Insights can help you only after you begin to act on them habitually. When you start acting on these insights every day, you'll turn them into personal beliefs and quickly get rid of your irrational fear. In the meantime, let's see if we can rationally add to your good start at rational thinking. Tell me, under what circumstances will you have proven to yourself that you're as good as they think you are?

DOUG: If I get promoted again.

DR. M: That's not true, and you know it. When you get promoted again, I'll bet a million dollars to a penny that you'll say: "Well, all I proved is that I'm still able to keep them fooled, but I know I'm still a phony, so I've got nothing to feel good about yet. Now I've really got to prove to myself that I'm as good as they think I am." Want to bet? (Laughing)

DOUG: (Laughing) You know, it really sounds stupid, but you're right. That's exactly what I say after every promotion. But before, it wasn't so bad because I never had more than a secretary and a part-time assistant working directly under me.

DR. M: Now you have over five times that many people "to fool" every day, and you are over five times as scared as before. Right?

DOUG: I hate to admit it, but you're right. What should I do about it?

DR. M: Before we get started on that, let's finish the RSA. Do you have any more "B's"?

DOUG: The last one is, "I wish I could just take off and go, but I feel trapped." I debated that with: "I can take off and just go, but I'm too scared to do it. I'm not objectively trapped, so feeling "as if" I were is like being afraid after I see that the noise that woke me up is just a harmless venetian blind."

DR. M: That was a good first attempt at RSA. We cleared away most of the psychological garbage that you've been filling your mind with. Now I think we can take a straight look at your basic problem.

DOUG: Which is?

DR. M: I think you know, so why don't you tell me. I think it's much better if you admit it, if you know it.

DOUG: As I see it, and I have known this all my life, I'm just a phony who has had a few lucky breaks, and it's just a matter of time before the one big fall that will put an end to my masquerade. I'm scared to death of it, but the way I feel now, I wish it would just happen and be over and done with.

DR. M: Tell me how you feel about phonies.

DOUG: I hate them. That's why I can't stand myself.

DR. M: I'd describe your problem a little bit differently from the way you did. I'd say your basic problem is that for as long as you can remember you've believed that you are a worthless, inferior human being who goes around pretending to be as good as everybody else. In your mind, it's bad enough to be inferior, but to pretend you're not is the worst possible sin. So you hate yourself on two counts. Then the more successful you are in life, which in your mind means the more successfully you fool people, the more convinced you are that you should hate yourself. You ignore your real successes because, in your mind, achieving success while you're just pretending doesn't really count. If they knew the real you, they'd hate you as much as you hate yourself. Then you conclude that if they hated you as much as you do, they'd also make you feel as bad as you already make yourself feel. That's why you are so scared and paranoid about the world and everyone in it. It really doesn't matter whether you run off or not; wherever you go, you'll be there, and *you* are *your* problem. Until you stop being your problem, you are going to continue to be miserable.

DOUG: Unless I've had a few drinks. Doc, I hate to admit it, but you really have got my number. How can you help me?

DR. M: I can help you *only* if you are willing to help yourself.

DOUG: Well, if you'll just tell me what to do, I'll do it.

DR. M: All you have to do is give up a couple of irrational, as well as useless, beliefs.

DOUG: Just give up a couple of beliefs? Is that all? That's hard to believe. What are they?

DR. M: The first is your belief that you are a phony. What's a phony?

DOUG: Aw, come on, Doc. You know what a phony is.

DR. M: That's right, I do know, but I don't think you do. That's why I want you to describe a phony to me so that I can recognize him or her before they tell me that's what they are. You see, I never would have recognized you as one, so there must be something about them that I don't know about.

DOUG: Well, a phony is someone who pretends to be something he isn't. Take me, if you'd talk to anybody at the office, they'd tell you that I'm Mr. Successful Executive. But the fact is, I'm just a frightened kid.

Author's Note #3

The fear of being a phony and feelings of worthlessness are both self-created, self-maintained, self-image problems. Neither has anything to do with objective reality. The objective cause of those

emotional problems is the irrational habit of masquerading ignorance or utter nonsense about oneself as being useful knowledge.
Doug knowingly mislabelled himself and then reacted to himself
emotionally as if his silly label were correct.

Doug was not a frightened kid. He knew it and I knew it.
Yet, he insisted upon seeing himself as a frightened kid, then
reacting with logical emotions to that irrational self-image.

My job now was to get Doug to stop seeing himself as a
frightened kid. Because he and I both knew that he was a thirty-
year-old frightened adult, you'd think my job would have been
easy. But notice how stubbornly he clung to that ridiculous self-
image.

DR. M: What about the fellow who had your job before you
          got it? Was he a phony?
DOUG: No, he was for real. I mean, he really knew his stuff,
          and he knew that he knew it, and everybody else knew it
          too. He was what you call a real "blue chip" executive.
DR. M: If your boss were to do a really thorough objective check
          of all your work of the past six months and compare it to
          the last six months of the other guy's work, what would
          be the results?
DOUG: Well, we did just that and found that I have caused
          a twenty percent overall increase in business.
DR. M: Well, if you have objectively produced twenty percent
          more than the previous guy, how is it that he was a "real"
          executive and you're just a phony executive?
DOUG: Well, you see, you can't just look at that. I mean, how
          do you know it will last? I mean, what if six months from
          now productivity is down fifty percent?
DR. M: Is there any objective evidence that that's likely? What
          do the latest two monthly reports show?
DOUG: Well, month before last it was off three percent over
          the previous one, but last month we were up five percent.
          So, I'd say things look stable right now.
DR. M: Well, it seems to me that if a person were just pretend-
          ing to be a successful executive, you could look at the quality
          and quantity of his work and see it. I mean, if I weren't
          a real psychiatrist, the departmental peer review board would
          see evidence of that fact right away. So if you know your
          executive job so well that all an expert evaluator can find
          is that you are producing twenty percent more of the same

type work than a "real" executive did, how do you justify calling yourself a phony? Better still, under what circumstances would you be willing to call yourself a "real" executive?

DOUG: Oh, that's easy, when I feel it.

DR. M: Feel what?

DOUG: That I'm for real. Okay, I know you're going to say that there's no such feeling.

DR. M: That's right, and that's why you haven't felt it and never will feel it. You're trapped by your sloppy use of language. You're not going to solve your problem until you clear it up. A person who pretends to be what he isn't is not a phony human being; he's a real human being impersonating another human being.

DOUG: I guess next you're going to tell me there's no such thing as a phony.

DR. M: No, there are lots of phony human beings in the world. Department store windows are full of them. They're called mannequins. They are *not* alive, so you can't possibly be one. Even when you die, you won't be one. You'll just be a real dead human being.

DOUG: That's all well and good, but it doesn't change my feeling that I'm just a frightened kid pretending to be a successful executive.

DR. M: And it won't change it; you'll have to change it. And all you have to do to change it, is give up the idiotic belief that you are a frightened kid. If you were to clear up your sloppy thinking, you'd say that you are a 30-year-old frightened adult making himself feel like he thinks a frightened kid feels. But I doubt that there are any frightened kids who are afraid of what you are afraid of. If that's true, you're not even doing a good job of impersonating a frightened kid. That's one of your major problems; you are a 30-year-old competent, successful, irrationally frightened executive trying to impersonate a frightened kid. And the tragedy is that you don't realize that it's all an irrational game of pretense. So you insist on holding on to the irrational belief that you really are a frightened kid. That's the second irrational belief you are going to have to give up if you are going to get rid of your self-hate rationally.

DOUG: But how can I give it up when I have this feeling? You don't understand, this is a real feeling. I can't just turn it off.

DR. M: You can if you are willing to be as logical about it as you said you'd be about your fear of a harmless venetian blind.

DOUG: But this is different.

DR. M: The only difference is the length of time you've held this belief. In the example of the burglar you would have held the belief that there was a burglar only a few minutes — just long enough to check it out against objective reality and then get rid of it. You've held the belief that you're a frightened kid for as long as you can remember, and you've never checked it out against objective reality. Tell me, how does that belief help you? Does it help you get your goals in life? Does it help you feel the way you want to feel or help you stop drinking too much? How does it really help you?

DOUG: It doesn't. It's just the opposite.

DR. M: Yet you are trying to convince me that it's a good idea to hang on to it. And I'm telling you that it's the main irrational as well as useless belief you have to give up in order to help yourself. Now, are you willing to help yourself or not?

DOUG: I guess so, if you think I can do it.

Author's Note #4

Even now, after having treated hundreds of bright people for feelings of inferiority and worthlessness, I am still amazed at how stubbornly they insist on holding on to the irrational beliefs that cause their problems. Almost all of them, however, find the following argument gives them a challenge they can't refuse.

DR. M: I know you can. Now let's see if I can help you make up your mind to really try it. Just for the sake of this conversation, let's assume that for just one week — not forever now — just one week, that you give up the belief that you are a phony. What would you lose?

DOUG: Well, nothing really.

DR. M: That's not quite true. You'd lose all your morning depression and chronic fear of being found out. Now, is that worth your personal effort?

DOUG: Of course.

DR. M: Now, during this *one* week that you actually gave up the belief that you are a phony, would you gain anything?

DOUG: Yeah, a much better feeling about myself, and that in itself is reason enough to do it.

DR. M: Wait a minute. Now, let's not be too hasty. Let's consider the possibility that I'm wrong. Maybe I am psychotic and I'm hallucinating a 30-year-old competent successful executive when in fact you really are a frightened kid. Now, let's suppose that at the end of that week of having given up the belief that you are a phony, you then learn that I really was wrong, that you really are a frightened kid impersonating a 30-year-old man. Would you be any worse off then than you are right now?

DOUG: No, I don't see how.

DR. M: Would you be any better off?

DOUG: (Pause) Yeah, I would have had one happy week. That's something I can't remember the last time I had.

DR. M: Okay, so you have here a situation where you have nothing but unwanted emotional pain to lose and lots of happiness to gain, plus you can't possibly be any worse off in the end, even if you have made a mistake. And all you have to do is just give up an irrational belief that's not worth having in the first place. Now, if you are not willing to take that kind of risk for your own happiness, then you deserve every second of every minute of every hour of your misery. How can you lose?

DOUG: (Laughing) I don't see how, so I'll do it.

DR. M: Great. Now, let's look at the other aspects of your problems. This business about being a phony was just a secondary offshoot of your core irrational belief that you are just a plain old worthless, inferior human being. We usually call it having an "inferiority complex." Giving up the belief that you are a phony won't help much unless you get rid of your belief that you are an inferior person. The rational way to do that is give up the belief that anyone can be inferior as a human being. (Doug gave me a wide-eyed look of disbelief, but I continued.) Yeah, that's right. There are no inferior human beings — only fallible human beings. It's true that some people show their fallibility more than others. But that doesn't mean that any one of them is less or more fallible than another.

DOUG: I don't buy that at all. You're saying that a person who hardly ever does anything right is no more fallible than a person who hardly does anything wrong. I don't see that at all.

DR. M: Okay, look at it like this. Let's say that you have two guys, Jack and Bill, both seven feet tall. Now let's say that Jack butts his head against doorsills and low hanging objects five times as many times per day as Bill. Now, does the fact that Jack demonstrates his unusual height five times more than Bill prove that Jack is five times or even 1 1/5 times taller than Bill? Or does it merely mean: Jack and Bill are the same height; Jack is just more careless than Bill; Jack could probably become less careless if he worked at it?

DOUG: What you're saying is a man's acts don't make the man?

DR. M: Exactly. Human beings are not the same as their acts. They are responsible for their acts in that they cause them; and they deserve all the rewards and penalties their acts produce. But people are always different from their acts. That's why no matter how many promotions you get or don't get, you will *never* be a better nor worse person. You'll always remain *only* a fallible human being just like all other human beings. That's why I suggest that you give up the belief that you are inferior. You can't prove that it makes any more sense to hold that belief than it does to hold the belief that you are a frightened kid. Any facts or evidence that you believe prove you are inferior as a human being, to a rationally thinking person, would merely prove that you're a fallible human being.

DOUG: Man! That's a mind blowing concept. But can you prove it?

Author's Note #5

Rational self-counseling causes you to see that there are many common ideas about mankind that can't be proven or disproven. One such commonly believed idea is the idea that some people are inferior to others as human beings. When rational people are faced with such ideas, they decide to hold or dismiss them on the basis of how useful they are for rationally pursuing life. From a rational point of view, the idea that some people are inferior to others is much *less* useful for rational living than the idea that there are no inferior people. So, instead of trying to prove what hasn't and probably can't be proven, I tried to get Doug to see that the idea of inferior people is useless and that he'd be better off if he gave it up.

DR. M: No, I can't prove it any more than you can disprove it. But from a rational point of view, the belief in inferior people is *no more* useful for the rational pursuit of life than

the belief in Santa Claus and the Easter Bunny. Do you believe in Santa Claus and the Easter Bunny?

DOUG: (Laughing) No, of course not. There's no such thing.

DR. M: How do you know? When you really stop and think
about it, you'll see that no one has ever proven that there's
no Santa or Easter Bunny. All anyone has ever done is stop
believing in them. For all anyone really knows, there may
well be both a Santa Claus and an Easter Bunny. It's unlikely,
but possible.

DOUG: I see your point. But I don't see where believing in inferior people is quite the same.

DR. M: Well, it's the same in the sense that just like you can't
prove to me that there's no Santa or Easter Bunny, I can't
prove to you that there are no inferior people. But I still
recommend that you give up that belief because it can't help
you with your problem of self-hate. But, once you give it
up, you'll stop hating yourself because of it. Then, you'll
stop believing that you *don't* deserve the rewards that your
hard work entitles you to. Finally, you'll stop being afraid
to let people get close to you. Those are the advantages of
believing that there are no inferior people.

DOUG: Man! You have really given me a lot to think about.
But I just can't believe that it's that simple.

DR. M: What do you mean?

DOUG: You're telling me that after just one week of giving up
my beliefs that I'm a frightened kid and that inferior people
exist, I'm not going to be depressed and scared anymore?
That's just impossible to believe!

Author's Note #6

Doug has the common but *incorrect* belief that giving up a well
learned irrational belief is a three step process consisting of:

    (A) making the valid insight that the belief is irrational;

    (B) making the sincere announcement that you've given
       up the belief; and

    (C) never admitting even to yourself that you still have the
       belief.

The real process of giving up a belief is a five step process.
A and B are the same as above. But the other three are quite
different from C above. You must:

    (C) refuse to use the old belief any more to explain your
       present life experience;

(D) explain your old and present life experiences using your new belief;

(E) continue to think in terms of the new belief, while acting "as if" you believe it. That's just another way of saying that you must habitually practice believing the new belief.

My job now was to get those five points across to Doug.

DR. M: No, absolutely not. I predict that you will be depressed and scared tomorrow simply because that's your well learned morning habit. Long standing emotional habits don't just roll over and die merely because you *don't* want them any more. The human body does *not* work like a faucet. You can't just turn it on and off like hot and cold water. Furthermore, you have not yet given up your beliefs in inferior people and that you're a frightened kid.

DOUG: What do you mean? Don't you believe me? I said I'd do it for a week and see what happens.

DR. M: I know what you said, but that's not all there is to giving up a belief. That decision is just the first step. But because of the way the human brain works, you always change your mind much faster than you change your habitual emotions. So I predict that you'll feel depressed and scared in the morning. But you won't feel as depressed or scared and you'll get rid of both with less or no alcohol, if you do exactly what I say, the way I say do it. Are you willing to do that?

DOUG: Okay, that seems more reasonable. Yeah, I'm willing to try anything for a week.

DR. M: Now you're not going to be completely cured after just one week. That'll take three to six months of diligent daily practice. But at the end of a week, if you have done what I'm about to say, in the way I say it, you'll be feeling a hell of a lot better about yourself than you were this week. I believe that fact will get you to see the personal value of continuing a second and a third week, etc. until you have cured yourself. Now, are you still interested?

DOUG: I'm more interested now than ever before, because it's really beginning to make sense.

DR. M: Time is running out, so I'm going to quickly run through what I want you to do. Didn't you tell me you have a cassette tape recorder at home?

DOUG: Yes.

DR. M: Well, I'm going to break my own rule and let you take the tape of this session home with you. I want you to listen to it night and morning for the next week. Now, that means changing your daily routine so that one hour before you go to bed at night and one hour before you get up in the morning you can listen to the tape. Then, all day long, act on all the insights and advice given in the tape.

Author's Note #7

Doug was typical of most people who need emotional self-improvement. They see the need for it. They want it. But they want to get it while continuing to do everything else exactly the way they always have done it. Self-improvement can't occur in that way. Therefore, it's irrational to desire it. Yet, many people insist upon hanging on to that irrational desire. All they get is the painful frustration caused by sincerely wanting personal change while being stubbornly committed to refusing to make personal changes. Watch.

DOUG: Doc, I don't think that I can find that much spare time.

DR. M: Doug, who is the time for?

DOUG: Me, I guess.

DR. M: I don't guess, I know it's for you. So what you are saying is that you can't find time for yourself. That is the most irrational thing you've said yet. You're bright enough to see where the road you've taken the past six months will lead you. If you keep on like you are going, how long do you think you will last? How long do you give yourself before it all catches up with you?

DOUG: If I'm honest, I'll be lucky to last a year.

DR. M: Well, I don't see how you can afford not to find the time. Just think of what you're saying. You're saying that you're not worth a fourteen hour investment of your time. When you were taking the business management courses to help get this promotion, how many hours on the average did you spend studying?

DOUG: About two and a half to three hours a night.

DR. M: So you willingly spent two and a half to three hours per night for a whole year to get good grades in courses that last week you said have nothing really to do with your doing your job. Yet you're not willing to make a fourteen hour investment in *you* — the most important person to you that you now know and ever will know. If you're not willing to be that rationally concerned about yourself, then this is a waste of your money and my time. I'm not a magician. If you get rid of your problems, you will be the one who takes the time and does the work. I can't do it for you.

DOUG: Will I only have to do it for one week?

DR. M: No. But with a week of hard work, you'll be off to a running start. After that, I expect your own self-interest and greater personal satisfaction to keep you going at whatever rate you want to stop being miserable. Like everything else, the more you practice, the quicker you'll get better at it. And the better you get, the less practice time you'll need. But if you're not willing to even get started, I suggest that we wait until you get miserable enough to be willing to help yourself.

DOUG: Okay, I'll do it. I'm tired of the way I am. What do I have to do?

DR. M: First, rearrange your schedule so that you can give yourself an hour just before bed. First, listen to this tape completely. That'll take a half hour. Then reread one of the nine articles I gave you. After you read it, write the date on it so you'll know the ones you haven't reread yet. Right beside your bed, put this RSA we just went over today. Then go to bed and begin the deep breathing exercises described in the article on rational emotive imagery (Chapter 7). After five to ten deep breaths, picture yourself the next morning waking up feeling well rested and calm; then see yourself getting up and going through your whole daily routine, as if you were already as rational as you want to be. Before each new scene, ask yourself: "Now, if I were really serious about practicing being rational, what rational thoughts would I have when I do this?" Then answer yourself based on these two sessions and the five rules for rational thinking. Then see yourself in your mind doing those things and feeling rationally calm doing them. Keep doing that type of REI until you fall asleep. As soon as you wake up the next morning, reach over, get your RSA, read it; then do ten minutes of REI; again see yourself, calmly going through the day doing all the things you want to do and feeling the way you want to feel while doing them. As I said, you're going to still feel somewhat depressed and scared at first. But if you ignore those feelings and concentrate only on thinking rationally, you'll feel much less depressed and scared each morning. Are you willing to do that every day for just one week for yourself?

DOUG: I'll do it. Is that all?

DR. M: No, not quite. At work, no more beer breaks. Take an REI break at ten o'clock. And don't tell me you don't have time because you've been making time for morning beer for the last six months. So, just sit in your office alone and repeat your rational emotive imagery. Start by asking yourself, "If I were behaving as rationally as I want to, would I sneak out for a beer or would I stay here and do my work without alcohol?" Then answer the question with an honest and sincere, "yes." If you can't make it honest and sincere, then you'll be wasting your time. There's no magic in rational emotional re-education, just sincere, diligent practice. At lunchtime, spend ten minutes in your office doing REI before going to lunch. At five o'clock, instead of dashing across the street for your five o'clock martini, stay in your office and do another ten minutes of REI. Then go home.

Now, I know that seems like a lot of time to spend practicing behaving rationally. But if you stop and think about it, you'll see that I haven't suggested any more time for your emotional re-education than you have already been spending drinking irrationally and suffering unnecessarily. Right?

DOUG: Yes, I see your point.

DR. M: One last point — no more nightcaps. To get to sleep, use the rational behavioral approach to insomnia that's explained in this article. (See Chapter 7)

Emphasis Questions

(1) Just because you don't notice the perceptions involved in your emotions, that does not prove they are not involved. True   False   (P-157)

(2) Like most adults, most of Doug's habitual emotions were controlled by the thought-shorthand of his _____. (P-157)

(3) By feeling as if he couldn't do his job, Doug's feelings were contrary to the objective reality that he _____ _____ the job.   (P-157)

(4) When Doug said "It's (i.e. My job's) too much," what he meant was that he was _____ himself too much about the _____.   (P-157, 158)

(5) Doug had some objective evidence that the people at the office were just waiting for him to make a mistake so they could take advantage of him.
True   False   (P-158)

(6) Doug was lucky because he was winning the rat race.
True   False   (P-158)

(7) Positive thinking is trying to _____ yourself into _____ better without really _____ better.
(P-158)

(8) By refusing to worry any more about the rat race, Doug was behaving rationally for _____ reasons.   (P-158)

(9) To be rational, thinking must obey at least _____ of the _____ rules for rational thinking and be _____ and _____ to solving some problem.
(P-159)

(10) When people ignore that fact, they often _____ themselves with _____ and useless facts.   (P-159)

(11) When Doug said "I feel I can't quit," what he meant was "I'm too _____ to quit."   (P-160)

(12) Considering Doug's objective situation, it really was rational for him to feel trapped.   True   False
(P-161)

(13) Doug's RSA was useful because it cleared away much of the psychological _____ he had been confusing himself with.   (P-161)

(14) One of Doug's basic problems was his belief that he was a _____.   (P-162)

(15) Both of Doug's main problems (fear of being a phony and feelings of worthlessness) were self _____ and _____ _____.   (P-162)

(16) Doug really was a frightened kid.
True   False   (P-163)

(17) Doug was trapped by his _____ language.   (P-164)

(18) There really are no such things as phony people.
True   False   (P-164)

(19) Believing in inferior people is rational because it's a useful idea.   True   False   (P-167, 168)

(20) Usually people can achieve self-improvement without changing their daily routine.   True   False   (P-170)

CHAPTER 13

THE RATIONAL APPROACH TO DRUG AND ALCOHOL ABUSE

1. DR. M: Well, Doug, it's been two weeks since your last session; let's start with you telling me how you have been handling yourself.
2. DOUG: (With a big smile) Rationally, of course. Is there any other way?
3. DR. M: Oh, I can think of a few other ways if I work at it. But I want to hear about what you've been doing.
4. DOUG: Well, for the first week I did exactly what you told me. And just like you said, it did feel kind of odd at first, like I was just playing a game with myself. But I felt so much better than I usually felt that I thought: "Well, if this isn't the real me, I need to make it the real me." Reading your article on cognitive dissonance three or four times was a big help too; so I didn't have much trouble with it; I just ignored it. (Then with a big smile) My muscles stayed sore for a whole week from doing push-ups the first three or four nights of trying to go to sleep without drinking. But after the third or fourth night, just the thought of push-ups and my sore muscles put me right to sleep.
5. DR. M: Did you listen to your tape?
6. DOUG: Seven days in a row; then I dreamed about the session, so I figured that was enough. Besides, by then, I knew it by heart. But I think the REI's every day are what help me the most. When I catch myself tensing up, I just stop right there and take a few deep breaths and think: "If I were really practicing being rational I'd go about this calmly." And like magic, it calms me right down.
7. DR. M: No, "it" never does anything; you calm you right down; and it's not magic. It's merely the rational use of your brain. And I agree that once you've listened to a tape every day for a week, that's probably enough for that session.

But I hope you realize that the reason your REI's are so effective now is *only* because you diligently kept feeding rational insights into your brain every day with the tapes, the self-help articles and your RSA's. That's what kept your brain filled with rational material to work with. If you had just tried to do REI's without that rational input, you wouldn't have progressed as fast. That's an important point, and I want you to remember it so you won't be tempted to take short-cuts. As soon as most people start making rational progress, they usually want to take short-cuts. But there are no short-cuts in emotional re-education. It always follows an inflexible order of stages, first, intellectual insight, then cognitive dissonance, finally emotional insight. Did you do any new RSA's?

8. DOUG: Not on myself. I mean, things are just going so great that I didn't have anything to analyze.

Author's Note #1

"Things" is merely a plural form of "it." Where rational emotional control is concerned, neither *it* nor *things* ever do anything. *You* always do everything. When you do things well, you get good results, *plus* the most rational reason to give yourself credit and make yourself feel good about your achievements. It's both illogical as well as irrational to give credit *to things* for the results that you work to achieve. That fact is so important that I always make a special effort to get people to see it.

9. DR. M: "Things" is just another way of saying "it." But neither it nor things ever do anything. You always do everything. Therefore, you are entitled to full credit for your efforts.

10. DOUG: Things, it, what's the difference if I feel good? Feeling good is all that really counts, right?

11. DR. M: Wrong, that is if you want to go on feeling good. To see clearly why I say that, you must keep in mind that the same principles of motivation apply when you interact with yourself as apply when you interact with other people.

12. DOUG: I don't follow you.

13. DR. M: Suppose your secretary voluntarily puts in extra work without pay, just to help you get some important work done; would you ignore her and praise your boss's secretary for the work that your secretary did?

14. DOUG: Not on your life. I'd never be able to get her to do anything ever again. She hates my boss's secretary.

15. DR. M: But even if she didn't hate her, unless she's crazy she wouldn't keep doing work for you if you ignored her and gave all the praise for her work to someone else, do you think?

16. DOUG: No, I guess not.

17. DR. M: And the same is true of you about you. If you keep giving *things* all the credit for the good results of your hard work, P.D.Q. you're going to decide to stop working and let *things* keep up the good work. But since things can't do anything, in nothing flat, you'll end up right back where you started. Then you'll probably say: "Well, things went well for awhile, then for some strange reason they just stopped working. I can't figure out why; I guess I'm just not lucky." Then you'll settle back into your old miserable ways and say: "It sure would be great if I could just get rational self-counseling to work for me, but I can't. I tried it, and it worked for awhile, then it just quit." To avoid that irrational trap, I advise you to always remember that where your emotional control is concerned you always do everything, and you deserve all the credit for both the good and bad results. Otherwise, you'll end up back where you started, blaming your job, fate, alcohol, etc. for the things you alone do.

18. DOUG: That's one of the few things I really question. I honestly feel (smile) think that you make too big a deal of the way I talk. I mean, is it really necessary to be that concerned about words?

19. DR. M: Yes! Yes! Yes! for two very important reasons, if you want permanent rational emotional control. First and most important, your words are essentially the same as your thoughts. And that fact is so important for rational self-counseling that I'll try to prove it to you now. For the next twenty seconds, try to have a thought, any thought about anything and hold it for twenty seconds without using a word. Try it. (After ten seconds Doug gave up, saying: "I can't do it; it's impossible.") Right, it's impossible except for unusual circumstances. And even then you can't use that type of thinking for rational emotional control nor to solve personal problems. That requires the use of words, which brings us to the second reason your choice of words

is so important: Since your words are your thoughts and because the thoughts you believe cause and control both your emotional feelings and your physical actions, that means your *self-control* is the result of your *choice* of words. When you are *neither* lying nor joking, you react *logically* to your words. Now do you see why it's so important to be as careful when you talk to yourself as it is when you talk to other people?

20. DOUG: I hear what you are saying, but it just doesn't seem like that big a deal. I mean, everybody talks the way I talk.

21. DR. M: That's right, and because of that, every day you spend at least a few minutes to several hours trying to figure out the most appropriate words to say to certain people. For example, do you ever joke about fat people in front of your fat boss?

22. DOUG: Hell no, he'd fire me on the spot, best office manager or not.

23. DR. M: That's what I'm trying to get you to see. You and anybody else who understands people at all, know darn well that it makes a hell of a difference what words you say to other people. But you stubbornly ignore that the same is equally true of the words you say to yourself. Like most unhappy people, when you talk to yourself, you act as if it doesn't make any difference at all what you say. And that's your biggest mistake. The reality is, just like other people feel positive, negative or neutral when they accept and believe the words you say to them; *you* also feel positive, negative or neutral when you accept and believe the words you say to yourself. The only exception is when you are joking or lying.

24. DOUG: What you're saying makes sense, but I'll still have to think about it some more.

25. DR. M: Fine, I'm always all for thinking, especially if it's rational. Tell me, did you practice on any of the "as-if" RSA's?

26. DOUG: Oh yeah, I did the two on drinking too much. They helped me, (smile) I mean I used them to help myself stop drinking at work. That's something I want to talk about. Can this rational self-counseling really help people solve a drinking problem?

27. DR. M: Not only can rational self-counseling help them, in my opinion, it's the only thing that will help them. Talk

to any *former* problem drinkers and you'll find that their
present thinking about their drinking, *obeys at least three
of the five rules* for rational thinking about alcohol for them.
Any time your thinking about any subject obeys at least
three of the five rules for rational thinking, then your
thinking is rational about that subject. And when you act
on that rational thinking, you are doing rational self-counseling. Do you think that you have a drinking problem?

28. DOUG: Well, I don't know. That's what I want to talk
about today. For the past five or six months, every time
I go to a party, I've blacked out.

29. DR. M: Do you mean you pass out or you just don't remember what happens after a certain time?

30. DOUG: That's it, I keep right on talking and having fun,
at least everybody says I have fun, but I don't remember
it. I can even drive without any trouble and not get arrested
and still not remember it. Just last Saturday my wife and
I went to a party, and according to her I drove home. Actually, she said I insisted on driving just to prove I wasn't drunk.
But I don't remember anything about it. In fact, that was
about one o'clock in the morning and I don't remember
anything that happened after about eleven o'clock. So there
is a good two hours gone, just lost. Another thing, after
I stop remembering, I start making phone calls, usually long
distance calls. I plan trips, tell people I'm coming to see
them, and things like that. Then a week or so later I'll get
a call or letter asking me why I didn't come, or telling me
I'm expected or telling me that they're taking me up on
my invitation to them to come visit, and I won't remember
a thing about ever having talked to them. Would you say
that's a problem?

31. DR. M: Yes, it does sound like you are in the early phase
of a drinking problem.

32. DOUG: Are you sure it's early?

33. DR. M: I can't be certain at this point but if you are giving
me all the facts it sounds somewhat early. Early to me is
when you are still able to function; that is, hold your job,
stay out of jail, that kind of thing. That usually shows that
you still have the upper hand so to speak, or more specifically it means your major problem is still just *irrational* emotional control. That's when rational self-counseling can give
the fastest and best results. But in my opinion, early or late,

the best solution to a drinking problem is still the same, rational self-counseling. And because a drinking problem is like any other problem, the earlier you start to solve it, the easier the problem usually is to solve. Also, early problem drinkers who are honest with themselves usually work harder and therefore get over their problem quicker than people who have been abusing alcohol for so long that they can't hold a job, or they have been arrested five or six times for intoxication and things like that. Even then, the rational approach is still the best answer, but it takes longer.

34. DOUG: Do I have to stop drinking altogether?

35. DR. M: Not necessarily, that is, if it's really an early drinking problem. What do you want to do?

36. DOUG: I'd like to get back where I was say two years ago.

37. DR. M: How was that?

38. DOUG: I felt good most of the time. When I went to a party I'd expect to have a good time. I might get a little high, but never drunk, and I never forgot anything. I'd drink just enough to get a little glow and feel free to act a little foolish and have a little fun, but never enough to lose control or get obnoxious. But now my wife says I get mean and sarcastic. All our friends are wondering what's come over me. To be perfectly honest, we don't get invited out near as much as before, and Candy is kind of sensitive about that. You know, she's a fun person, and she sort of blames me, and rightly so I guess.

39. DR. M: You guess?

40. DOUG: Well, like I said, I don't remember saying or doing all the things she says I do. But it's a fact that we don't get invited out anymore. Last week was the first time we've been invited to a party in three months. And that really doesn't count because it was Candy's brother that invited us. But she said we probably won't be invited back there either. It seems I insulted her brother's wife; but I honestly don't remember a thing about it. The last thing I remember was catching a little bit of the ten-thirty news on TV.

41. DR. M: What kind of party was that with the TV going?

42. DOUG: Oh, well you see, that's something else; parties don't really interest me anymore. They depress me (smile). I mean, I get depressed with them.

43. DR. M: Are you depressed before you get there?

44. DOUG: Well, yeah, I guess you could say that. But mostly it's like I'm afraid they won't like me. I never used to be

that way. But now, I feel about going to parties almost like I used to feel about going to work three weeks ago. I dread it.

45. DR. M: How has getting to work been the past two weeks?

46. DOUG: No problem at all; that is, no problem compared to what it was last month. That REI is magic.

47. DR. M: No, not magic; just the rational use of your brain.

48. DOUG: Right! I mean it's really great. After the fourth or fifth day of doing it, it was like I could feel the depression and fear just peeling away. Now I hardly notice it at all because as soon as I wake up I go right into my rational images. And it just vanishes before it starts.

49. DR. M: You mean you stop the depression before you start it.

50. DOUG: Yeah! That is, I stop it before I start it.

51. DR. M: Good! And you say you have completely stopped drinking at work now?

52. DOUG: Yeah! I haven't even had a beer at work for, let's see, this is the eighth day. Instead of dashing across the street to a bar for lunch, I stay behind in my office and do ten minutes of REI seeing myself going to the canteen thinking: "I don't need a drink. I don't really even want a drink. It's just that I have taught myself to control my anxiety with alcohol. So I foolishly call my anxiety a desire for a drink when in reality it's an anxious feeling that I create with my irrational thoughts. So if I rationally stop scaring myself I can skip the drink and keep a sober mind. I work much better with a clear head." After four or five minutes of that plus the deep breathing, I'm just as calm as can be. Then I picture myself calmly doing my work and liking it, like I used to. It's like magic (smile), I mean like really great.

53. DR. M: The belief in magic dies hard doesn't it? (laughter) Well, let's get back to the parties; what have you been thinking when you have gone to parties during the past several months?

54. DOUG: There haven't been too many, parties I mean; and actually I can't remember thinking any one particular thing. It's more like a feeling that I have to watch it or they'll see through me.

55. DR. M: A feeling or an attitude or belief plus a feeling?

56. DOUG: It's like you said; I feel as if I'm thinking they don't really want me there, not the real me — they just want

the old me, the clown. And I'll be damned if I'll be their clown. Then there's another part of me that would like to calmly spit in their eyes. But there's not much of that. I guess I get kind of scared that if I think about it too much, I might do it. So I put it out of my mind fast.

Author's Note #2

A brief review of the dynamics of gut thinking might be helpful here. Otherwise, some readers may not see the importance of the following discussion on biofeedback that I'm about to have with Doug.

First, let's look at a typical gut-thinking statement. If, for example, Bill says to Harry: "Harry, I feel that you are being unfair to me, and you had better stop it right away; otherwise you'll be sorry." Everything that follows, "Harry, I feel..." is merely subjective opinion or belief. But because Bill preceded the statements of his opinion or belief with the clause "I feel," he made his subjective opinion appear to him to be an objective fact. That's because (if Bill is being sincere) he really does have a real, logical and correct feeling. BUT his feeling is the real, logical and correct ONLY for the suspicious attitude that he is now expressing as a belief. Bill hides that fact from himself by putting an "I feel" in front of his subjective opinions. Then, like most gut-thinkers, Bill mistakenly believes that if he really weren't being treated unfairly, he wouldn't feel that he is being treated unfairly. That would be crazy and Bill is definitely not crazy. So "Damnit! Harry damn well better stop it, if he knows what's good for him." The awareness of his real, correct, intense emotional feelings prevents Bill from seeing any reason to look for objective evidence to prove unfair treatment. He believes his feeling is all the proof he needs. It's only natural that he would then angrily demand that Harry stop doing what Harry may not be doing in the first place — unfairly treating Bill. This type of irrational behavior is quite common when people: (a) don't know that their own attitudes and beliefs (and not other people) cause their emotional feelings, and (b) don't realize that emotional feelings can't prove whether an attitude or belief is valid or not.

Some readers might wonder, "But what if Harry was in fact treating Bill unfairly?" In that case, Bill would not need to refer to his feelings; he could point to the objective evidence of unfair treatment. Emotional feelings are merely impulses to act; they are never proof that the action is objectively justified.

In addition to being ignorant of how their emotions work, gut-thinkers usually are naively, but stubbornly committed to magical thinking. They usually insist the most strongly on believing that "he, she, they and it" magically make (That's the only way it could happen.) them have the emotions they have. That's why Bill (in the example) would be so sure that he was being unfairly treated; he would be convinced that *only* unfair treatment would and could make him feel unfairly treated. In other words, in Bill's mind: *"If there were no unfair treatment, there would be no feeling of unfair treatment."* Fortunately Bill is wrong.

What if Bill had said, "Harry, I believe that you are treating me unfairly and I feel bad about my belief." That would have been a much more useful statement of the facts as Bill saw them—more useful because rational beliefs can be checked against reality. Then Bill could make an objective decision about whether or not his belief was worth having. Then, Harry could sincerely reply: "I can certainly understand your feeling; I would probably feel the same way if I believed about you what you believe about me. But your belief is mistaken; the facts are . . ." etc. That type of rational exchange would solve the problem fast. It *wouldn't* help the situation if Harry replied: "Well, Bill, I feel that your feeling is wrong." Feelings are never wrong. They are always correct for the beliefs or attitudes that trigger them.

Opinions or beliefs that begin with "I feel that you are. . . ." are merely confusing ways of saying, "I feel the way I think I would feel if you really were doing what I think you are doing." But if Harry (in the example) is innocent, then Bill's feeling is clearly his own problem and has nothing to do with Harry. Yet, by saying "I feel that you are. . . .," Bill blinds himself to the fact that his feelings are his own problem and convinces himself that Harry is his problem. But if Harry is innocent, he is put to a big disadvantage.

Remember! An emotional feeling is never mistaken; and it is its own proof. It doesn't make sense, therefore, to look for evidence to prove that an emotional feeling is real or correct. That's like asking yourself for the evidence that you feel a real or correct pain when you stick a burning cigarette to your hand. The feeling is its own proof. That fact lets you see that the common saying, "I really feel that such and such is true," is most often just a meaningless statement, designed to give more weight to a subjective opinion than it objectively deserves.

Rationally thinking people avoid such irrational situations by habitually saying: "I feel..." *only* when they mean physical sensations like pain, heat, etc., or emotions like sadness, happiness, etc. Rather than preface a belief or opinion with "I feel," rationally thinking people say "I believe..." or "I think..." etc.

The most important insight to add to all this is: Normally, self-control is based on continuous brain-body feedback. I call that feedback process your cognitive-biofeedback system. It means that your perceptions, thoughts, attitudes and beliefs (i.e. your cognition) cause your brain to trigger emotional and physical (i.e. biological) reactions which are both *registered* in your brain and *controlled* by your brain on the basis of further perceptions, thoughts, etc. This cognitive (i.e. brain action) and bio (i.e. body reaction) process are the basis of most learning, including the learning that leads to habitual alcohol abuse.*

If you remember those facts, you will be able to see why I was able to teach Doug to overcome his drinking problem.

57. DR. M: It seems fair to me to say that you probably do have at least an early drinking problem, and I strongly recommend that you admit to it as the first step in rationally working on it. It's a waste of time to try to solve a problem that you refuse to admit exists.

58. DOUG: Oh! I'll admit to it; I have no problem with that. My problem is I don't know what to do about it.

59. DR. M: Well, after having admitted to a drinking problem, the next thing to do is discover the obvious, namely why you drink too much. Why do you do it?

60. DOUG: If I knew that I probably wouldn't have my problem. I sure don't want to drink too much. I know it's a stupid thing to do, and every time I do it I tell myself I'll never do it again; but I do it again anyway. I can't figure it out. Can you?

61. DR. M: It really is quite simple. You drink too much for the same reason you do everything else you do.

62. DOUG: I don't follow you.

63. DR. M: If you think about it objectively, you'll see that you do everything you do primarily for one of three reasons:

---

*Alcohol is a drug. So everything I say about alcohol abuse can be applied to the learned aspects of hard drug abuse. The most important differences between alcohol and other drug abuse are largely *legal* rather than *biological*.

You are trying to avoid something you don't want, or you are trying to get something you want, or you are trying to do both at the same time.

64. DOUG: I don't buy that at all; I'm not trying to get or avoid anything when I help a stranger, stranded on the highway, whom I've never seen before and will never see again, and from whom I refuse to accept any pay for my favor. I'm not trying to get something when I see to it that my kids have a good home and education.

65. DR. M: Of course you are, in both cases. In the case of your kids, you provide for them the way you do *primarily* to get or keep the positive self-image you have of yourself as a good father and provider, and at the same time you avoid the negative self-image you are sure you would have if you didn't care for your family the way you do. In the case of the stranger on the highway, you stop to help primarily to avoid feeling toward yourself the way you probably feel toward others when you are stranded on the highway and cars pass you by. You are also trying to get or keep the good feeling you have when you think of yourself as a concerned citizen, a person who really cares about other people and who is willing to act to prove it. If you'd just think about it, you'd see that I'm right. You wouldn't stop to help someone if you knew beforehand that you'd hate it and that you'd feel better if you didn't stop. Right?

66. DOUG: (Pause) Yeah, I've got to admit that you're probably right.

67. DR. M: You got confused because you thought I meant that people only act to get material things like money, etc. Those are just secondary motivations; the single most important factor in human motivation is *emotional feeling*. Money *means* nothing if you *have no* desire for it. It's only because desires are merely emotional urges to act that money gets you to act, if, and *only* if, you have the proper emotional feeling or urge (i.e. desire) for money. Do you follow me so far?

68. DOUG: Yeah, but what has that got to do with my drinking?

69. DR. M: *ONLY Everything.* You drink both to avoid the feelings you try to drown with alcohol and to get the *illusion* of feeling better. I say illusion of feeling better because when you are high on alcohol, you probably don't really feel bet-

ter; you are merely less aware of how miserable you were. In either case, though, you end up with a mental dependence on alcohol.

70. DOUG: Are you saying that my drinking problem is all in my mind?

71. DR. M: Not really, but in one sense, yes. Your problem with drinking is in your brain, or more specifically, how you are using your brain.

72. DOUG: I thought alcoholism was a physical problem.

73. DR. M: Yes and no. To understand alcoholism or alcohol dependency as I like to call it, you must first understand the brain-body feedback system that your brain uses to control both your emotional feelings and your physical actions.

74. DOUG: Brain-body feedback?

75. DR. M: Yes, you see, the brain not only works like a camera, it also works like a programmed computer. Your brain programs are your well-learned attitudes and beliefs. That's the brain's part of the feedback system. It causes your body to have specific reactions which generate feedback information to your brain. Then your brain uses that feedback information as the basis for continuing or stopping the original reactions or for starting new reactions by your body. That's why it's called brain-body, or as I call it, cognitive feedback.

76. DOUG: Cognitive feedback — I've never heard of that before.

77. DR. M: Most people haven't. It's my original idea based on interpretations of my own clinical observations and the recent research on alcoholics done by Dr. Arnold Ludwig, Professor and Chairman, Dept. of Psychiatry, University of Kentucky Medical Center. Our data clearly show that people teach themselves to be addicted or mentally dependent on alcohol (and all drugs for that matter); they do it with their continuous but irrational attempt to feel better *without* thinking better. That fact makes the solution to alcohol and other drug addiction simply a matter of learning to think better. That's what rational self-counseling teaches best: how to feel better by thinking better without alcohol or other drugs. Once you start feeling better without alcohol, then your drinking problem will be no more severe than your habit of smoking. That is, all you'll have to do to get rid of your learned desire or craving for alcohol is change your habit of thinking alcohol abuse thoughts, and you'll stop drinking too much.

78. DOUG: But there has to be more to it than just the mental part. I mean, when I want a drink I feel it. Last month when I was still having martini lunches, my body literally cried out for a drink; I really felt a need, just like the need for food. That was my problem; I really needed it.

79. DR. M: That's where you are mistaken. You created the appearance of a need by suppressing or interrupting your irrational cognitive-biofeedback that caused your irrational brain-body interactions. Let's go back to the time when you were still having martini lunches and take a rational look at what was happening. Keep in mind what I have told you and what you have read about your brain being divided into two parts.

80. DOUG: You mean the neocortex and the, what was it, the feeling part?

81. DR. M: Right! The neocortex or thinking part and the limbic system or feeling part. As I told you before, the thinking part is the boss; it controls everything else, and it does it on the basis of incoming information; information from the world outside and from your body, your bodily feeling as well as your memory and imagination. After your brain uses the same information over and over, always causing the same bodily reactions, your brain converts that repeated information into attitudes and beliefs. They in turn exert a kind of semi-automated or computer-program type of control on your brain. Do you follow me so far?

82. DOUG: Yeah, I think so, but it sounds so mechanical.

83. DR. M: To the contrary, it's not mechanical at all.

84. DOUG: Of course it is; you make my brain sound like it's a machine.

85. DR. M: Come on now! You can't be serious! That makes no more sense than accusing me of calling you a fish just because I say that you can swim under the water. There is not and never will be a machine that can do what I have just described. Have you ever heard of a machine that, without any outside influence, can teach itself a new response, then rationally decide to get rid of that response and replace it with another one?

86. DOUG: No, I can't say that I have.

87. DR. M: Neither can I. So, if I'm saying your brain is a machine, it would have to be a machine that neither you nor I have ever heard of. And since all rational discussions start with and stay with objective reality, as best we know

it, I wouldn't waste time talking about things neither of us has ever heard of. Just as it is useful to realize that your brain works like a camera, it is equally useful for your rational self-counseling to realize that your brain works like a self-teaching and self-programming computer. But that fact doesn't stop it from being the *most* important organ any human being can have. I think you're reading things into what I'm saying, rather than listening objectively to what I'm saying.

88. DOUG: Yeah; maybe you've got a point. Okay, I'll try to be more objective.

89. DR. M: Good! Now up until four weeks ago, you'd wake up every morning with your brain under the influence of your well learned attitude that you were a worthless, inferior frightened kid and this might well be the day you'd be exposed, and wouldn't that be terrible. Your terrible attitude automatically triggered a logical, terrible depressive dread in you of facing the day without any conscious thoughts or self-talk by you. Just waking up had become your well learned or programmed cue for that attitude to take over control of your morning emotional feelings. Now what is your normal evaluation of situations in which you feel a terrible depressive dread?

90. DOUG: That they are awful or dangerous places and I should try to get out of them.

91. DR. M: Right! Or try to avoid them. Now we can put your morning depression, feeling trapped, etc. in rational perspective. Waking up in the morning was the mental cue that put your brain under the influence of your fearful, depressive attitude or brain program, and your limbic system or the feeling part of your brain responded with what kind of feelings?

92. DOUG: Like a black hole in the pit of my stomach and feeling weighted down.

93. DR. M: Right! And you'd want to go back to sleep, but you weren't sleepy. You wanted to get up and run away but you felt?

94. DOUG: Weighted down, chained, trapped.

95. DR. M: And that information was registered in your neocortex or thinking part of your brain as the idea or belief that you were in an objectively dangerous life situation. That reinforced the initial feeling of dread and depression

produced by your limbic system, and you'd just lie there immobile, suffering, wishing you could feel better and never dreaming that you had started and were then keeping your suffering going.

96. DOUG: That's the part I have trouble with. I don't see how I could hate feeling that .way as much as I did and still not see that I was causing the whole thing. Could it be that unconsciously I really wanted to suffer?

97. DR. M: That's one way to explain it, but it *doesn't make scientific sense* to explain it that way. Why not just accuse the devil of having made you do it? It would make as much sense as saying some unconscious wish made you do it. If you really were making yourself suffer because of some uncontrollable unconscious desire, why did you so willingly reverse the process in the past two weeks? What happened to the unconscious desire to suffer then?

98. DOUG: I don't know.

99. DR. M: I don't know either. That's why it makes *more* rational as well as scientific sense to say that you made yourself suffer because you were ignorant. You didn't know that you were causing your suffering. And because your feelings all happened so fast, came so automatically, it appeared that you had absolutely nothing to do with them. It was only natural for you to assume that the external world was causing your feelings. That's because, like most gut-thinkers, you were convinced that because you didn't want to feel afraid and depressed, because you didn't like to feel that way, those facts proved that you wouldn't feel that way if you *were not* really in some hopelessly dangerous situation that was making you feel that way.

100. DOUG: Well why didn't I just point out to myself that I was *not* in an objectively dangerous situation?

101. DR. M: Because human emotional feelings are usually real, logical, appropriate and correct for what people believe. And when people who don't know how their emotions work have an emotion that *they don't have any* objective evidence to rationally justify feeling, they usually make up believable, but in fact, pseudo-evidence that their situation or some other person is making them feel that emotion.

In your case, you used the fact that you habitually woke up afraid and depressed as pseudo-evidence that you were in the dangerous situation of possible exposure as a phony. Because no human being can ever be in such a situation, the danger that you feared, was really a pseudo-danger that you responded to with a real feeling of fear. Then you used your real fear and depression to convince yourself that it really would be awful to be exposed as a phony. Your fear plus the fact that other "real" people didn't seem to have it, convinced you that you really were a phony.

102.   DOUG: Why was that?

103.   DR. M: I just told you. Like most normal people, you erroneously believed that you would *not* continue to feel afraid of being exposed as a phony if you were not in fact, a real phony and if it were not in fact really terrible to be exposed as a real phony. But what you didn't know, is that it's not facts that make people feel afraid, it's *merely* their beliefs about facts. Consequently, your irrational belief about phony human beings kept you from benefitting from the fact that you were not and could not ever be a phony human being. Blinded by your irrational belief that you were in this terribly dangerous situation, you'd lie there in bed morning after morning practicing your habit of feeling depressed and afraid.

104.   DOUG: What do you mean, practicing?

105.   DR. M: Just that, practicing. Emotions are merely learned habits. Everytime you repeat a specific emotion, you are practicing having that emotion in that situation. That's how your habit of morning depression and fear got to be so intense and automatic; you diligently practiced it every morning. Now do you follow me?

106.   DOUG: I never thought of it like that before.

107.   DR. M: I know, but that's the way it was. And by being fully aware of doing it every morning, you proved that there was *nothing* unconscious about it. So, after your conscious morning practice in being afraid to face the day, you'd consciously get yourself out of bed by consciously and actively distracting yourself with your series of irrational "have-to's." I have to get up; I have to hurry up; I can't be late; Candy is calling, I better get up, etc. That distraction caused an immediate decline in your fear and you'd get up, shower, shave, etc., and go to work. But your fearful attitude was always there to take over as soon as you stopped concentrating on your distracting "have-to's."

Once you got to your office, you'd give free rein to your fearful attitude because you were then in the lion's den, so to speak. In addition, most of the alcohol that you had drunk the night before to get to sleep would be just about all burned up. So you'd have mild alcohol withdrawal symptoms that intensified your feeling of fear and impending doom. That, plus the pressure or anxiety triggered by your "have-to do this and got to do that" approach to your work, caused you to feel more and more uptight with each staff meeting, telephone call, etc.

Past experience told you that alcohol seemed to make you feel better, less tense, more confident. But you also knew that alcohol and work don't mix over the long haul. So in the beginning, when you first got promoted, you'd only drink beer at lunch. You probably figured that beers were not that strong, so you could probably handle it. And you really believed that as soon as you got over the pressure of your new job, you wouldn't need to drink at work any more and everything would be fine. And you would have been right too, except for one thing: There was no job pressure. There was *only* the pressure you created with your perfectionistic "have-to's," "got-to's," "should's," "ought's," etc. Does that sound like what you use to say to yourself?

108. DOUG: Almost to the word! I said beer would calm me down, and if I used certs and cigars nobody would notice. (Laughter) The first time I smoked a cigar on top of two beers on an empty stomach, it made me so nauseated I threw up.

109. DR. M: But you see, the beer didn't calm you down; it didn't give you more confidence; all it did was temporarily weaken or disrupt your fearful cognitive-biofeedback mechanism. In other words, the beer made you less aware of your feeling of fear. It was like breaking your toe and *not* being able to walk on it because it hurts. The pain from your toe goes to your neocortex (thinking brain), which in turn causes your limbic system (feeling brain) to make you feel afraid to step down on your hurt toe. That's normal *healthy* cognitive biofeedback. Now, suppose you inject novacaine into your toe. The novacaine either stops or dampens the flow of pain impulses to your thinking brain. That weakens your healthy cognitive-

biofeedback and you feel less afraid to step down on your hurt toe. Your toe will still be hurt; but you will *be less* painfully aware of it. That increases the unhealthy probability of now walking on your hurt toe and making it worse. Do you follow that?

110.   DOUG: Yeah, but it's kind of hard to see how that's like drinking beer.

111.   DR. M: You have to keep in mind that your feeling of fear is your body's "gut" or emotional reaction to your attitudes about your life situation. Because you didn't know that before, you thought your fear was your body's reaction to a *real* external danger. That belief caused you to maintain and continue to practice your fearful emotions because the human brain does *not* automatically distinguish between fearful beliefs triggered by an objectively dangerous situation and fearful beliefs triggered by subjective nonsense. The feeling of fear is the link in your feedback system that your beers dampened or cut. When you no longer felt afraid, you'd ignore your fearful attitudes and beliefs temporarily. But you never gave them up; so they were always available to make you afraid when your body burned up the alcohol. Your quick but temporary relief with beer, led you to try stronger martinis. Also, vodka martinis didn't smell very strong, and didn't make you go to the toilet as much as beer did. By the time your body had burned up the martinis, you'd be home trying to catch up on work you thought you should have done at the office. Being irrationally perfectionistic, you ignored the fact that you had already put in more than a good day's work. You kept thinking, "I've just got to do more; I can't fall behind," etc. Right?

112.   DOUG: Right. I thought: "I've got to keep everything in front of me; can't let anything pile up or I might get behind." Then I worked and drank until I got sleepy.

113.   DR. M: Once I got you to try rational thinking, you began each day by replacing your irrational fearful attitudes with rational ones. That broke the fearful cognitive biofeedback cycle at the thinking link in your feedback system. And because your alcohol withdrawal symptoms were mild, you didn't need alcohol to control them, especially since you were using REI's at work. They kept the fear cycle broken and at the same time put a rational cognitive biofeedback

cycle in motion. That's why you are now able to handle your work without drinking. Do you understand that?

114. DOUG: Yeah, I think so.

115. DR. M: Good, because your social alcohol abuse is essentially the same as your work alcohol abuse plus four added emotional features: first, is your relatively persistent anger at the people at the parties. You said you'd like to spit on them, right?

116. DOUG: But I never dwell on that; I mean, the thought just sort of flies through my mind sometimes.

117. DR. M: But it's still there. The second added feature to your social drinking problem is that you don't have your work at a party to distract you when the alcohol dampens or stops your fearful cognitive-biofeedback cycle. Third, at work you know two or three martinis will take the edge off so to speak, so you drink them and stop. But at a party you rapidly and continuously drink one drink after another, trying to feel better in a hurry but with no thought of stopping. The fourth and final extra feature of your social alcohol abuse is that you have both hostile and fearful attitudes toward the people at parties whereas you only have fearful attitudes toward the people at work. Rather than rationally challenging and getting rid of your hostile attitude, you ignore it because you believe it's justified and you are afraid that if you dwell on it you might behave hostilely and create a scene. But what happens as soon as you have had three or four stiff drinks?

118. DOUG: I stop feeling afraid.

119. DR. M: Exactly. And because it was *only* your fear that caused you to ignore your hostile attitude, once you no longer feel afraid, your hostile attitude or hostile brain program is still there to trigger your suppressed feelings of self-righteous anger. Self-righteous anger feels more manly and desirable to you than fear; and since the drinks seem to have made it happen, you drink more to keep your anger going. Your angry feelings are a stimulus to your neocortex to release angry thoughts which lead to angry talk. Because of your fast drinking pace, you quickly build up amnesic blood levels of alcohol. So you continue to act angrily even though you don't remember having done it. Because you basically are *not* a physically aggressive type person, your anger leads only to verbal fights instead of fist fights. Since

your friends were probably only interested in having a good time, they just got angry at you, ignored you and made a mental note not to invite you back.

120. DOUG: Do you think I can ever get back to social drinking?

121. DR. M: Sure. All you have to do is get rid of your irrational hostile attitudes and go back to your social drinking attitudes. That means going back to seeing parties as places to have fun with friends rather than as battlefields full of enemies. After you do that, the next and equally important step is to relearn rational (or social) drinking skills by practicing them.

122. DOUG: Rational (or social) drinking skills? I've never heard of that before.

123. DR. M: Rational (or social) drinking is a learned skill; it requires three things: a rational plan, a personal preference for the feeling of a sober brain over the feelings of a drunk brain, and a continuous stream of rational drinking self-talk.

124. DOUG: Sounds complicated.

125. DR. M: It's really simple. The only problem is getting yourself under enough rational self-control to follow a rational drinking plan.

126. DOUG: Where do you get this rational drinking plan?

Author's Note #3

Only when a patient is clearly in the early phase of alcohol dependency, will I agree to making rational drinking the first treatment goal. When people are in the late phases of alcohol dependency, I insist that they first learn to live happy, productive lives without any alcohol. Only then will I try to teach them rational drinking skills.

Interestingly enough, after practicing rational self-counseling long enough to get dry and happily stay that way, most people lose interest in trying to learn to drink rationally. But if those who keep their interest in rational drinking can stay with the following plan diligently, they learn to be rational drinkers again.

127. DR. M: I'm going to give you the rational drinking plan I recommended right now. It's really quite simple:
Never take more than one ounce at a time of anything stronger than beer. *Always* drink it *straight* with or without ice and *never faster than one ounce per hour.*

128.   DOUG: Straight! I never drink anything straight. I don't like the taste. I drink for the feel.

129.   DR. M: I know; and that's why you drink so much so fast that you lose your memory. To solve your drinking problem rationally and still drink, you have got to learn rational drinking attitudes. That means preferring a sober mind to a drunk mind. That means being constantly aware of your drinking behavior, so that you will not slip up and drink more than you want to without realizing it. Drinking mixed drinks you lose track fast. Rational drinkers don't want that.

130.   DOUG: But drinking it straight! Ugh!

131.   DR. M: Not only are you to drink it straight, you are to sip it; hold it in your mouth and savor it like fine wine; run it around between your teeth like a mouthwash. Hold each sip in your mouth for at least a full minute. By then, your saliva will have diluted it and it won't taste so bad. Use the same drinking technique for beer as well as wine. Remember, rational drinkers don't primarily drink for feel; for them drinking is largely a social amenity, like eating with a fork rather than their fingers. So much for how to drink, now let's talk about drink strategy. At a party, let your wife get your drink for you, if she's willing. Needless to say, you can cheat. Neither I nor your wife nor anyone else can stop you. But just keep in mind that if you cheat, you are cheating only yourself and you are the only one who really loses. Although your wife is *not* your watchdog, she is expected to feel free to make any comment she wants to about how well or poorly you are following your one-ounce per hour schedule. You, in turn, are to sincerely welcome her reminders with the same honest gratitude you would show to her for pointing out that you are about to trip over an unseen chair. Understand?

132.   DOUG: (Pause) Yeah, I guess so.

133.   DR. M: Well, don't worry about it. If you are sincere in your desire to become a rational drinker, you will listen to this tape every day until you get it.

Author's Note #4

I have never seen a problem drinker (even an early one) who sincerely accepted the facts about his or her problem as soon as I described them to them. At first, they all (in my experience) want to cling to the irrational belief that they are the exception to the rule, that they can continue their drinking behavior as usual and still somehow (magically) get rid of their drinking problem. I no longer waste their time trying to get them to change their minds. If they are sincere and they are *not* babbling idiots, they will listen to the tape of their sessions over and over until they learn. Otherwise they'll go on as they always have. I was sure that Doug was not a babbling idiot, so I was willing to trust him to do the necessary listening and learning to solve his problem. I could do that because I sincerely believe that every sane individual has the right to be a drunk and I can't stop them. *ONLY THEY CAN STOP THEM.* All I can do is show them how to stop; but they must be willing to *SEE.*

My job, as I see it, is to make it as difficult as possible for problem drinkers *NOT* to see the easy solution to their problem. In my experience, one of the most effective ways to get them to see what they need to see to solve their drinking problem is to get at least one significant other (wife, husband, parent, lover, friend, etc.) rationally involved in helping the problem drinker as much as the drinker will permit and the significant other is willing to be rationally involved.

By rationally involved, I mean first and foremost, calmly accepting the objective fact that the problem drinker's problem is their problem. In no way is that problem the problem of the significant other. That's important! Remember it. The most appropriate as well as helpful attitude for significant others to have toward problem drinkers is the *Tight-Shoes Attitude.*

The Tight-Shoes Attitude

Suppose Mary goes with Richard, her husband, to buy new shoes. Richard likes a pair of shoes that is a little too tight for him. However, the shoes feel okay when he first puts them on; still, both he and Mary know that after a half hour or more, the shoes will be painful. Mary calmly tells Richard not to buy those shoes. But Richard buys them anyway and insists upon wearing them every day. What would be the most logical attitude and reaction for Mary to have when Richard comes home every day limping on painful feet, but still insisting on wearing those shoes? Would it help for Mary to nag and scream at Richard, get suicidally depressed, miserably angry or otherwise chronically upset when Richard insists on making himself miserable by wearing shoes that are too tight? Of course not! A rational Mary would sympathetically advise irrational Richard to soak his feet in hot water; she might even prepare the water for him sometimes, if she felt like it. *BUT* even though she is convinced that Richard's behavior is silly, if she has the *appropriate rational attitude,* she will not call him a fool nor try to embarrass him in front of the kids, his family or friends. On the other hand, she will *not* injure her back trying to pick him up and carry him upstairs just because his feet hurt when he tries to walk. She'd probably insist that he either carry himself, sleep downstairs or stop wearing those shoes. That would be the most *rational involvement* she could have in Richard's shoe problem. And that's the same calm acceptance, or calm rejection, that I recommend to a rationally involved person for a problem drinker.

As it turned out, Doug's wife, Candy, was an ideal significant other for a problem drinker. She was sincerely concerned about him, but she was rationally *unwilling* to upset herself significantly about his drinking problem. Yet, she willingly followed my instructions to the letter. She was secure in her decision to stay with Doug as long as she was personally *more* satisfied with him, drinking problem òr not, than she was with thoughts of living without him. Whether Doug solved his drinking problem or not would certainly have a significant bearing on her decision; but it wouldn't have any greater bearing than whether or not she enjoyed him *more* as a person when he was drunk than as a person when he was sober.

At the time of this session, I had not had time to get to know Candy. But, in my experience, inviting a potentially helpful significant other person to listen with the patient to an *appropriate* one of the patient's therapy tapes has proven to be a good way to learn quickly whether or not that person will prove to be helpful. So I told Doug to let Candy listen to this tape with him.

133. *cont'd.* DR. M: I want your wife to listen to this tape with you and discuss it with you every day for at least a week. Are you willing to do that without explanation, just because I said so? If you are not, we may as well stop therapy now.

134. DOUG: Since you put it that way, I'll do it.

135. DR. M: Good! Now, let's do your rational self-talk. This is the most important part of problem drinking re-education. It's also where even the most *sincere* efforts to regain rational control of drinking usually fail. After the first or

second drink, the problem drinker falls into the pitfalls of his old attitudes and beliefs about drinking. In the professional jargon, we call this "state dependent learning." But that's just a fancy way of saying nothing that you need to be concerned with. I mention it only because I realize that you either have or might check out my program for you with other mental health professionals. After you have had four stiff drinks you have learned to think: "One more won't matter; I can handle it now. I'm here to have a good time. One more won't hurt; I hardly feel it at all." Because you have usually had those thoughts *only* after you have already drunk three or four drinks, the feel of having that much alcohol in your body is now a cue to start thinking "One more won't hurt," etc. Because you got into the habit of thinking those thoughts only after you had put your body in an alcoholic state, we call that state dependent learning. All it means is that you have conditioned or programmed your brain to respond to alcohol in your blood with alcohol abuse thoughts that lead quickly to drinking more alcohol and a secondary loss of memory. That's why you may not remember having those thoughts, even though you act in light of them. So, before you know it, you wake up the next day with a first prize hangover and you can't understand how it happened because the last thing you remembered was your intention never to get drunk again. The key insight is that you have made drinking three or four drinks a learned cue to think thoughts that lead to alcohol abuse. Now, in order to drink rationally, you will have to eliminate that by erasing your brain program for your habitual alcohol abuse thoughts and replacing it with a brain program for rational drinking thoughts. *BUT*, there is no point in going into that unless you are convinced that you are willing to stick with the rational drinking program that I have already described.

136.   DOUG: How long will I have to stay on it?

137.   DR. M: That depends on whether you want to become a rational drinker or just give yourself a rest until you go back to problem drinking. If you are serious about rational drinking, in six to nine months on my program you'll probably be at the point where you are doing rational drinking as effortlessly as you now drink too much.

138. DOUG: Okay, I'll do it.
139. DR. M: Okay, but sincere desire is just the first step. Now, you must give yourself a personally meaningful group of rational drinking thoughts that you are willing to use to consistently challenge *and dismiss* your old irrational alcohol abuse attitudes and beliefs. That's because your old alcohol abuse attitudes and beliefs won't just roll over and die. Instead, they will come out just like clockwork every time you've had that third or fourth drink. So you will have to have your brain already programmed beforehand with rational ideas that you are willing to act on or more specifically drink on. From this point on, it's your responsibility to come up with rational drinking plans and thoughts that I'm willing to agree to, based on my knowledge of you as a person. We'll start with your rational plan to stay sober with straight drinks.
140. DOUG: Well, first off, I'm going to tell myself the truth: "I hate straight drinks, but I'm paying to learn to drink rationally. So I'm going to do exactly what Dr. Maultsby says, come hell or high water. He said to sip it straight; and I'm going to sip it straight, one ounce per hour."
141. DR. M: How many times?
142. DOUG: Every time I take a drink.
143. Dr. M: Right. Okay, what'll you say when your wife says, "Doug, you're drinking too fast; you're getting off schedule. It's only been fifteen minutes, and your glass is empty."
144. DOUG: I'll say: "Hey, you're right. I wasn't paying enough attention. How about getting me a plain coke or plain mix to sip on until time for my next drink. For the next drink I think I'll try a beer. That way I won't run out so fast."
145. DR. M: Good thinking; but are you willing to do it every time? Notice, now, I didn't ask are you willing to try to do it. I'm asking you if you are willing to actually do it. If you aren't, then don't try it.
146. DOUG: I'll do it.
147. DR. M: Okay, so you are now home after the party and sober; how will you handle this common idea: "Well, now that I've proved I can handle it, I'll just reward myself with a couple of my favorite nightcaps. Dr. Maultsby shouldn't mind that."

148. DOUG: You sure know me well, don't you?

149. DR. M: Not really; I just know the kind of self-talk that causes alcohol abuse.

150. DOUG: Well, I'll just tell myself that I don't need to drink as a reward. The success of carrying out my plan is all the reward I need. It's irrelevant that Dr. Maultsby won't mind my drinking, but since nightcaps *are not* part of my rational drinking plan, I won't do it. If I have trouble going to sleep, I'll do push-ups. That plus my bedtime REI will put me to sleep.

151. DR. M: Great! Now if you'll just follow through on that plan every time; you'll soon become a rational drinker. But *remember!* Good intentions are not enough! You have to actually do it every time. Daily REI's will be a big help. I suggest you do them at least four times a day every day. Then, a full half an hour before you leave your house for a party do REI's on your complete plan for rational drinking that evening. Be sure and include your wife in the REI's; see yourself gladly paying attention to her advice to stick to your schedule. Finally, and very important, never go to a party feeling depressed or angry or otherwise bad. A party is for celebration. Rational drinkers go to a party feeling good with the idea of sharing their good feelings. Only alcohol abusers go to a party feeling bad, hoping to drink themselves into better feelings. So never leave your house until you are feeling the way you would want to feel even it you didn't have a drink. I see our time is up.

152. DOUG: Doc, do you think I need to come back? I think I've got the hang of this rational thinking now and I'm having one hell of a time finding time to see you.

153. DR. M: I'm glad you mentioned that because I want to encourage you to begin keeping your weekly appointments. It takes time to get rid of life long emotional habits. Although you seem to have made tremendous progress, it's unrealistic to expect that you are all over your problems. In fact, you are probably just now at the point where you can benefit most efficiently from regular individual and group sessions.

154. DOUG: Group! You mean where people sitting around and screaming at each other tell people off. No thanks. I've been that route.

155. DR. M: No, I don't mean that at all. I mean group rational self-counseling. I recommend it to all people receiving indi-

vidual consultation. Group rational self-counseling has helpful features that the individual experience can't duplicate. Seeing and interacting with other people at varying stages of rational progress with varying types of problems is a tremendously stimulating rational growth experience. And there's no screaming or telling people off. There's only ten to twelve people trying to help each other develop greater skill in rational personal problem solving.

156. DOUG: Well Doc if you say it's good then, I believe you. You have sure showed me that you really know how to help people; but I just don't see how I can afford to take the time; I mean I've got a pile of work a mile high on my desk that I just walked away from to come today, and I have the tape. Don't you think, I could do it by myself if I do everything just like you said to do it?

157. DR. M: Yes, I think that's theoretically possible but, in my experience, if it's necessary to consult a psychiatrist at all the person usually needs at least three months of diligent individual and group work, but preferably six months.

158. DOUG: Okay Doc. If you say so. I mean I'm sure you're right. I'll see what I can do. Okay?

159. DR. M: Fine.

Emphasis Questions

(1) At first, some people believe that thinking rationally is just playing a game with themselves.
True   False   (P-175)

(2) REI's are most effective when you use rational insights from tapes, readings, and RSA's every day.
True   False   (P-176)

(3) As soon as most people start making rational progress, they usually want to take _____.   (P-176)

(4) The same principles of motivation apply when you interact with yourself as when you interact with other people.   True   False   (P-176)

(5) Your self-control is the result of your _____ of _____.   (P-178)

(6) It's not necessary to be concerned about the words you use.   True   False   (P-177, 178)

(7) The best solution to a drinking problem is rational self-counseling.   True   False   (P-178)

(8) REI is magic.   True   False   (P-181)

(9) By preceding a statement with the words "I feel," you make your subjective opinions appear *to you* to be objective facts.   True   False   (P-182)

(10) Gut thinkers believe their *feeling* of being treated unfairly is proof of unfair treatment.   True   False (P-182)

(11) Emotional feelings *can't* prove whether or not an attitude or belief is valid.   True   False   (P-183)

(12) It makes more sense to look for evidence to prove or justify your beliefs than to justify emotional feeling. True   False   (P-183)

(13) Your thoughts cause your brain to trigger reactions which are both _____ in your brain and _____ by your brain. This process is the basis of most _____. (P-184)

(14) The first step in rationally working on a problem is admitting the problem exists.   True   False   (P-184)

(15) The most important factor in human motivation is _____ _____.   (P-185)

(16) It's not facts that make people afraid, it's merely their beliefs about facts.   True   False   (P-190)

(17) The human brain doesn't automatically distinguish between fearful beliefs triggered by an objectively dangerous situation and fearful beliefs triggered by subjective nonsense.   True   False   (P-192)

(18) Replacing irrational attitudes with rational ones breaks the cognitive biofeedback cycle at the thinking brain link.   True   False   (P-192, 193)

(19) Rational or social drinking is a learned skill. True   False   (P-194)

(20) In order to drink rationally (socially), a problem drinker has to replace his habitual _____ _____ thoughts with thoughts and beliefs that cause rational (i.e. social) drinking. (P-198)

CHAPTER 14

DOUG IN THE FIVE STAGES OF RATIONAL DRINKING RE-EDUCATION

Introduction

In my experience chronic alcohol abuse is learned in two phases: (1) an obsessive phase and (2) a compulsive phase. In early problem drinking, these two phases often overlap. But the obsessive phase comes first and gets the abusive process going. Drinkers then drink primarily to get a better feeling fast, and almost any negative emotion can be a mental cue to take a drink. Their usual thought is: "All I need is a drink or two to fix me up, make me feel better." You know that thought has become an obsession when drinkers no longer try other methods of feeling better. They stop trying to philosophically accept unavoidable frustration; they stop thinking things like: "Okay, so I don't like it; but I refuse to make a federal case of it. It's not the end of the world just because I got turned down." Instead, they think: "I can't stand it without a DRINK." And they drink.

Doug's work-drinking was obsessive drinking. He was obsessed with feeling better fast and getting his work done. Alcohol let him do that. But once he learned to feel better with rational self-counseling, he no longer had an urge to drink at work. That's why he could stop his work-drinking so easily. Unfortunately, however, Doug's nighttime and party-drinking proved to be compulsive drinking. That phase of alcohol abuse requires a bit more work than either Doug or I first imagined he needed.

From Doug's story alone, no one could have told beforehand whether or not his drinking was all obsessive. That's why at the end of session three (Chapter 13) I encouraged Doug to keep making regular appointments with me. The rational approach to alcohol abuse is the same in both phases. But compulsive drinkers need more consistent guidance and support than most obsessive drinkers.

Compulsive drinking means alcohol addiction. The drinker has then trained his body to crave alcohol in certain situations. His crave seems like an overwhelming compulsive urge to drink. And the more he drinks, the more he wants to drink. This is the opposite of what happens in the obsessive phase. That's why Doug usually got drunk at night and at parties; but he never got drunk at work.

The five stages of rational drinking re-education are the same as in any other re-education. Like most compulsive drinkers, Doug tried to ignore that fact and got into trouble.

Doug in the Intellectual Insight Stage

At the end of session three (Chapter 13) Doug had both intellectual insight into his drinking problem and a mental map for solving it. He listened to his tape with his wife several times. She agreed to help him in the rational way I had described. So, Doug cancelled his next appointment with me and began stage two of his drinking re-education: Practice.

Doug in the Practice Stage

Because Doug and Candy were not being invited to parties, they began to give them. They gave four in a row. In the first two, everyone was subdued, a bit apprehensive, wondering what Doug would do. He followed his rational drinking program to the letter and was an excellent host. And at the third and fourth parties Doug was an even more pleasingly entertaining host and everyone had a ball.

By then, Doug and Candy were being invited out again. At the first two such parties Doug blew it, got drunk, blacked out, had angry arguments, the whole bit. Candy cancelled their plans to go to a third party. She also insisted that Doug start consulting me again.

Doug in Cognitive Dissonance Stage

The following are excerpts from Doug's fourth session, three months after his last one (Chapter 13).

1. DOUG: Did my wife call you?
2. DR. M: Yes, she wanted me to consider putting you in our intensive outpatient treatment program. I was quite surprised, and I told her I'd talk to you about it.
3. DOUG: Do you think I'm that bad?

4. DR. M: It's not a question of being good or bad. It's more a question of giving people one or two weeks of concentrated rational self-counseling so that they have a running start, so to speak, in terms of getting immediately on top of their problem. It's particularly good for people like you who tend to put work and everything else ahead of the daily practice they need in order to resist slipping back into their old habits.

5. DOUG: Would I have to go in the hospital?

6. DR. M: No, but it would mean taking off from work, because our intensive patients come to the clinic at 8 a.m. and are given an intense emotional re-educational experience until 5 p.m. every day, and some days 'til 9 p.m. Then they go home for the night or to their motel if they are from out of state. But before we go into that, let's see what your present situation is.

7. DOUG: I just blew it; I mean I was doing great and then I got too confident I guess, I don't know, but I really think I can handle it if I give it another try.

8. DR. M: That may be. Suppose you tell me exactly what you did at those last two parties.

9. DOUG: Well at the first one as soon as I walked in they had a double black Russian waiting for me. I knew I wasn't supposed to drink mixed drinks and Candy even told me that I shouldn't. But Jack was making such a big thing about having remembered my favorite drink, and he's so super sensitive I was afraid I might hurt his feelings; so I felt that one wouldn't hurt.

10. DR. M: There's no such feeling. There is the thought, attitude or belief that one won't hurt and a neutral to positive feeling about those ideas.

11. DOUG: Yeah, I really believed that I could handle it with no trouble, and I did but no sooner than I finished it, Jack stuck another one in my hand. But this time I told myself: "No you better not drink it. You know you can't handle it." And I could almost hear your voice telling me to sip it straight and that's what I intended to do. But you know how it is; you get to dancing and talking with your friends and before you can change your order, they've brought you another one and you keep saying you're going to start the program after this one, but you just don't get around to it.

12. DR. M: Who? Me?
13. DOUG: What do you mean?
14. DR. M: I'm wondering who you are talking about. You keep saying you, as if you are telling me what I do.
15. DOUG: Awww, come on doc, you know I mean me.
16. DR. M: Well if you mean you, then why not say I?
17. DOUG: (Smiling) Okay, I kept saying: "I'm going to start Dr. Maultsby's program after this one."
18. DR. M: My program? I thought it was your program.
19. DOUG: Okay okay, (smiling) my program.

Author's Note #1

Saying "you" when you are talking about yourself, is probably the most common, yet irrational way normal people confuse themselves. By using this second person "you" instead of "I", they try to make their irrational ideas and fears appear more logical and rational than they really are. For example, a person who is afraid to ask his boss for a promotion will often excuse himself with: "You can't just go in and threaten to quit if you don't get promoted." In fact, you most certainly can do that, and the people who say "you can't" know they are lying. But their lie feels better to them than the truth: "I'm afraid to threaten to quit."

Much more important than their irrational self-deception, by using "you" when they mean "I", such people attempt to disown their behavior. Doug didn't say, "I kept lying to myself that I was going to start my rational drinking program after this one." In effect he said "You did it." (item #11 above) He didn't say "No, I had better not drink it. I know I can't handle it." He said "you" and that made it seem as if a rational Doug was advising an irrational Doug. Then rational Doug took the credit by saying "and that's what I intended to do."

Having shown himself that he could rationally tell irrational Doug what to do, rational Doug patiently waited for irrational Doug to follow the rational advice. In the meantime rational Doug *saw no reason* why he shouldn't rationally enjoy his black Russian. But, there was no other Doug; there was only one Doug confusing himself with irrational second person "you's."

Rationally thinking people own up to all their behavior. So they say "I" when they mean "I." If you think I'm making too big a deal of this point, answer these questions. Have you ever had a person who has just found $10.00 or has just gotten a big raise, rush up to you and say "You just found $10.00," or "You just got a big raise."? If not, why not? I say it's because they are proud to own up to that behavior; and they refuse to give anybody else credit for it.

Doug knew all that. We had gone over it in detail in one of his other sessions. But like many people, he was not convinced that his language was that important, so he ignored it. But he needed to remember it; so I reminded him.

20. DR. M: Now don't tell me you have forgotten the time I got you to see how different you feel when you say I, instead of you, when you mean I.
21. DOUG: Yeah, I guess I need to watch my language.
22. DR. M: I agree. Now suppose you tell me the story again in the first person.
23. DOUG: Okay. No sooner than I had finished the first one, Jack stuck another one in my hand and I thought "No, it would really be better for me not to drink this. I have gotten off my program already. Two wrongs don't make a right. Maybe I can handle it, but maybe I can't. Anyway, I promised Dr. Maultsby, Candy and most important, I promised myself to follow my rational drinking plan.
24. DR. M: Hey, that's not what you said before.
25. DOUG: Yeah, but that feels more like what I would have said if I had stayed with I. It sounds funny I know, but that's the way I feel.
26. DR. M: I don't think it sounds funny; it sounds rational to me. It seems funny to you because you haven't yet made it your habitual way of thinking. That means you are in . . .
27. DOUG: Cognitive dissonance?
28. DR. M: Right, but instead of resolving it in favor of new learning you resolved it by feeling right, but thinking and drinking wrong or at least irrationally. Let's see what happened at the next party.
29. DOUG: Well at the next party I was determined not to let it get the best of me. I told myself that if I'm as rational as you say I should be I could handle it. So I . . .
30. DR. M: Abandoned the rational drinking program and tried to do it on good intentions. Right?
31. DOUG: Right, and I blew it.
32. DR. M: I wouldn't say you blew it, I'd say you did what was necessary to get drunk and you succeeded. And you

should have succeeded. But that wasn't anything new, that was your old, irrational business-as-usual; you didn't . . .

33. DOUG: Have enough will power, right? I just don't have enough will power. Right?

34. DR. M: I don't know because I don't know what will power is. So, let's get back to rational thinking. As I recall, there was nothing in the rational drinking plan that called for will power, just rational thinking. Did you do a rational self-analysis of your failure?

35. DOUG: I intended to but I just . . .

36. DR. M: Didn't take the time, right?

37. DOUG: I guess.

38. DR. M: Well, let's take the rest of this session to do the RSA you would have done had you done one.

Author's Note #2

We used the remainder of the session to write a RSA of his failure to follow through on his rational drinking plan. The Db section was essentially the first person self-talk that Doug describes in item #23 above. I had him actually write in the insight that, now that he had *sincerely decided* to cut down on his drinking, his drinking problem was no different from a cigarette problem. All he had to do to go back to rational or social drinking was be careful *not* to confuse his crave for a drink with a desire for a drink. If you smoke three packs of cigarettes per day, that means you want and crave a cigarette about every fifteen minutes. If you are satisfied with that much smoking, you don't have a cigarette problem. So, it's *not* necessary to distinguish your want for a cigarette from your learned craving for a cigarette. But even if you sincerely desire to cut down to a half a pack of cigarettes per day, your new sincere desire *will not* instantly stop your well learned crave for a cigarette every fifteen minutes. The crave will continue even though you *only* want to smoke every one and one half to two hours.

To get rid of those extra craves every fifteen minutes, you must consciously remind yourself every fifteen minutes that you *don't want* a cigarette then; you merely crave one. But, if you ignore that crave and concentrate on other rational things that you want more than the cigarette, the crave will gradually disappear. Each time you rationally refuse to smoke in less than one and one half to two hours the fifteen minute craves will become weaker and weaker and gradually stop for good. Then you will have changed from a three pack a day smoker to a half a pack a day smoker. But you have to work at it daily. The same is true of any drug habit. However, some drugs, like narcotics, cause such strong craves, it's impossible to get rid of them without complete abstinence. Fortunately *that's not the case in early* alcohol addiction.

39. DR. M: Now, I want you to go back to your four times per day rational emotive imagery routine using this RSA. In addition, carry this RSA with you to every party and read it over after each drink. Most important of all, make and keep an appointment with me every week until I tell you to stop. If you do that, I think you can succeed rationally without the intensive program. Are you willing to do that?
40. DOUG: Yeah, and this time I'm going to make it work.

Author's Note #3

This is how Doug went from cognitive dissonance through emotional insight to the social drinking trait: He followed through with his rational plan. He did his REI's and kept his appointments. Because he was only a fallible human being he did not follow the whole program *perfectly* well all the time. Sometimes he confused his craves with an overwhelming want, which he *incorrectly* called a *NEED*. But he did RSA's on his failures and we went over them in his weekly sessions. So each failure was less significant than the last one. After six months of this he rarely had craves and he was drinking solely for the sake of social drinking. He said "I can take it or leave it." And he'd prove it to himself by alternating parties at which he drank (but always rationally) with parties at which he rationally enjoyed himself without drinking at all. After doing that for several parties, he began to enjoy the non-drinking ones as much or more than the drinking ones. Then I discharged him to the local ART chapter. A year later, he reported drinking only beer with certain meals and an occasional party cocktail. He also had switched from cigarettes to an occasional pipe.

Doug tried to kick his irrational drinking habit by himself and failed. Does that mean he couldn't have succeeded without my continued help? No. It only means that he didn't succeed without my help. There is considerable scientific evidence that alcoholics can use rational thinking by themselves to stop abusing alcohol (see references at end of book).

It is a fact however that most alcohol dependent people *do not* and *will not* succeed alone. Most just haven't developed strong enough habits of self-discipline toward their alcohol habit to make it alone. They at least need the help of rational peers such as they find in chapters of ART (Association for Rational Thinkers).

The problem of rational drinker re-education is like the problem of a college education. You *can* get a college education by studying alone at home, never setting foot on a college campus. But you are much more likely to succeed in getting a college education if you attend college. By the same logic, alcoholics are more likely to succeed at rational drinking or rational non-drinking if they meet regularly with rational peers as in ART or with a rational mental health professional.

Programmed Rational Thinking for Rational Sobriety

When problem drinkers want to stop drinking completely, in the fastest way possible, I put them on this routine. I have them buy a copy of my standard tape recording that explains the important difference between wanting a drink and craving a drink.* Then I have *them* make a tape recording of my following standard rational sobriety script, using their normal conversational voice. (See page 212) Each night they set a half pint of their favorite soft drink and a half pint of their favorite alcoholic beverage in front of them. While looking at each bottle, they listen to both tapes. When both tapes are over, they slowly sip two ounces of their favorite soft drink while listening to both tapes again. They repeat that exercise up to four times each night. Four repeats take about two hours. If you are not worth two hours per day of your time, you probably won't succeed with this method.

Sincere people who follow through as directed, usually eliminate their alcohol craving completely in a few weeks. If they give in and start drinking the alcohol they probably need professional help.

---

*That tape can be purchased for $6.95 from the Intensive Rational Behavior Therapy Training Section, UKMC Psychiatric OPD, Lexington, Ky. 40506. Make checks payable to University of Kentucky.

Emphasis Questions

1. Chronic alcohol abuse has _____ phases.   (P-203)
2. The _____ phase comes first and leads to the _____ phase.   (P-203)
3. In the obsessive phase the belief that only _____ or _____ drinks can cause a better feeling keeps the drinking habit in force.   (P-203)
4. In the _____ phase the learned _____ for alcohol is the main reason the person keeps on drinking.   (P-203)
5. Compulsive drinking means _____.   (P-204)
6. Rational drinking re-education is different from other re-education.   True   False   (P-204)
7. If you ignore the fact that all re-education is the same, you may slip back into your old habits.
   True   False   (P-204)
8. At the end of his third session Doug had _____ insight into rational drinking re-education.   (P-204)
9. When Doug practiced rationally he succeeded.
   True   False   (P-204)
10. Doug got into trouble in the stage of _____ _____.   (P-204)
11. Intensive rational self-counseling solves your problems in one week.   True   False   (P-205)
12. On the night Doug gave up his rational drinking plan he was thinking rationally.   True   False   (P-206)
13. When people say you when they really mean I, they are just being modest.   True   False   (P-206, 207)
14. Saying you when you really mean I, is often an irrational way of trying to _____ your irrational _____.   (P-206)
15. When people find money, they often run up to others and say: "You found this money."   True   False   (P-207)
16. If you have good intentions, it doesn't really matter how you choose your words.   True   False   (P-207)
17. Because Doug tried so hard and still failed, that proves that at that time rational self-counseling failed.
   True   False   (P-209)

18. Alcohol addiction is different from any other type of addiction   True   False   (P-208)

19. Alcohol dependent people are not special people and therefore deserve to be treated like other otherwise normal people who have an irrational problem.
True   False   (Chapter 14)

20. Just because you crave something, that does not mean that you want it.   True   False   (P-208)

NON-DRINKING SCRIPT
Used by
Maxie C. Maultsby, Jr., M.D.

That's the most sensible talk I have ever heard about alcoholism. He sure is right about that first drink. If I don't drink it I can't get drunk. That bottle sure looks good. I want to take a drink right now. Nope that's not right. I don't want a drink. In fact, I really don't want a drink. I really want to stop drinking. I just feel like I want a drink because I have trained my body to crave a drink when I see or smell alcohol. But I see now that my crave is not my want. My want is to stop drinking. So I will just ignore that stupid crave in my gut and think with my mind.

My mind tells me that I don't want a drink. So I will follow my mind and take a drink of that nice cold (*read in your favorite soft drink*). I used to think it was hard for me to refuse a drink. Now I see that it's really easy. All I have to do is keep thinking rationally and sipping my nice cold (*read in your favorite soft drink*).

Hey! That stupid crave has started to go away already. That guy on the tape was right, by just taking my mind off my crave, I make it start going away. It's really true that all I have to do to refuse that first drink is think straight; just concentrate on what I really want instead of the stupid gut feelings that used to confuse me. By doing that, I make the craving go away fast. It's really great to know that I really can control myself. Never again do I have to be a slave to my gut. I have a good mind, and I am going to use it to retrain my gut. I don't want a drink; I don't need a drink and I will refuse to take a drink. I will drink some more nice cold (*read in your favorite soft drink*). That's all I need. This is really great! I have actually started getting over my drinking habit already. Now, I can start thinking about my future. Now that I know how to stop being a slave to alcohol I am free to do whatever I want and am able to do. Never again will I have to get drunk just because I get mad or bored or depressed. I can just turn on my rational thoughts, like I am doing now, and honestly tell myself that I don't want a drink even though I'm mad. It's just that I am used to drinking when I am mad. But the only person I hurt by such stupid drinking is me. And that's really stupid. I don't have to drink just because I'm mad. Before I started to drink, I used to get over being mad without drinking and I can still do it now.

The same thing is true when I get to feeling like I am no damn good. I see now that, no matter how badly I feel, I really don't have to drink to feel better. I can get rid of my bad feelings by just thinking rationally. I am not going to get confused anymore. I'm just going to tell myself that drinking is bad for me and I honestly don't want what's bad for me. I don't need it, so I'll refuse to drink it. I feel badly because of my stupid habit of self-pity. But I am going to stop that irrational crap right now. I am as good as anybody. It's just that I have had the stupid habit of drinking more than most people. But starting right now I am giving up that stupid habit. I will refuse this first drink and I will feel good about myself for refusing it. I really don't want to drink; so I'll just ignore all my feelings that seem like I want to drink; and just refuse to drink. It's just like that guy on the tape said. It really is as easy to stop drinking as it is to stop smoking. I see that now. All I have to do is just refuse this first drink one more time. Stopping drinking is easy, just refuse one more time. This could get to be fun. I feel better already. I don't want a drink. I don't need a drink and I refuse to take a drink. I don't care how my stupid gut feels. I have a brain. I have a rational mind and I am going to follow my rational mind.

Now that I have cleared up my confusion about my want for alcohol and my stupid craves for it, I will be able to stay out of drunk tanks, and stop wasting my money paying for bail and jail fines, and hospital bills. My liver is half gone already, but doctors say all you need is half of a good liver to go on living as long as anyone else. So, I can start planning my future to start enjoying life. Since I now know how to resist that first drink, I won't have anymore hangovers and Monday, Tuesday and Wednesday morning shakes. So I'll be able to work as well as anybody and I won't have to worry about embarrassing myself and my family anymore.

If I would just keep my thinking straight about my true want, which is not to drink, and if I just ignore my stupid crave just one more time, I'll have it made. I'll get my self-respect back and I won't be ashamed of myself anymore. I'll be able to look anybody in the eye and honestly believe I'm as good a person as they are. All I have to do is keep thinking about these three facts. The fact that I don't want to drink; the fact that my crave for a drink is stupid and irrational and it would be best for me to ignore it and the fact that I don't need a drink. By keeping these three facts in mind I can easily refuse that first drink just one more time and enjoy my nice cold (*read in your favorite soft drink.*)

CHAPTER 15

THE CLASSROOM AS AN EMOTIONAL HEALTH CENTER

Students today face many problems that were hardly known to their parents. Consequently, it is unfair to blame those parents for having failed to teach their children to cope satisfactorily with the emotional stresses of modern living. Caught between those heretofore unknown emotional stresses on the one hand and their healthy striving for mature independence on the other, many students seek pseudo-relief in alcohol and other drug abuse.

If emotional self-help could be taught in the classroom, students could learn to solve for themselves many of the emotional problems for which they now seek scarce, expensive, professional help. With their new, self-created freedom, students should then recognize the futility of searching for emotional stability outside themselves. Reliance on alcohol and other drugs should decrease as students involve themselves in self-reinforcing personality expansion.

CLASSROOM RATIONAL SELF-COUNSELING

All the people described in this book probably could have solved their emotional problems using rational self-counseling alone, if they had had this book. But, that *does not* mean that RATIONAL SELF-COUNSELING is a cure-all for all emotional problems. It *IS NOT.*

A great many emotional problems are too severe to be solved with rational self-counseling alone. I advise and encourage people who have such severe problems to get professional help. Indeed, failure to help oneself with a sincere trial of rational self-counseling usually means that person needs professional help. Even then, rational self-counseling usually helps that person benefit most in the shortest amount of time from professional help.

Throughout this book I have shown that regardless of the source of your outside help, you have to process it in *your* brain;

that means Rational Self-Counseling. To demonstrate that fact scientifically I formulated and tested a rational self-counseling course for high schools and colleges. I could do that easily because rational self-counseling has the three essential features required for classroom instruction in emotional self-help techniques. Those essential features are:

a) Has a scientifically valid explanation of human emotions that people of high school level or above can readily understand and use.

b) Is a simple yet effective technique of emotional self-analysis that people of high school level or above can easily learn.

c) Fits easily into the usual school and classroom routine.

The course is structured around this book and a series of audio or video tape recordings of people who are successfully using rational self-counseling to solve various common emotional problems, such as exam anxiety, feelings of inferiority, common depression, poor self-motivation, romantic hang-up, irrational fears, etc.

Using the college computer system we randomly selected fifty students from the total (1150) enrollment of a midwest, religiously affiliated, liberal arts college. The college counseling center sent a letter to the selected students inviting them to take the rational self-counseling course for three college credits at the regular college credit tuition charge. Thirty student enrolled. The course met for one hour and a quarter twice per week for fifteen weeks.

Psychological testing was done before and after the rational self-counseling course, using the Shostrom Personal Orientation Inventory (POI) and the Rotter Internal versus External Locus of Control Scale. The same tests were given to a second year organizational psychology class of thirty students, which served as a control group.

Approximately the same number of males and females were in both classes; their grade point range was evenly distributed; their modal educational level was sophomore year and they were predominantly single and Catholic.

At the beginning of the two courses there was no significant difference between the two classes on either the POI or the Rotter I-E tests. But after the two courses ended, the post course test scores of the rational self-counseling class showed highly significant improvement in emotional health as it is measured by eight of the twelve POI scales. This improvement was apparent both when the rational self-counseling class was compared to itself as well as to the psychology class. The same was true for the Rotter I-E test.

This study is important for two major reasons. First, it confirms what repeated emotional health surveys show; namely most normal people can improve their emotional health, if they are shown how. Second, the regular school classroom is a practical, economical and efficient approach to mass mental health improvement. In addition, there are three major advantages for using the classroom.

   a) The classroom approach, using rational self-counseling, is efficient. One regular teacher (with *no prior training* in rational self-counseling) can teach thirty to forty students at once, to solve their own emotional problems.
   b) With the classroom approach it becomes possible to establish uniform minimum standards of institutional and community emotional health, similar to institutional and community standards for education.
   c) Willing (normal) students will learn to accept full responsibility for their own emotional feelings. Since students always decide how much and how well they will learn anything, they will also decide how much and how well they emotionally re-educate themselves. Because of that, they will have fewer inappropriate fears of being "brainwashed" by the so-called establishment. Students will then have the greatest possible freedom of choice to get rid of or keep whatever emotional habits they desire.

This rational self-counseling course is now offered for college credits at the University of Kentucky, Lexington Technical College, and Rockhurst College in Kansas City, Missouri. It is also being offered regularly in two high schools.

Because of our success with the classroom approach to improved emotional health, we formulated and perfected two intensive one to two week rational self-counseling courses. One is for normal people (non-students) who don't need professional help but who want to start getting more joy in living as fast as possible. The other is for business executives who have one or more of the following causes of executive failure:

   a) Chronic procrastination and frequent missed deadlines;
   b) Frequent breaches of company policy;
   c) Supersensitiveness and inappropriate suspiciousness;
   d) Frequent feelings of inadequacy;

e) Inappropriate stubbornness
f) Refusal to accept new ideas;
g) Inappropriate acceptance of new ideas;
h) Frequent overuse or abuse of alcohol or tranquilizers;
i) Chronic job resentment or other dissatisfaction;
j) One or more psychosomatic disorders (hypertension, ulcers, asthma, colitis, etc.)

You can obtain further information about these courses by writing to me (Dr. Maxie C. Maultsby, Jr.) Director, Psychiatric OPD, UKMC, Lexington, Ky. 40506

SECTION V

THE ART OF SMALL GROUP AND COMMUNITY SELF-HELP

I wrote this book primarily for people who want to help themselves by themselves. I know, however, that most people learn best by combining individual and complementing small group learning experiences. That's why one appendix of this book describes in detail the history and activities of ART (Association for Rational Thinking). ART enables interested people to combine their individual self-help efforts with the self-help, small group approach. In another appendix you will find interesting case histories of the ART group approach to overcoming drug abuse, marital problems, worry about a physical handicap and the fear of flying. And if you happen to function best in small group activities, you will learn how you can contact some of the most rational small groups in the world, ART GROUPS!

CHAPTER 16

WHAT ART IS AND WHAT ITS CHAPTERS DO
By Connie Walling

ART is a non-profit, self-help organization, classified by the federal government as a public charity. ART's primary purpose is research and education about rational emotional self-help aids and techniques found in this book.

ART has over 1,200 members in the U.S. and several foreign countries, including India, Germany, Britain, Australia, Tasmania . . . yes, I said Tasmania, and Israel. We now have 22 active chapters and about 30 groups in some stage of formation, and new requests are coming in every day.

An ART chapter can begin any time ten or more people contact the ART national headquarters, P.O. Box 159, Lexington, Ky. 40501, describing an interest in the rational approach to living and requesting ART chapter status. While many new members in ART are unhappy people who want to learn how to increase their joy in living, equally as many new members are relatively satisfied with their lives but want to learn a systematic way to continue their personal growth. ART welcomes both groups of people with open arms and a sincere desire to help.

Since the first of the four main goals of ART is helping people help themselves, we think the best people to talk about ART, are ART members. Let's listen now to a former Viet Nam veteran who joined ART.

"It seems as if I've always had a lot of problems. I've been really shy most of my life. I've always had a lot of trouble getting along with people. I decided to major in psychology in college. Mostly, I think, because I wanted to find help for myself. I started to be more out-going and when I was a sophomore, I was elected to a student council office.

"But that was about the time they started the draft lottery. I thought my number was coming up soon and heard that if you enlisted they wouldn't send you overseas. So I enlisted. And they sent me overseas to Viet Nam. The weird thing is that my draft lottery number never even came close to being chosen. Boy! was I angry then — at the world, the government, the army and myself!

"While I was in Nam, I started messing around with drugs —, all kinds. I tried heroin, thinking I wouldn't get addicted. But, sure enough, I got addicted. I never used a needle, but I snorted it. A few months before I was going to come back to the States, I came down off the big "H". I knew I'd better get off for good, because "H" just wasn't available in the States and I knew I'd really mess myself up if I stayed on it. So I came down, and started helping other guys come down so I wouldn't forget just how bad coming down was, and be tempted to go back on it.

"I was OK when I got back. I had a few months left and was stationed in the States. I got to know some people near my new base and I spent all my spare time with them smoking grass and taking pills to get high and pills to calm down. When I got out of the Army, I moved in with my friends. We spent most of our time on one thing or another. In some ways I liked it, but I was getting to the point that I didn't want to talk to anyone much.

"Then I heard about some job openings in my home town, so I went back there. I got a job that paid well in a factory and started saving money. But I still spent a lot of my spare time getting high. I wasn't exactly what you'd call happy then. I knew I didn't want to keep working in the factory, but I didn't want to go back into school either; and I was scared shitless of going out with women.

"Then a friend of mine from another city told me about ART and invited me to one of their marathons. I figured I had nothing to lose but a week-end and a little cash, so I went. I really liked it — had a lot of insights that week-end and learned a lot about what I was doing. I guess the most exciting thing I learned was that even though I'd had a lot of problems, that didn't mean I had to spend my whole life being messed up.

"Since there wasn't an ART group in my town, I moved to a town where I could join one. First I went to rational self-counseling classes, and then I was assigned to a group and a rational associate (RA) to talk to individually. My experience in ART has been the best thing that has happened to me. The first thing ART helped me to do was to get over my irrational fear of women and start dating. Sure, I had some really heavy problems with it at first, but with the help of my RA and my ART group, I was able to work it through and start tackling my other hang-ups. Right now I'm involved in a relationship I enjoy a lot. In fact, I'm even considering a permanent arrangement with this woman and I'm even handling the whole thing pretty rationally: no panic or changing my mind back and forth or any of my old irrational games.

"I decided that taking drugs is not in my best interest, so I quit. Besides, just by deciding to use my brain for a rational turn-on, with REI's, I can "feel as high" as I want to without dope.

"Oh, I still have a few hang-ups I'll probably be working on for some time to come. I mean, you just can't revolutionize your whole life in one or two months. But with rational self-counseling and ART, you can get started any time you want to. I know there's nothing special about me; so since ART could help me, I'm sure it can do the same for anyone who is willing to be helped."

Another ART member tells this success story:

"I'm in my early twenties. I've got impaired hearing and a slight speech problem. I'd been married for three years when I became pregnant. Early in my pregnancy I began feeling afraid of just about everything about childbirth. I was making unneccessary visits to the doctor, calling his office every day and often even his home late at night; all for repeated reassurance. I wanted to know every detail about when the baby was coming, how long it would take, how would it feel; would I suffer, etc., and I got extremely upset because the doctor couldn't give me the answers. I also worried about gaining weight and getting fat and ugly and losing my husband's affection. I worried about my hearing loss and worried that the baby would be born deaf. Late in the pregnancy I began to worry about not being a good enough mother, about maybe even harming the baby out of stupidity. Whenever I thought about going in the delivery room, I'd go into panic. I was afraid that because I can't hear well, I wouldn't understand the nurses and do stupid things and make everybody disgusted with me and maybe they wouldn't want to help me and I'd be left alone to have my baby without any help.

"Finally, in self-defense as much as anything, my doctor suggested that I go to ART and learn to use rational self-counseling to deal with my worry problems. After going over a few of my RSA's in group and with my RA in individual sessions, I began to get rational control of my irrational worry; I stopped worrying about questions that only time could answer. I stopped worrying about when and how the baby would come. I just kept pointing out to myself: 'I can't control that, but when it comes, I'll deal with it, as rationally as I can. That's all I or anyone can do, so irrational worry is a big waste of time and emotional energy.'

"I began to accept the fact that weight gain during pregnancy is normal, natural and desirable and labeling myself "ugly" didn't change that fact; nor did it make me an ugly person. I began to accept myself as only a fallible human being who is ugly to some people and beautiful to others. That had always been the case and I had no rational reason to believe that it had changed. I taught myself to rationally accept the probability that my baby would not be defective and that even if it were, it would not be awful or catastrophic. After all, I'm living proof that a handicapped person can live and enjoy life as much as anyone.

"I even began to be calm about what might happen in the delivery room. I pointed out to myself that thousands of partially and even completely deaf women have babies every year. My most helpful insight was that even if the doctors and nurses had to repeat things to me, that wouldn't mean I was stupid; and if they got angry, that would be their problem, which I was determined not to let become my problem.

"In fact, my labor went very quickly and uneventfully. Thinking rationally helped me tremendously in the delivery room. At first, I had a mild panic; I wanted to just get off the delivery table and forget about having the baby. But then I started to think rationally, telling myself that I was going to have the baby whether I wanted to or liked it or not; so upsetting myself now was only going to add to my problem. No possible benefit to me could come from that.

"So I calmed myself down and stayed that way as the doctor delivered a beautiful little girl. She's normal, and healthy and I'm now making plans to use my newly learned rational self-counseling to help me deal with my child-raising problems as rationally as I can."

The second main goal of ART is to provide on-going problem-solving groups. The groups are guided by our trained lay leaders, called Rational Associates or RA's. Wherever possible, we encourage (but don't require) the ART members who are mental health professionals to consult with our ART chapter groups and RA's thereby helping ART maintain the highest quality of self-help possible. The following is a typical example of an ART group problem-solving session in one of our chapters:

How an ART Group Handled the Irrational Fear of Flying

Harriet, a new member of the ART group in Madison, had recently finished the introductory course in RBT and had attended a few group meetings. This was the first RSA she presented in group.

A Facts & Events	Da Camera Check of A
I want to visit my daughter in Ceylon, but I'm afraid of flying. Since Ceylon is 10,000 miles from Madison, I'll have to fly in order to get there and back in a three-week vacation. I had a bad experience during college on a flight from Pittsburgh to Washington, D.C., when a sister flight went down in Virginia during a severe thunderstorm that knocked our plane all over the sky.	Factual

B Self-Talk	Db Rational Debate of B
B-1. The plane might go down.	Db-1. This is true.
B-2. If it crashed, I'd probably be killed.	Db-2. This is true.
B-3. Even if I get the courage to get on the plane, if I change my mind about flying, they won't let me off.	Db-3. That's true but it also is good because once I make the decision to fly and get on that plane, the results of that decision are out of my hands.
B-4. Maybe I'll get a poorly trained flight crew.	Db-4. I have no rational reason to believe that there's much chance of getting a poorly trained flight crew. There is a lot of competition for positions on flight crews, so there should be very competent people around who want to fly.

B-5. It's a day and a half of actual flying time, and if I'm too scared, it'll be the worst experience of my life.

Db-5. Thirty-six hours is a long time to fly, but can seem to go quickly if I don't sit there paralyzed with fear. I wouldn't frighten myself so much if I'd enjoy the beautiful scenery I'll be able to see and think about the good ethnic foods that I will be able to eat. Also, just being scared isn't the worst thing I can think of. Torture or prolonged physical pain would be much worse.

B-6. I'm ashamed of myself for being afraid of flying. The rest of my family and most of my friends accept getting places by plane as a matter of course.

Db-6. I do not need to be ashamed of anything I do because I am a fallible human being. I tell myself a lot of negative things about flying and scare myself. My family and friends who aren't afraid of flying don't do that. They aren't any better than I am; they just tell themselves different things than I tell myself.

B-7. I might not be so scared when the plane is up in the air, but there are 14 take-offs and landings from here to Ceylon, so I'll be a nervous wreck when I get there.

Db-7. It's a good thing there are take-offs and landings or we'd run out of gas with 10,000 miles to cover.
    There's no getting around the length of the trip, but if I can get over being apprehensive about take-offs and landings, they can break the monotony.

B-8. Even if I get enough nerve to fly there, I will have to fly back, and I may think about the return trip so much that it will spoil my vacation.

Db-8. If I get enough nerve to make the trip to Ceylon, I should feel reinforced that it isn't all that bad and therefore be able to view the return trip with more composure.

B-9. I took flight lessons during WW II, so I know how

Db-9. I'm not a trained pilot, and what was hard for me

mixed up you can get with all those instruments in front of you — and the plane I flew was only a Piper Cub. How can anybody fly those big planes?

isn't necessarily hard for another person to do. I had only 10 lessons in a Piper Cub, and flight crews get thousands of miles in the air before they get licensed.

C	E
Emotion	Emotional Goal for Future A's
Fear of flying	Indifference to flying

After an RSA is presented to an ART group, the group members are invited to make rational comments they think might be helpful.

LARRY: I have an addition to the "B" section. Sentence #2, as stated, is probably objective. If the plane did crash, the passengers *would* probably be killed. But your fear makes it seem that you believe that it would be awful to die.

HARRIET: I wasn't aware of that; but perhaps so. In that case the entire B-2 sentence would actually be: "If it crashed, I'd probably be killed, and that would be awful."

BETTY: That's a good point. If no one else wants to add anything, I think it would be good for Harriet to review the five rules for rational thinking.

HARRIET: Oh, I remember those from the classes. Does what I'm doing make sense in view of the objective reality? Is it life-preserving? Is it likely to aid me in reaching my goals? Is it likely to help me avoid significant personal conflict? And is it likely to help me avoid significant conflict with my environment?

BETTY: Great. Now can you do a camera check of your "A" section?

HARRIET: I think the "A" section is OK.

BETTY: Well, the distance and time involved are objectively verifiable. And we'll take your word for it that you're fearful — otherwise I doubt that you'd be doing this RSA. But I question whether the last part of your "A" section about a previous flying experience is relevant here.

HARRIET: Well, I'm trying to show what the fear's based on. You see, the flight I was on almost did *crash*. There were two sections of the flight, and the second section crashed and ours got through. It was a terrible storm and the other flight went down, and I've had this fear ever since. I didn't see the other plane go down, but it was just a few minutes from us. So doesn't that belong in the "A" section?

BETTY: Not necessarily. What's past is past.

HARRIET: But my memory of it isn't past . . . it's current.

BETTY: That's because you continue to think about it.

LARRY: The only way your past can affect you now is through your feelings about your memories. If you remember using fearful thoughts, you will recreate the fear. But past events can't be here now to make you afraid.

HARRIET: It still seems as if it's important to my fear of flying.

BETTY: Only because you make it important by continuing to use your fearful memory to produce fearful thoughts about flying. But your logical concern now *is not* a flight several years ago, but the flight you wish to make now to Ceylon.

HARRIET: I see. You could do that with almost any experience in life, couldn't you? I mean, you could end up with past experiences kind of controlling your present.

BETTY: Yes, and many people do. They think their past experiences *cause* their present thoughts and feelings. But as Larry pointed out, it is your current thoughts *about* the past event that cause your present fear. By putting that in your "A" section, you make it appear that just because you had one bad experience, you will have to have it again.

HARRIET: Actually, I wasn't afraid during the flight. But when I got on the ground, my roommate ran up to me and said, "Oh, we thought you'd crashed!" And that's when all the fear hit me.

BETTY: The fear didn't "hit" you then, that's when you began to make yourself fearful about flying. And you have kept yourself fearful by continuing to think fearful thoughts about flying and accusing the past event of doing it. You won't get over this fear until you see that you are causing it with your fearful thoughts and then stop having those thoughts.

HARRIET: I wish I'd known RBT then — I've wasted all these years not flying!

BETTY: Let's go on now to the "D" section and discuss the challenges to your "B" sentences. In #1, you say it's true that the plane might go down. Strictly speaking, you're correct. But if you feel afraid, that shows that you believe the plane will *probably* go down. It's a good idea to distinguish between what is possible and what is probable. If you look at objective reality, almost anything is possible . . . but that doesn't mean that everything that's possible is actually likely to happen. If you concentrate on what's possible, you could make yourself fearful most of the time. It's possible that you could be hit by a car any time you cross the street. But that doesn't mean you will *probably* be hit every time you cross. And it's because you see that it's not likely that you'll get hit by a car, *if* you take reasonable precautions, that you don't think much about it when you cross the street.

FRAN: Another thing, everybody tends to over-emphasize the probability of planes crashing because we only hear about the ones that crash. You never see headlines that say: Five hundred planes took off and landed safely today at Chicago O'Hare Airport.

HARRIET: I see what you mean.

LARRY: What do you think now about your B-2?

HARRIET: Well, as you pointed out, I guess I do believe it would be awful to die. Yet I know that everyone has to die some-time . . . and I guess dying in a plane crash would be pretty quick . . .

LARRY: But right now you're challenging the process of dying. What you seem to think is awful is not the way you'll die — whether it is quickly or slowly — but the fact of your death.

HARRIET: Well, I can *say* that people have to die sometime, but I don't think I can face it calmly.

BETTY: That's because with regard to this particular idea, you are in the stage of cognitive dissonance. In other words, you know intellectually that death occurs and is not awful — but you react emotionally to your belief that death *is* awful.

HARRIET: How can one get apart from one's self long enough to look at one's own death with no emotions?

LARRY: You can't get apart from yourself.

FRAN: And if you are healthy, it's impossible not to have some type of emotions. So we *wouldn't* suggest that you look at your death with no emotions. We are just trying to get you to be less afraid of flying.

HARRIET: But you're saying I shouldn't think it's awful. But it would be awful if I lose me.

PAT: How can you lose yourself?

HARRIET: Well, if I'm all gone, I've lost myself.

LARRY: Are you saying that you'd be alive and dead at the same time?

MIKE: As far as we know, death is just the absence of life. You don't know whether you're going to be aware of your death or not. So worrying about it is a waste of time, it seems to me.

HARRIET: Well, maybe my fear of flying is really a fear of the unknown.

ROBIN: That may be part of it, but there are many things that you don't know, that you are not afraid of. Right?

HARRIET: But I have more control over them.

PAT: Not if they are really unknown.

DAVE: Do you know what's going to happen tomorrow?

HARRIET: Well, some things.

BETTY: But not everything, right?

HARRIET: No, not everything; you can't know everything.

MIKE: Well, are you scared about what you don't know about tomorrow?

HARRIET: No, not really.

BETTY: So what's going to happen on your trip is unknown, and what's going to happen tomorrow is unknown. Since you can rationally keep yourself from being afraid of the one, you could rationally keep yourself from being afraid of the other, if you thought about it rationally.

HARRIET: But you've got to admit, it's not like driving a car. You are able to get out of a car when you want to; you can't do that when you are up in a plane. I don't like that much loss of control.

PAT: I know what you mean, Harriet. I get nervous sometimes flying when I think about not having any control. But since I see I can't control the airplane I control my fear with rational thinking.

BETTY: Actually, when you get nervous in a plane you are just trying to get some control magically, when in fact no personal control is possible.

PAT: But you don't want to think you're just helpless.

DAVE: But the fact is that you are helpless, and it doesn't make any difference how nervous you get, the airplane won't know it. So all you prove is that you believe in magic

HARRIET: I never thought of that. It's like trying to pull some invisible strings; like when you know someone who is going in the hospital for surgery and you feel you have to worry about them to make sure they get through the operation okay.

JOHN: But the only thing that will really help that person is the surgeon and the nurses.

HARRIET: Yeah, . . . but it's so boring when you take off; there's nothing to look at but the runway.

JOHN: You could close your eyes and think rationally about your trip.

LARRY: Or read something.

FRAN: Or pray. (laughter)

JOHN: Not prayer — that makes it look like there really is a real danger.

BETTY: Rational thinking would be best, and when the plane is in the air, you'd see that it got there without you worrying about it, and you could congratulate yourself for your rational self-control. Let's go on to your next "D" sentence about dying if the plane crashes.

HARRIET: I still think my challenge is true, but I see now that even though it's possible, it's unlikely that I would get a poorly trained crew.

LARRY: Why do you think you worry about these possible but improbable things in the first place?

HARRIET: Maybe I just want a good excuse not to fly.

LARRY: I think it's because you believe it would be awful to die.

HARRIET: It seems as if everything goes back to the ideas in #1 and #2. I guess I'm really afraid to die.

BETTY: I agree. But you also said that you see intellectually that dying isn't awful; that's the first step in learning not to fear death. But intellectual insight is not enough; so after we finish with your RSA, we'll talk about rational emotive imagery and how it will help you get over your fear of flying and your fear of death. What's your next "B" sentence?

LARRY: Something about it being a long flight.

HARRIET: But it *is* a long time to fly.

PAT: "Long" is an arbitrary opinion. If someone really enjoyed sitting on an airplane and didn't get to do it more than once in awhile, they might think that 36 hours was a *short* time to fly.

HARRIET: Yes, but most people I tell about my trip say that it's a long time.

MIKE: No matter how many people agree, they are still just stating their arbitrary opinions; and fifty million can be and frequently are wrong.

HARRIET: You sound like Dr. Maultsby.

MIKE: That must mean that Dr. Maultsby is really getting rational. (laughter)

HARRIET: But it is an objectively long trip.

BETTY: But so what?

HARRIET: Hmmm. Yeah, thinking about it negatively won't shorten it, will it?

JOHN: I want to know why she's ashamed of her fear of flying. Can we talk about that now?

HARRIET: Well I put in my challenge that I know I'm a fallible human being and my shame is silly. But I still feel ashamed.

BETTY: I think that's just cognitive dissonance. I think you need to point out to yourself that you aren't any the "worse" as a person because you are afraid to fly.

HARRIET: Right. Other people aren't any better just because they aren't afraid to fly . . . they just feel better because they don't worry the way I do.

BETTY: I think your challenge to B-7 is good. But I think you're prophesying, and if you keep it up you may, in fact, fulfill the prophecy by making yourself afraid and arriving in Ceylon in panic. I think it would be better to remind yourself that you don't have to be anxious about the trip and that you can arrive in Ceylon weary but calm.

LARRY: Harriet, in the next challenge, you talk about getting enough nerve. I don't think that's very rational since objectively, nerves don't increase or decrease at will, and "enough" is highly arbitrary. I would rephrase that idea to say, "If I do go to Ceylon . . ."

JOHN: Another idea that you seem to have is that you don't control your thoughts; but that's not true. You always control them, both to your advantage and disadvantage: that is of course, unless you are on dope.

HARRIET: No, I don't use drugs.

JOHN: Good! So even if you do make yourself afraid on the way to Ceylon, you could still have rational thoughts about the return trip and fly back with much less fear. Your insight about positively reinforcing yourself about flying there is good.

HARRIET: I wasn't sure about my next challenge. What do you think about it?

BETTY: Well, for one thing, you ask the question, "How can anybody fly those big planes?" Whenever you ask a question in "B", it's a good idea to answer it in "D."

HARRIET: The answer would be that many people fly planes, so obviously it's possible.

PAT: You're also ignoring the objective reality that the pilots who fly for the airlines are very well trained and have to practice flying those large planes all the time.

LARRY: I think you're projecting your own fears about the difficulty of flying (based on the few flying lessons you had years ago) onto other people and saying that because you wouldn't be good at flying a large plane that *no one* can be good at doing it.

BETTY: Harriet, what kind of work do you do?

HARRIET: I'm an editor at the university.

BETTY: Do you think an airline pilot would think your job is easy?

HARRIET: Well, I think he could edit faster than I could fly a plane.

LARRY: You have no objective evidence for that idea.

BETTY: In fact, Harriet, an airline pilot might pick up a magazine and think, "How can anyone put a whole magazine together?"

HARRIET: Yeah, I see what you mean.

BETTY: Tell us your E section.

HARRIET: Well, I want to be indifferent about the actual flight to Ceylon but feel good about going there.

The group then had Harriet review the ideas she had found to be most helpful, and got her to promise to listen to the tape recording of the group meeting at least once and to do rational emotive imagery on feeling calm during her trip.

Harriet came back to group four weeks later and gave this report.

HARRIET: I just got back from Ceylon, and it was such a good trip. I want to thank you all for the help you gave me when I was trying to decide whether or not to go.

BETTY: Tell us about the trip.

HARRIET: We flew a total of 20,000 miles ... and I was calm at almost every takeoff and landing. All 28 of them! We had a little plane trouble on the way there — and I really used my rational thinking then. I just kept thinking about what Larry said about how it wouldn't be *awful* if we crashed, and I stayed pretty calm. My husband was amazed at how well I handled myself and after that I just settled back and enjoyed the trip, all 36 hours of it. And Ceylon was wonderful; I'm so glad you all helped me decide to go.

BETTY: That's just great, Harriet. Sounds like you're really on top of your fear of flying.

HARRIET: Yes, and I don't ever intend to stop myself from flying anywhere any more.

This RSA *isn't* proposed as the answer to all irrational fears of flying: there are probably many other irrational ideas people use to make themselves afraid to fly. But this RSA and the ART group discussion were all Harriet needed to get her in rational control of her fears about flying and death. The group discussion was fairly typical of how an effective ART group operates.

For people who don't have an ART chapter to go to or who need extra help with their fear of flying, we recommend the book, *How to Overcome the Fear of Flying*, by Dr. Albert Ellis, Director of The Institute for Rational Living, 45 E. 65th St., N.Y., N.Y. 10021.

A third main goal of ART is to help willing members get involved in their community to promote a rational and pleasant environment for everybody. For example, in response to the request of a local hospital, my staff and I taught the principles of rational self-counseling to the staff of the psychiatric unit of that hospital. We gave them our standard eight week course with excellent results. They now have on-going RBT groups on the wards and, when aftercare is needed, discharged patients are often referred to the local ART chapter. Next is a success story in the person's own words that resulted from that community involvement:

"As I sit here and consider what ART has done for me in the past five months, I can see that I have much more to say than I realized when I was first asked to write this. Probably the best way to explain what has happened would be to describe myself in May, 1974, and then again in October, 1974, just five months after becoming acquainted with ART and rational self-counseling.

"In May, my husband and I had been going to couple and group counseling for four years. We didn't seem to be progressing at all and nothing had really changed. I got so depressed, I took an overdose of pills and ended up in the hospital for two weeks. I was uncertain what purpose life had for me. It seemed that my children and my husband were so involved in their lives that they didn't need me. Whereas I didn't use to have any trouble with decision making and problem solving, then when decision or problem solving came up, I just couldn't cope; I'd spend most of my time crying. The little time my husband and I spent together was spent arguing, with me always ending up in tears. Though I hated myself for doing it, I was ignoring my household responsibilities. It just seemed that there was so much to do that I wouldn't be able to do it all anyway; so why bother?

"I learned about rational self-counseling and ART in the hospital. After just five months in our local ART chapter, I have replaced my crying spells with the rational insight: 'Pat, you have control over your emotions, and this is *not* going to get you what you want.' Sure, I still cry sometimes, but now it's just for moments whereas before it was for hours. Now when I have a problem to solve or a decision to make, I sit down and write an RSA, consider my alternatives and rationally choose one. All the while, I remind myself that getting upset will not help me solve my problem and it'll make me feel bad.

"I'm getting myself out of the house more and I've begun some volunteer work for ART which I enjoy very much, working with the people there.

"I've improved my relationship with my husband considerably. We now sit down and discuss and solve our problems, instead of arguing about them with me upsetting myself and withdrawing to cry. I find it much easier to deal with the hassles of raising my teenagers. In short, life is beginning to be fun again. It's really great!"

A fourth goal in ART is research and teaching in the field of self-help. The foregoing success stories show that we do have our share of successes. But, we also have our share of failures and of people who are not helped as much as we would like to help them. Therefore, we are constantly looking for and testing new approaches to emotional self-help. To that end we invite mental health professionals to study and evaluate our programs. We constantly review and improve our self-help techniques and educational materials. Finally, we welcome the opportunity to cooperate with other self-help or professional groups in mental health research projects.

For people who *are not* interested in ART chapter activities, we have and enthusiastically encourage individual memberships in National ART. As an individual member of National ART, you are eligible for all the services for individual members that ART chapter members receive. You will receive our newsletter, *ART in Daily Living.* If you want someone to exchange rational ideas with, National ART will try to put you in mail contact with someone who shares your interest. One example of this is the ART Chapter at Levenworth Prison, Levenworth, Kansas. The members there have volunteered to correspond with individuals in and out of prisons around the country. We have put them in touch with several inmates here in the Wisconsin prison system who are also trying to learn and practice rational self-counseling in and out of prison.

We are busily helping to develop self-teaching educational programs under various topic headings, so that our on-going chapters can offer their members and communities continuous training in emotional self-help for dealing with common but troublesome emotional problems in everyday living. These courses are structured around self-teaching video and audio tape recordings, demonstrating real people rationally eliminating their unwanted emotional habits. All of the self-help programs are formulated and tested for effectiveness by the Rational Behavior Therapy (RBT) Training Section of the University of Kentucky, Psychiatric Outpatient Department.

To pursue ART's continuing education goals both for professionals and lay people, National ART, in cooperation with interested local Chapters, present Dr. Maultsby and Dr. Albert Ellis as workshop leaders several times per year in all parts of the country. Our popular workshops include: Rational Emotional Self-Help Techniques, the Rational Approach to Love and Marriage, The Rational Approach to Raising Children, Eliminating Irrational Fears, The Rational Approach to Non-voluntary Clients, and many other common problem areas.

One of our biggest problems is chronic shortage of lay people who have been trained to teach rational self-counseling. To attack this problem, National ART and the Rational Behavior Therapy Training Section of the U. of Kentucky Psychiatric O.P.D. have created a one-week intensive para-professional training course in RBTT for lay people. This course teaches the basic principles of rational self-counseling and how to teach them to others. Several scholarships to these courses are available through National ART for ART members. Graduates of this course can get jobs as para-professionals in hospitals and mental health clinics that use the

Rational Emotive Therapy and Rational Behavior Therapy techniques in their psychotherapeutic programs.

Our oldest and still most important educational activity is the sale of self-help materials. We distribute almost all the books, pamphlets and tapes that rational therapists have made available to the public.

One of our most rewarding discoveries is that every ART member has something to offer the organization, and the organization has something to offer each ART member. It's a rational "mutual aid society." We openly admit that we need all the help we can get, and we try to benefit others with the help we can give. I would like therefore to invite you to join with us in helping others help themselves to improved emotional health and happiness. If you are interested in receiving self-help or in helping to give it, please write to:

Association for Rational Thinkers
117 W. Main Street
Madison, Wisconsin 53703
or call (608) 256-4851.

We will be glad to hear from you.

CHAPTER 17
A BRIEF HISTORY OF THE ASSOCIATION FOR RATIONAL THINKERS (ART)
By Betty Mattingly Barry

The history of the Association for Rational Thinkers (ART) is something of an adventure story. National ART began in the fall of 1970, in the Psychiatric O.P.D. of University of Wisconsin Hospital, Madison, Wis. The first ART members were largely former members of Dr. Maxie C. Maultsby's Rational Behavior Therapy (RBT) groups, who no longer needed therapy. Still, they saw the great potential value in learning to use rational self-counseling in all areas of their daily lives. By actually doing it, they correctly expected to continue their own personal growth as well as improve their relationships with their families, other loved ones, friends and maybe even a few enemies.

With Dr. Maultsby's advice and encouragement, the group began to meet alone, using the RBT group structure and format learned in RBT. With the help of Drs. Maultsby, Slack, Kuperman, Graham, and Attorney Stroud (all then of Madison, Wisconsin) the group incorporated as Associated Rational Thinkers or ART.* Ms. Joyce Gram, (a founding member of ART and Canadian citizen spending a year in America) became the first editor of our news-letter, *ART In Daily Living*.

A year later Dr. Maultsby moved to the University of Kentucky Medical Center (UKMC) in Lexington, Kentucky. By then, however, ART was ready and able to function without his direct input. In addition, ART was slowly growing; as the original members left Madison, some started new ART chapters in their new communities.

As a faculty member of the Institute for Rational Living, Dr. Maultsby frequently visits New York City. During one of

---

*The name was suggested by Attorney Stroud.

his lectures there, he met Dr. Leonard Pickering, an orthopedic surgeon from Southgate, Michigan, and long-time friend of Dr. Albert Ellis. Fortunately, Dr. Pickering shared Dr. Maultsby's interest in the mass-mental-health potential of the rational approach to daily living. Dr. Maultsby introduced Dr. Pickering to the Association for Rational Thinkers (ART), which had recently received its tax-exempt, non-profit status from the IRS.

Dr. Pickering contacted the Madison ART chapter and arranged a weekend rational marathon encounter in Southgate, Michigan, designed to teach him and other interested people about the ABC's of rational self-counseling and ART chapter functions. After that marathon the Southgate chapter of ART was formed.

Mr. Murray Merrill, close friend of Dr. Pickering and marathon participant, became so excited about the potential of ART as a self-help organization, he volunteered to edit and publish our newsletter, when Ms. Gram returned to Canada later that year. When that happened National ART moved from Madison, Wis. to Southgate, Michigan.

For over two years, Dr. Pickering (then ART's National Coordinator) and Mr. Merrill traveled around the country at their own expense to help get other ART groups started by leading one-day marathons to introduce new chapters to the technique of rational self-counseling. More than any other single factor, Dr. Pickering and Mr. Merrill kept National ART alive and growing for over a year. Twelve new ART chapters in six states were the direct result of their personal expense and enthusiastic efforts.

The Madison ART group started to dwindle after Dr. Maultsby moved to Kentucky. Fortunately, however, Ms. Connie Walling, one of the first ART members, was determined to keep Madison ART going and growing. She worked tirelessly giving talks to anyone at almost any place about ART. In January 1972, Connie started offering introductory classes in rational self-counseling to all new ART members and any others interested in learning to help themselves rationally. Her classes lasted two hours, one night per week, for six weeks. At the end of the classes, participants were invited to become active in ART, if they wished to maintain and increase their skill in rational self-counseling.

About the time Connie was teaching her third or fourth introductory class, Fran Kaplan, Robin Alexander and I (all former students and close friends of Connie) had become thoroughly committed to the continued growth of Madison and National ART. We were all group leaders and also volunteered our time to work with group members individually if they desired it. Within a year, the Madison ART chapter was fairly strong, with weekly group attendance between twenty or thirty people in each of two groups.

News of the helpful activities of the Madison ART chapter began to spread to the mental health professionals in the area. Dane County Social Services promptly came forward requesting more information. Connie responded with a personal presentation to twelve Dane social workers. Several of them became so enthusiastic about ART as an additional community resource, they registered for Connie's next course in rational self-counseling. Their continued enthusiasm for ART led to an ART-sponsored workshop on rational emotional self-help techniques, conducted by Dr. Maultsby for the social workers from Dane County and the surrounding counties. After that, the Madison ART chapter began to receive continuous referrals from Dane County Social Services, people who were interested in emotional self-help.

Eight or nine months later, Connie, Fran, Robin and I decided to hold a large regional RBT conference to be led by Dr. Maultsby and Dr. Ellis. While putting the conference together, the group decided to petition the ART board of directors to move the headquarters of ART from Southgate back to Madison. That seemed to be a logical move since we four were willing to volunteer our time and effort to building the organization, and National ART had then grown beyond the limits of the part time attention Dr. Pickering and Mr. Merrill were able to give it. The board of directors agreed.

In August, 1973, Connie traveled to Southgate where she met with Dr. Pickering and Mr. Merrill and completed the details of transferring National ART. Back in Madison the National office this time was set up in a room at Adams House (a co-op owned by Betty and Mike Barry, Connie, Fran, Robin, and Carolyn and Gary Kraemer). There the organization began functioning on a full-time basis for the first time.

The initial activities of the new staff member included writing a brochure to describe ART, publishing a special edition of *ART in Daily Living* to alert ART members to the change in headquarters, defining the responsibilities of each staff member, etc.

For a time, the staff continued to work for both the local Madison chapter and National ART. That quickly created problems with divided loyalties and duties. Pat Patterson, a local chapter member, rationally solved our dilemma by volunteering to take over the duties of coordinator of the Madison chapter.

Through the efforts of Rod Kennedy (the coordinator of the ART chapter in Racine, Wisconsin) and Dave Goodman (an ART Board Member and co-author with Dr. Maultsby of the book, *Emotional Well-Being Through Rational Behavior Training*), the Johnson Foundation of Racine, Wisconsin, gave National ART a small grant to finance our first national convention. The meeting was held at Wingspread, the Johnson Foundation's national conference center in Racine, in November, 1973.

For three days, representatives of nine ART chapters as well as many people interested in forming new chapters of ART met at Wingspread with Dr. Maultsby, other board members and the national staff of ART. In addition, Dr. Robert Morse, psychiatrist from Mayo Clinic, and Mr. Len Boarman, Project Director for the Clement Stone Foundation, met with us as outside observers of the convention, invited by the Johnson Foundation. ART's first National Convention was a "smashing success" and everyone left with feelings of excitement and enthusiasm about the future of ART.

During the months that followed, a number of things happened. The National office was moved from its one room at Adams House to a more spacious suite in downtown Madison. ART began publishing and distributing two of Dr. Maultsby's emotional self-help books and ART's own journal, *Perspectives in Emotional Self-Help.* Also, at the requests of local ART chapters, National ART began to help them sponsor workshops and marathons on emotional self-help, directed by Drs. Maultsby and Ellis. Those activities now serve three important functions: (a) they produce much needed financial support for both National ART and local chapters, (b) they help "spread the rational word", and (c) they help get newly formed ART chapters off to a flying start in their communities. Consequently, we now have over 20 active chapters and another 30 in various stages of organization in the U.S., Canada, Australia, England and Mexico.

The rapid growth of ART is due to many factors. Three of them that immediately come to mind are (a) the excellent direction from our board of directors (Maxie C. Maultsby, Jr., M.D., Albert Ellis, Ph.D., Mr. David Goodman, Solomon Kuperman, M.D., L.M. Pickering, M.D., Warner Slack, M.D., Robert Hibbard, M.D.), (b) the continued financial aid and general promotional help from Dr. Maultsby, Dr. Ellis, Dr. Janet Wolfe and the board of directors of the Institute for Rational Living of New York City, and (c) the hundreds of hours of work without pay by the national staff plus the thousands of hours of enthusiastic work volunteered by the members of all the ART chapters.

Still, I believe that the single most important factor that will insure the continued growth of ART is the continuing discovery, by mental health professionals and lay people alike, that ART and its Rational Self-Counseling technique fill a pressing need for emotional self-help in our society. ART makes helpful emotional re-education available to needy people who otherwise would not have an opportunity for this type of helpful, low cost personal growth. I am confident therefore, that as long as people have problems in daily living, there will be a need for ART, and ART will be there to fill that need.

In August, 1975, the part-time national staff decided that National ART had grown to the point where it needed more direct, personal leadership from the founder, and national headquarters were moved to Lexington, Kentucky. Today ART is known as the International Association for Clear Thinking (INTER-ACT). INTER-ACT's national headquarters are located at 2036 Blairmore Road, Lexington, Kentucky 40502.

ANSWERS TO EMPHASIS QUESTIONS

Chapter 1

1. self
2. True
3. brain, human
4. self
5. correct, wrong
6. True
7. (a) based on objective reality and relevant facts
   (b) enables people to achieve their goals most quickly
   (c) enables people to protect their lives
   (d) enables people to keep out of significant trouble with others
   (e) enables people to prevent or eliminate significant personal emotional conflicts
8. three
9. False
10. True
11. emotional, behavior
12. significant
13. rational self
14. objective reality
15. camera or recorder
16. irrational
17. False
18. two
19. rational, analysis, emotional re-education
20. brain, emotions, work

Chapter 2

1. brain, emotions
2. believe, feel
3. thinking
4. neocortex
5. True
6. neocortex, True
7. True
8. suffer
9. limbic system, choose
10. choice, thoughts
11. True
12. False
13. True
14. True
15. False
16. False
17. True
18. believable
19. True
20. three, rational

Chapter 3

1. most, misunderstood
2. positive, negative, neutral
3. positive, negative, neutral
4. perceptions, thoughts
5. no
6. False
7. False
8. negative
9. True
10. True
11. False
12. True
13. True
14. True
15. True
16. True
17. True
18. True
19. step
20. True

Chapter 4

1. emotional
2. four
   (a) intellectual insight
   (b) correct practice
   (c) emotional insight
   (d) personality
3. intellectual
4. True
5. brain, map
6. emotional
7. True
8. actual, mental
9. emotive imagery
10. False
11. five
12. cognitive dissonance
13. True
14. limbic system, neocortex
15. False
16. see page 46
17. cognitive dissonance
18. incorrectly, can't
19. average intelligence
20. as long as it takes

Chapter 5

1. six
2. three, emotion
3. see page 56
4. facts & events
5. True
6. self-talk, thoughts, attitudes
7. emotional consequence, felt
8. you, you
9. five
10. Da
11. objective, subjective
12. True
13. False
14. emotional goals, future
15. False
16. emotion
17. False
18. True
19. phony
20. True

Chapter 6

1. True
2. True
3. feel
4. False
5. feel
6. ignorance
7. True
8. False
9. irrational
10. thinking, wanting
11. irrational
12. False
13. can't
14. True
15. communicate, yourself
16. thoughts
17. emotions
18. rationally, works
19. True
20. True

Chapter 7

1. emotional insight
2. True
3. True
4. practice
5. three, five
6. rational emotive imagery, re-education, private
7. True
8. camera
9. habit
10. want, rid
11. game
12. False
13. calm, instant, feeling
14. stop
15. False
16. vague, unclear, distracting
17. False
18. False
19. False
20. emotional, school

Chapter 8

1. True
2. pass
3. True
4. False
5. False
6. False
7. False
8. False
9. True
10. True
11. True
12. True
13. False
14. False
15. (a)
16. False
17. False
18. False
19. False
20. False

Chapter 9

1. False
2. True
3. True
4. False
5. False
6. True
7. True
8. False
9. True
10. True
11. False
12. False
13. True
14. irrelevant, irrational
15. True
16. False
17. False
18. False
19. False
20. False

Chapter 10

1. True
2. True
3. True
4. True
5. True
6. True
7. True
8. False
9. False
10. True
11. False
12. perceptions and thoughts
13. True
14. thought, talk
15. True
16. decisions, irrational
17. False
18. False
19. find, get, attitudes
20. attitude, belief, change

Chapter 11

1. True
2. believe
3. True
4. True
5. True
6. False
7. True
8. distorting, confusing
9. didn't
10. True
11. perceptions, thoughts, attitudes, beliefs
12. real, real
13. emotion
14. thoughts
15. add
16. attitudes, beliefs
17. True
18. True
19. learning, emotions
20. didn't

Chapter 12

1. True
2. attitudes
3. was doing
4. hassling, job
5. False
6. False
7. trick, feeling, thinking
8. irrational
9. three, five, relevant, useful
10. confuse, irrelevant
11. afraid
12. False
13. garbage
14. phony
15. created, self maintained
16. False
17. sloppy
18. False
19. False
20. False

Chapter 13

1. True
2. True
3. shortcuts
4. True
5. choice, words
6. False
7. True
8. False
9. True
10. True
11. True
12. True
13. registered, controlled learning
14. True
15. emotional feeling
16. True
17. True
18. True
19. True
20. alcohol abuse

Chapter 14

1. True
2. obsessive, compulsive
3. one, two
4. compulsive, crave
5. addiction
6. False
7. True
8. intellectual
9. True
10. cognitive dissonance
11. False
12. False
13. False
14. disown, behavior
15. you decide
16. False
17. False
18. False
19. True
20. True

REFERENCES

The particular chapter or chapters to which each of the below-listed publications is relevant is indicated in parentheses in bold type at the end of each listing.

Beritoff, J. S., *Neural Mechanisms of Higher Vertebrate Behavior* (Translated by W. T. Liberson) Boston: Little, Brown & Co., 1965. **(2, 5, 7)**

Eccles, J. C., "The Physiology of Imagination," *Scientific American*, Sept., 1958, Vol. 199, p. 135. **(7)**

Ellis, Albert, *How to Master Your Fear of Flying*, Philadelphia: Curtis Books, Inc., 1972. **(16)**

Ellis, Albert, *Reason and Emotion in Psychotherapy*, New York: Lyle Stuart, 1963. **(1, 3, 5)**

Ellis, Albert, "Toward a More Precise Definition of Emotional and Intellectual Insight," *Psychological Reports*, 1963, 13, pg. 125. **(4)**

Ellis, A., "Rational Emotive Therapy," Ch. 10 in *Operational Theories of Personality*, Edited by Burton, A., New York: Brunner-Mazel, 1974, p. 308–344. **(1, 3, 5)**

Epictetus, *Discourses of Epictetus* (translated by George Long) London: George Bell & Sons, 1888. **(1, 3, 4, 5, 6, 7)**

Gantt, W. H., "Principles of Nervous Breakdown," Ann. New York, Acad. Sc., 1953, 56, p. 146. **(2, 7)**

Grace, W. J., and Graham, D. T., "Relationship of Specific Attitudes and Emotions to Certain Bodily Disease," *Psychosom. Med.*, 1952, 14:243–251. **(3, 4, 5, 10)**

Graham D. T., "Some Research on Psychophysiologic Specificity and its Relation to Psychosomatic Disease", in R. Roessler and N. S. Greenfield (Eds.); *Physiological Correlates of Psychological Disorder*, Madison: University of Wisconsin Press, 1962. **(3, 4, 5, 10)**

Graham, D. T., Kabler, J. D., and Graham, F. K., "Physiological Response to the Suggestion of Attitudes Specific for Hives and Hypertension", *Psychosom. Med.*, 1962, 24:159–169. **(3, 4, 5, 10)**

Graham, D. T., Lundy, R. M., Benjamin, L. S., Kabler, J. D., Lewis, W. C., Kunish, N. Q., and Graham, F. K., "Specific Attitudes in Initial Interviews with Patients Having Different Psychosomatic Diseases," *Psychosom. Med.*, 1962, 24:257–266. **(3, 4, 5, 10)**

Graham, D. T., Stern, J. A., and Winokur, G., "The Concept of a Different Specific Set of Physiological Changes in Each Emotion," *Psychiatric Research Reports*, 12, American Psychiatric Association, Jan. 1960. **(3, 4, 5, 10)**

Graham, D. T., Stern, J. A., and Winokur, G., "Experimental Investigation of the Specificity of Attitude Hypothesis in Psychosomatic Disease," *Psychosom. Med.*, 1958, 20:446–457. **(3, 4, 5, 10)**

Hebb, D. O., *The Organization of Behavior*, New York: John Wiley & Sons, Inc., 1959. **(2, 7)**

Holland, J. G., and Skinner, B. F., *The Analysis of Behavior*, New York: McGraw-Hill, 1961. **(3, 4, 5)**

Hudgins, C. V., "Conditioning and Voluntary Control Reflex," *J. Gen. Psych.*, 1933, 8:1–49. **(2, 3, 7)**

Ludwig, Arnold, M. "Craving and Relapse to Drink," *Quarterly Journal of Studies on Alcohol*, March, 1974, Vol. 35, No. 1, pp. 108–130. **(11, 12, 13, 14)**

Ludwig, Arnold, M., Wikler, A., "The First Drink," *Archives of General Psychiatry*, April, 1974, Vol. 30, pp. 539–547. **(5, 8, 11, 12, 13, 14)**

MacLean, P. D., "Chemical and Electrical Stimulation of Hippocampus in Unrestrained Animals: II Behavioral Findings," *Arch. Neurol. & Psychiat.*, 1957, 78:128. **(2)**

MacLean, P. D., "Contrasting Functions of Limbic and Neocortical Systems of the Brain and Their Relevance to Psychophysiological Aspects of Medicine," *Am. J. Med.*, 1958, 25:611. **(2)**

MacLean, P. D., Flanigan, S., Glynn, J. P., Kin, C., and Stevens, J. R., "Hippocampal Function: tentative correlations of conditioning, E.E.G., drugs, and radioautographic studies:Yale," *J. Bio. & Med.*, 1955, 28:380. **(2)**

Maultsby, M. C., "The Pamphlet as a Psychotherapeutic Aid," *Rational Living*, 1969, 3(2), 31–35. **(1)**

Maultsby, M. C., "Rational Emotive Imagery," *Rational Living*, 1971, 6(1), 24–26. **(6, 7, 12, 13, 14)**

Maultsby, M. C., "The Relapse Patient in RBT," *Growth Through Reason*, Palo Alto, Calif.: Science and Behavior Book Co., 1971. **(1, 3, 4, 5, 7, 11)**

Maultsby, M. C., "Routine Tape Recorder Use in RET," *Rational Living*, 1970, 5(1), 8–23. **(1, 12, 13, 14)**

Maultsby, M. C., "Seven Reflections on Scientism and Psychotherapy," *Psychological Reports*, 1968, 22:1311–1312. **(1, 2, 3, 4, 5, 6, 7)**

Maultsby, M. C., "Systematic Written Homework in Psychotherapy," *Psychotherapy: Theory Research and Practice*, 1971 8(3), 195–198. **(1, 3, 5)**

Maultsby, M. C., "Written Homework for the Patient with an Emotional Crisis," *American Family Physician*, 1971, 4(6), 69–75. **(1, 5)**

Maultsby, M. C., and Graham, D. T., "Controlled Study of Effects of Psychotherapy on Self-Reported Maladaptive Traits, Anxiety Scores, and Psychosomatic Disease Attitudes," *J. of Psychia. Res.*, 1974, Vol. 10:121–132. **(1, 2, 3, 4, 5, 6, 7)**

Maultsby, M. C., and Gram, Joyce, "A Two Year Follow-up Study of Rational Behavior Therapy," Paper presented at the 5th Annual Meeting of the Behavioral Therapists in Washington, D.C., September 6, 1971. **(5, 8, 9, 11, 12, 13, 16)**

Maultsby, M. C., and Gramm, J. M., "Patients' Responses to the Use of Tape Recorders in Psychotherapy: A Clinical Study of 56 Patients," *J. of Nat'l. Med. Assoc.*, 1972, 64(4):375. **(12, 13, 14)**

Maultsby, M. C. and Stiefel, L., "A Theory of Rational Behavioral Group Process," *Rational Living*, 1972, 7(1):28–34. **(16)**

Maultsby, M. C., and Winkler, P. J., "Directed Rational Self-Counseling (A New Approach to Mass Mental Health)," 1972 ANA Clinical Sessions. **(1, 2, 3, 4, 5, 6, 7)**

Mowrer, O. H., *Learning Theory and Behavior*, New York: John Wiley & Sons, 1960. **(2, 3, 7)**

Mowrer, O. H., *Learning Theory and the Symbolic Process*, New York: John Wiley & Sons, 1963. **(2, 3, 7)**

Papez, J. W., "A Proposed Mechanism of Emotion," *Arch. Neuro. & Psychiat.*, 1937, 38:725. **(2, 3)**

Papez, J. W., In Jasper, H. H., et. al., "Reticular Formation of the Brain," Boston: Little, Brown & Co., 1958. **(2, 3)**

Piaget, J., *The Judgment and Reason in the Child*, New York: Harcourt, Brace & World, 1929. **(2, 3)**

Piaget, J., *Logic and Psychology*, New York: Basic Books, 1957. **(2, 3)**

Razran, G., "The Observable Unconscious and the Inferable Conscious in Current Soviet Psychophysiology: Interoceptive Conditioning, Semantic Conditioning and the Orienting Reflex," *Psych. Rev.*, 1961, 68:81–147. **(4, 7, 10)**

Rotter, J. B., *Social Learning and Clinical Psychology*, New York: Prentice Hall, Inc., 1954. **(3, 4, 5, 6, 10)**

Schachter, S., "The Interaction of Cognitive and Physiologic Determinants of Emotional States," *Ad. Exp. Soc. Psych.*, 1964, 1:49–80. **(3, 4, 5, 6, 7, 10)**

Skinner, B. F., *The Behavior of Organisms*, New York: Appleton-Century, 1938. **(3, 4, 5, 6, 7)**

Skinner, B. F., *Science and Human Behavior*, New York: The Free Press, 1960. **(3, 4, 5, 6, 7)**

Skinner, B. F., *Verbal Behavior*, New York: Appleton-Century-Crofts, 1957. **(3, 4, 5, 6, 7)**

Solnitzky, O., "The Limbic System: Its Relation to Personality," *Georgetown Med. Bull.*, 1964, 17:161. **(2)**

Tolman, E. C., "Cognitive Maps in Rats and Men," *Psychol. Rev.*, 1948, 53:189. **(2, 7)**

Wikler, A. "Requirements for Extinction of Relapse-Facilitating Variables and for Rehabilitation in a Narcotic-Antagonist Treatment Program," *Advances in Biochemical Psychopharmacology*, 1974, Vol. 8, p. 399–414. **(7, 11, 12, 13, 14)**

Wikler, A. "Some Implications of Conditioning Theory for Problems of Drug Abuse," *Behavioral Science*, January, 1971, Vol. 16, p. 92–97 **(7, 11, 12, 13, 14)**

Wikler, A., and Pescor, Frank T., "Persistence of 'Relapse — Tendencies' of Rats Previously Made Physically Dependent on Morphine," *Psychopharmacologia*, 1970, 16, 375–384. **(7, 11, 12, 13, 14)**

Wolpe, J. and Lazarus, A. A., *Behavior Therapy Techniques*, Oxford: Pergamon Press, 1966. **(7)**

Wolpe, J., Salter, A., Reyna, L. J. (Eds.), *The Conditioning Therapies*, New York: Holt, Rinehart & Winston, Inc., 1964. **(7)**

INDEX